82229

The GIF
Animator's Guide

D0851438

The GIF Animator's Guide

by Sandra E. Eddy

A Subsidiary of
Henry Holt and Co., Inc.

Copyright © 1997, by The Eddy Group, Inc..
MIS:Press is a subsidiary of Henry Holt and Company, Inc.
115 West 18th Street
New York, NY 10011

First Edition—1997

Printed in the United States of America.

Library of Congress Cataloging-in-Publication Data
Schnyder, Sandy Eddy.
   The GIF animator's guide/by Sandra E. Eddy.
     p.   cm.
   ISBN 1-55828-561-X
   1. Computer animation. 2. Computer graphics. 3. Web sites. I. Title.
TR897.7.S38   1997   97-28077
006.6'96--dc21   CIP

10 9 8 7 6 5 4 3 2 1

Associate Publisher: *Paul Farrell*

Managing Editor: *Shari Chappell*	**Production Editor:** *Kitty May*
Editor: *Debra Williams Cauley*	**Technical Editor:** *Adam Gerstein*
Copy Edit Manager: *Karen Tongish*	**Copy Editor:** *Sara Black*

Table of Contents

INTRODUCTION IX

CHAPTER 1 ◆ CREATING AND EDITING AN IMAGE 1

Learning About Graphics 1
Planning an Effective Image for the Web 5
Drawing or Painting an Image 10
Obtaining Images from Other Sources 10
Observing Copyright Laws 11

CHAPTER 2 ◆ CREATING AN ANIMATION 13

Planning and Designing an Animation 13
Creating an Animation 15
Manufacturing the GIF Animation 16
Inserting an Animation in an HTML Document 17
Testing an Animation 18
GIF Animation Programs 18
Animation Effects 19

CHAPTER 3 ◆ WORKING WITH MICROSOFT IMAGE COMPOSER AND MICROSOFT GIF ANIMATOR 29

Starting Image Composer 29
The Image Composer Window 30
Creating a Sprite—Example 1 43
Building a Composition 45
About This Animation—Apple Tree 47
Manipulating Sprites—Example 2 48
About This Animation—Rotating Beach Ball 51
Applying Colors—Example 3 51
About This Animation—Happy Dog 55
Tuning the Colors 56

Adding Text—Example 4 57
About This Animation—Flashing New Sign 58
Applying Patterns and Fills 59
Applying Warps and Filters 61
Applying Art Effects 64
Scanning and Animating a Sprite 66
Introducing Microsoft GIF Animator 67

CHAPTER 4 ◆ WORKING WITH PAINT SHOP PRO 73

Starting Paint Shop Pro 73
The Paint Shop Pro Window 74
Creating an Image—Example 1 87
Modifying an Image 90
Creating Images for Animation 97
About This Animation—Movie-Marquee NEW Sign 97
Manipulating an Image—Example 2 98
About This Animation—Crazy HOME Sign 106
Scanning and Animating an Image —Example 3 107
About This Animation—Animated Teeth 108

CHAPTER 5 ◆ WORKING WITH GIF CONSTRUCTION SET .109

Starting GIF Construction Set 110
The GIF Construction Set Window 110
Using the Animation Wizard 112
Modifying an Animation 115
About This Animation—Arrow Bend 119
About This Animation—Snapping Scissors Rule 122
Creating an Animation from Scratch 124
Creating Special-Effects Animations 125

CHAPTER 6 ◆ WORKING WITH ADOBE PHOTOSHOP 129

Starting Adobe Photoshop 130
The Photoshop Window 131
Preparing to Create an Image 141
Creating an Image—Example 1 152
About This Animation—Lighted Rule 162

THE GIF ANIMATOR'S GUIDE

Modifying an Image 163
Working with Layers 177
Transforming a Selection or Layer 179
Applying Special Effects—Example 2 182
About This Animation—Bouncing Ball 184
Scanning and Animating an Image— Example 3 185
About This Animation—Cool Faucet 185

CHAPTER 7 ◆ WORKING WITH ADOBE ILLUSTRATOR 187

Starting Adobe Illustrator 188
The Illustrator Window 189
Preparing to Create an Image 199
Creating an Image—Example 1 204
About This Animation—Rainbow Star 214
Modifying an Image 214
Transforming a Selection—Example 2 218
About This Animation—Snail Rule 223
Applying Special Effects 225

CHAPTER 8 ◆ WORKING WITH CORELDRAW 227

Starting CorelDRAW 229
The CorelDRAW Window 230
Preparing to Create an Image 244
Creating an Image—Example 1 252
About This Animation—Orange-Red-Yellow New 258
Modifying an Image 258
Transforming a Selection 262
Converting to a Bit Map—Example 2 267
About This Animation—Square-Square 269
Scanning and Animating an Image—Example 3 270
About This Animation—Accordion 271

CHAPTER 9 ◆ WORKING WITH GIFBUILDER 273

About the Frames Window 273
About This Animation—The Lighthouse 275
Getting Ready to Animate 276

TABLE OF CONTENTS

Starting GifBuilder 276
Editing an Animation 277
About This Animation—Deborah's Moon 279
Creating an IMG Tag Automatically 281

APPENDIX A ◆ AN INCOMPLETE HISTORY OF ANIMATION . . .283

The Persistence of Vision 283
Animation Devices 283
Photography and Movement 284
Experiments with Motion Pictures 285
The Early Films 286
Early Cartoons and Their Makers 286
Experimental Animation 288

APPENDIX B ◆ TRADITIONAL ANIMATION TECHNIQUES . . .291

Drawing and Painting on Cels 291
Stop-Motion Animation 292
On-Film Animation 293
Art under the Camera 293
Rotoscoping 294
The Optical Printer 294
Computer Animation 295

APPENDIX C ◆ A TIMELINE OF ANIMATION AND RELATED SUBJECTS 297

APPENDIX D ◆ COMPUTER-BASED ANIMATION 313

The Beginning 313
Advancing Toward Realism 313
Special Effects in Television and Motion Pictures 314
Programming Animations 315
Animation on the World Wide Web 315

INDEX 317

THE GIF ANIMATOR'S GUIDE

Introduction

Welcome to *The GIF Animator's Guide*, which is designed to demonstrate how easy it is to create eye-catching animations using a variety of popular art and animation programs. This book is for all levels of artists—ranging from rank beginners to professionals—who want to learn how to produce good-looking GIF animations quickly and easily.

The mission of this book is to provide the tools to help you produce high-quality GIF animations. Here you'll learn about GIF animation techniques, tips, and tricks. You'll also get detailed instructions on using popular art programs to create good-looking images. And you'll find out how to use several GIF animation programs to convert images into animations. Most chapters include examples of animations with notes and illustrations of each frame.

On the CD-ROM disk at the back of the book are trial or complete versions of most of the programs featured in this book, all example animations, and a large gallery of unique GIF animations. Feel free to use these animations on your Web pages or edit them to make them your own.

HOW THIS BOOK IS ORGANIZED

The GIF Animator's Guide is designed to be easy to use—especially for those who are new users of art programs, beginners in GIF animation, or novices in animation techniques. The book is organized as follows:

- ◆ Chapter 1, "Creating and Editing an Image," presents information about standard graphics file formats and design basics, emphasizing how to produce an image suitable for animation.

- ◆ Chapter 2, "Creating an Animation," discusses the most efficient methods for creating animation files. Subjects include planning, techniques, and effects suitable for GIF animation.

The remaining chapters cover several popular art and GIF animation programs, their features, and how to use them to produce images and animations. Each chapter helps you learn the basics and important features of a particular program:

◆ Chapter 3, "Working with Microsoft Image Composer and Microsoft GIF Animator," explores a sophisticated Windows-based art program you can use to create transparent sprites and compositions and a Windows-based animation program you can use to construct animations from Image Composer and other art programs.

◆ Chapter 4, "Working with Paint Shop Pro," examines an easy-to-use Windows-based shareware art program with all the tools you need for creating and editing images in a variety of graphic formats.

◆ Chapter 5, "Working with GIF Construction Set," covers a Windows-based shareware program you can use to create, edit, and manage GIF animations.

◆ Chapter 6, "Working with Adobe Photoshop," explores a commercial program you can use to draw and paint images and apply art effects. Adobe provides Windows and Macintosh versions of Photoshop.

◆ Chapter 7, "Working with Adobe Illustrator," describes how to use this drawing program, its tools, and art effects. Adobe provides Windows and Macintosh versions of Illustrator.

◆ Chapter 8, "Working with CorelDRAW," explores this drawing program and its features. Corel provides Windows and Macintosh versions of CorelDRAW.

◆ Chapter 9, "Working with GIFBuilder," provides you with information on a Macintosh-based freeware program you can use to create, edit, and manage GIF animations.

In preparation for writing this book, I spent many enjoyable hours researching animation and related subjects: basic animation techniques, experimental animation, photography, animation devices, and the early days and development of motion pictures, full-length animated features, and, of course, cartoons—from *Little Nemo* to *Beavis and Butthead*. The appendices provide some of this information.

◆ Appendix A, "An Incomplete History of Animation," discusses the events that have led to the current state of animation—in movies, computer graphics, and Web animation.

◆ Appendix B, "Traditional Animation Techniques," covers all types of animation methods, especially for film and fine art.

◆ Appendix C, "A Timeline of Animation and Related Subjects," lists important events in the history of visual studies, photography, animation machines, early film, cartoons, and the associated inventors, scientists, and artists.

◆ Appendix D, "Computer-Based Animation," is a brief history of computer graphics and animation.

The CD-ROM disk in the back of this book includes trial, demo, or complete versions of the programs featured in this book, other GIF animation programs, and a gallery of unique GIF animations.

CONVENTIONS USED IN THIS BOOK

This book uses several special conventions and features.

 NOTE
A note provides general information about a function or feature.

 SHORTCUT
A shortcut is a tip or hint about performing an action more quickly or efficiently.

 WARNING
A warning alerts you to a potential pitfall in taking a particular action.

This icon indicates that you can perform a particular action using a computer running under the Windows operating system.

This icon indicates that you can perform a particular action using a computer running under the Macintosh operating system.

ABOUT THE PARTICIPANTS

The following people have generously contributed animations for the CD-ROM disk bundled with this book.

Deborah Eddy is a landscape painter living in Satna Cruz, California. Her work has been exhibited extensively, and she has been Artist in Residence at Yosemite National Park twice. In addition, she has been a commercial artist, package and display designer, and has written and illustrated several books. Her animations for this book are debbug.gif. debmoon.gif, landscap.gif, and debyes.gif.

T. Allen Barnes is a paramedic and a rhythm guitarist for the band, *The Stumble*. His anmimation is stum_rot.gif.

Michael Schnyder is a paramedic. He has over ten years of experience using computers. His animation is hello.gif.

ACKNOWLEDGMENTS

Writing any computer or Internet book is a team effort, bringing together people who many times have never met face to face. For example, those individuals working on this book live and work in various areas of New York, California, and Delaware. In this section, I'd like to thank all the people whose efforts have been so important.

Special thanks go to Debra Williams Cauley, who is a wonderful editor and an outstanding person.

I especially thank the other people at MIS:Press for all their help and extremely hard work. Special thanks go to Sara Black, Matthew Casper, Kitty May, and Karen Tongish.

For accuracy and attention in reviewing every page, figure, and graphic, I offer a special thank you to the Technical Editor, Adam Gerstein.

As always, thanks go to Michael Swertfager, my friend, occasional coauthor, super Web master, and world traveler, who introduced me to GIF animation.

I have perpetual thanks for the patience and persistence of my agent, Matt Wagner of Waterside Productions.

There are also thanks for the special efforts of Steven Lurie of Microsoft, Amy Morris and Sonya Shafer of Adobe, and Jill D. Ryan of McLean Public Relations on behalf of Ulead Systems, Inc.

For their continued encouragement, I thank my family and friends—you know who you are.

For their special and continuing contributions, I thank Toni, Bart, and Eli—and always in loving memory of Indy.

Dog. A kind of additional or subsidiary Deity designed to catch the overflow and surplus of the world's worship.

—Ambrose Bierce

DEDICATION

For Deborah Eddy, Margaret Cusick, Christine Brennan, and Kathryn McCue.

> For there is no friend like a sister
> In calm or stormy weather;
> To cheer one on the tedious way,
> To fetch one if one goes astray,
> To lift one if one totters down,
> To strengthen whilst one stands.
>
> —Christina Rossetti

HOW TO REACH THE AUTHOR

I would like to hear from you—especially if you can furnish tips, shortcuts, and tricks that you have used to create imaginative and innovative animations for the Web. If I have missed an important fact or should include a particular art program, GIF animation program, or utility in the next edition of this book, be sure to let me know. My email address is **eddygrp@sover.net**, or you can send a note in care of MIS:Press.

Creating and Editing An Image

The basic building blocks of good GIF animations are individual frames and the images within those frames. Before you plunge into your first animation, you should be familiar with at least one drawing program, know both the benefits and limitations of working with GIF files, and understand how to use the benefits and work within the limits.

The first part of this chapter introduces you to graphics for the World Wide Web. In this section, you'll learn about the two basic graphics types, graphic formats supported by popular art programs and those used for Web graphics—especially the GIF format, its history and standards.

The following pages cover planning and developing the best possible images with a minimum of mistakes and frustration. You'll find out about selecting colors, specifying height and width, working with transparency, and more. Finally, you'll learn about the variety of methods used to create and obtain images for use in animations.

LEARNING ABOUT GRAPHICS

This section starts with a basic overview of computer graphics and gradually narrows down to the GIF standard with which you will create frames for animations. Before you focus on GIF images, you'll learn about the two types of computer graphics—bit maps and vector. Art programs support particular formats within the two graphic types. You'll find out the formats supported by each of the programs covered in this book. Then, you'll learn about JPEG and GIF, the two Web-graphics formats, and the reason for using the GIF format.

About Bit-mapped and Vector Graphics

Art programs produce two types of graphics:

♦ *Bit-mapped* or *raster* graphics generate images on a grid of columns and rows. The smallest element in an image is a *pixel*, the intersection of a column and row. A bit-mapped image is made up of dots, which look smooth when running in a horizontal or vertical direction but which are jagged when forming arcs or diagonal lines. *Scaling*, or changing the size of a bit map, may result in distortion and an increased amount of jaggedness. Bit mapped file formats include GIF, BMP, and TIF.

♦ *Vector* graphics generate images mathematically, using shape and size in the calculations. A vector image is made up of lines rather than individual dots, resulting in a smoother look. Scaling a vector does not change the sharpness of the image. Vector file formats include CGM and PCX.

NOTE   Computer monitors display their contents in pixels. This means that art programs producing vector graphics must convert them to bit maps for onscreen display. However, vector images generally look better than bit maps.

Formats for Graphics Files

Through the years, software developers have produced many graphics file formats—many times designed to work on a computer or printer manufactured by a particular company or group of companies. As a result, most popular art programs support many formats. Simply draw or paint a picture using a program with which you are comfortable and save the file using almost any format. Table 1.1 shows the formats supported by the programs featured in this book. For more information about a particular format, see the chapter devoted to the program that supports it.

Graphics for the World Wide Web

Because the best Web pages load quickly, the best graphic formats support small files. The two formats that currently meet the small-file criteria are JPEG and GIF.

Developed by the Joint Photographic Experts Group, JPEG, or JPG, is the best format for photographic or near-photographic 24-bit images (that is, images that can use up to 16,777,216 different colors). JPEG files compress very efficiently and lose very little image quality. However, whenever you save and/or compress a JPEG file, it loses slightly more quality. Also, you cannot currently animate a series of JPEG files.

Table 1.1 Graphic Formats Supported by Popular Graphic and Animation Programs

Program	Reads These Formats	Writes to These Formats
Microsoft Image Composer	.GIF, .ACC, .BMP, .JPG, .MIC, .PSD, .TGA, .TIF	.GIF, .BMP, .JPG, .MIC, .PSD, .TGA, .TIF
Microsoft GIF Animator	.GIF, .AVI	.GIF
Paint Shop Pro	.GIF, .BMP, .CDR, .CGM, .CLP, .CMX, .CUT, .DIB, .DRW, .DXF, .GEM, .HGL, .IFF, .IMG, .JIF, .JPG, .LBM, .MAC, .MSP, .PBM, .PCD, .PCT, .PCX, .PGM, .PIC, .PNG, .PPM, .PSD, .RAS, .RAW, .RLE, .TGA, .TIF, .WMF, .WPG	.GIF, .BMP, .CLP, .CUT, .DIB, .EPS, .IFF, .IMG, .JIF, .JPG, .LBM, .MAC, .MPS, .PBM, .PCT, .PCX, .PGM, .PIC, .PNG, .PPM, .PSD, .RAS, .RAW, .RLE, .TGA, .TIF, .WMF, .WPG
GIF Construction Set	.GIF, .ART, .BMP, .CUT, .HRZ, .IFF, .IMG, .JPG, .LBM, .MAC, .PCX, .PIC, .PNG, .RAS, .RLE, .TGA, .WPG	.GIF
Adobe Photoshop	.GIF, .AI, .AI*, .BMP, .EPS, .FLM, .ICB, .JPE, .JPG, .PCD, .PCT, .PCX, .PDD, .PDF, .PIC, .PNG, .PSD, .PXR, .RAW, .RLE, .SCT, .TGA, .TIF, .VDA, .VST	.GIF, .BMP, .EPS, .ICB, .JPE, .JPG, .PCT, .PCX, .PDD, .PDF, .PIC, .PNG, .PSD, .PXR, .RAW, .RLE, .SCT, .TGA, .TIF, .VDA, .VST
Adobe Illustrator	.GIF, .AI, .BMP, .CDR, .CGM, .CMX, .DOC, .EPS, .FLM, .IFF, .JPG, .MAC, .PCD, .PCT, .PCX, .PDD, .PDF, .PNG, .PSD, .PXR, .RLE, .RTF, .TGA, .TIF, .TXT, .WMF, .WP7, .WPG	.GIF, .AI, .BMP, .CDR, .CGM, .CMX, .DOC, .EPS, .FLM, .IFF, .JPG, .MAC, .PCD, .PCT, .PCX, .PDD, .PDF, .PNG, .PSD, .PXR, .RLE, .RTF, .TGA, .TIF, .TXT, .WMF, .WP7, .WPG
CorelDRAW	.GIF (imports), .AI (and imports), .BMP (imports), .CDR (and imports), .CDT, .CMX (and imports), .CPT (imports), .DOC (imports), .EMF (and imports), .EPS (and imports), JPG (imports), .PAT, .PRN (and imports), .PS (and imports), .RTF (imports), .TIF (imports), .TXT (imports), .WI (imports), .WMF (and imports), .WP7 (imports), .WPG (and imports)	.GIF (exports), .AI (and exports), .BMP (exports), .CDR (and exports), .CDT, .CMX (and exports), .CPT (exports), .DOC (exports), .EMF (and exports), .EPS (and exports), .HTM (exports), .JPG (exports), .PAT, .RTF (exports), .TIF (exports), .TTF (exports), .TXT (exports), .WI (exports), .WMF (and exports), .WP7 (exports), .WPG (and exports)
GIFBuilder	.GIF, .PCT, .TIF, .PSD, .PDD	.GIF

Most graphics on the Web are two-dimensional images using relatively few colors. For this reason, GIF (Graphics Interchange Format) is ideal: GIF files are 8-bit; that is, GIF images are limited to 256 colors. However, the GIF format provides many advantages:

◆ GIF files are small. Therefore, they will load quickly.

◆ You can specify colors that will become *transparent* on the Web page. (In other words, you can see part of the page underneath the transparent part of the graphic.) This means that, instead of every image having to be rectangular, you can insert irregularly shaped images on a Web page.

◆ A GIF can be *interlaced*; that is, it can appear on the page in stages. This means that visitors to your site can see the image as it loads rather than stare at a blank frame.

◆ You can insert comments that visitors to your site won't be able to see but that can help you when you want to edit the file in the future.

◆ GIF files are easy to edit.

◆ Most importantly—at least for the purposes of this book—you can animate a GIF file. An animation results from embedding several images within one file, defining transparency, specifying the amount of time between the display of the current image and the next, setting the number of times the images will be shown, and adjusting each image's location onscreen.

GIF History and Standards

The online service CompuServe developed GIF87a, the original GIF standard in 1987, and followed it with the improved GIF89a in 1989.

GIF87a supported the following:

◆ many images embedded within a single file (that is, animation)

◆ a range of 2 (black and white) to 256 (red-green-blue or RGB) colors

◆ the ability to interlace an image

◆ the ability to set the position of an image from the upper-left corner of the screen

◆ file compression, using the popular LZW (Lempel-Ziv-Welch) compression *algorithm* (set of computer instructions).

 NOTE Unisys Corporation owns the patent to the LZW algorithm. Most companies that use GIF LZW must license its use. However, online services, nonprofit organizations, and individual users can use GIF LZW without a license. CompuServe has made GIF royalty-free.

In addition to GIF87a features, GIF89a supports the following:

- the definition of a color that will become transparent when displayed
- a set delay between the display of the image following the current image
- nonreadable comments inserted within image files
- text displayed from within image files

PLANNING AN EFFECTIVE IMAGE FOR THE WEB

Creating a graphical image for Web animation involves several factors: selecting the best combination of colors, specifying dimensions of a reasonable size, setting an appropriate resolution, and using other techniques to keep the size of the file as small as possible. The best images load quickly and look good in most browser windows on most computers.

 NOTE In Chapter 2, you'll learn about other ways to reduce file size.

Selecting Colors

The starting point for planning an image is to choose a color *palette* (a set of colors) that results in the desired effect. Obviously, your best and safest bet is a black-and-white palette, which results in about the same effect, regardless of computer platform, monitor, or video card, and gives you the extra bonus of an extremely small file. (When you reduce the number of colors in an image, the size of the GIF file also decreases.) However, most people find a steady diet of black-and-white images somewhat boring.

The best choice is to select a palette that contains colors recognized by most browsers and computers that run the Windows and Macintosh operating systems. Although GIF files can use 256 colors, only 216 colors are common to both platforms. However, under most circumstances, 216 colors are enough. Figure 1.1 shows two three-color images created in Adobe Photoshop. The image on the left used a 216-color palette, and the one on the right used slightly different colors. Table 1.2 illustrates each color in the palette and provides its red-green-blue (RGB) value.

 SHORTCUT The LZW algorithm compresses each horizontal line in an image, so if you have the choice between an image with horizontal or vertical lines of varying colors, choose horizontal arrangements of colors.

On the CD-ROM disk, you will find 216-color palettes for Adobe Photoshop and Paint Shop Pro. The file names are **216color.aco** and **216color.pal**, respectively.

Figure 1.1 Two images—one with colors from a 216-color palette and the other with slightly different colors.

Table 1.2 The 216-Color Palette

Color	RGB Value	Color	RGB Value	Color	RGB Value	Color	RGB Value
■	0-0-0	■	51-153-0	■	153-0-0	■	204-153-0
■	0-0-51	■	51-153-51	■	153-0-51	■	204-153-51
■	0-0-102	■	51-153-102	■	153-0-102	■	204-153-102
■	0-0-153	■	51-153-153	■	153-0-153	■	204-153-153
■	0-0-204	■	51-153-204	■	153-0-204	■	204-153-204
■	0-0-255	■	51-153-255	■	153-0-255	■	204-153-255
■	0-51-0	■	51-204-0	■	153-51-0	■	204-204-0
■	0-51-51	■	51-204-51	■	153-51-51	■	204-204-51
■	0-51-102	■	51-204-102	■	153-51-102	■	204-204-102
■	0-51-153	■	51-204-153	■	153-51-153	■	204-204-153
■	0-51-204	■	51-204-204	■	153-51-204	■	204-204-204
■	0-51-255	■	51-204-255	■	153-51-255	■	204-204-255
■	0-102-0	■	51-255-0	■	153-102-0	■	204-255-0
■	0-102-51	■	51-255-51	■	153-102-51	■	204-255-51
■	0-102-102	■	51-255-102	■	153-102-102	■	204-255-102
■	0-102-153	■	51-255-153	■	153-102-153	■	204-255-153
■	0-102-204	■	51-255-204	■	153-102-204	■	204-255-204
■	0-102-255	■	51-255-255	■	153-102-255	■	204-255-255
■	0-153-0	■	102-0-0	■	153-153-0	■	255-0-0
■	0-153-51	■	102-0-51	■	153-153-51	■	255-0-51
■	0-153-102	■	102-0-102	■	153-153-102	■	255-0-102
■	0-153-153	■	102-0-153	■	153-153-153	■	255-0-153
■	0-153-204	■	102-0-204	■	153-153-204	■	255-0-204
■	0-153-255	■	102-0-255	■	153-153-255	■	255-0-255
■	0-204-0	■	102-51-0	■	153-204-0	■	255-51-0
■	0-204-51	■	102-51-51	■	153-204-51	■	255-51-51
■	0-204-102	■	102-51-102	■	153-204-102	■	255-51-102

Table 1.2 The 216-Color Palette (continued)

Color	RGB Value	Color	RGB Value	Color	RGB Value	Color	RGB Value
	0-204-153		102-51-153		153-204-153		255-51-153
	0-204-204		102-51-204		153-204-204		255-51-204
	0-204-255		102-51-255		153-204-255		255-51-255
	0-255-0		102-102-0		153-255-0		255-102-0
	0-255-51		102-102-51		153-255-51		255-102-51
	0-255-102		102-102-102		153-255-102		255-102-102
	0-255-153		102-102-153		153-255-153		255-102-153
	0-255-204		102-102-204		153-255-204		255-102-204
	0-255-255		102-102-255		153-255-255		255-102-255
	51-0-0		102-153-0		204-0-0		255-153-0
	51-0-51		102-153-51		204-0-51		255-153-51
	51-0-102		102-153-102		204-0-102		255-153-102
	51-0-153		102-153-153		204-0-153		255-153-153
	51-0-204		102-153-204		204-0-204		255-153-204
	51-0-255		102-153-255		204-0-255		255-153-255
	51-51-0		102-204-0		204-51-0		255-204-0
	51-51-51		102-204-51		204-51-51		255-204-51
	51-51-102		102-204-102		204-51-102		255-204-102
	51-51-153		102-204-153		204-51-153		255-204-153
	51-51-204		102-204-204		204-51-204		255-204-204
	51-51-255		102-204-255		204-51-255		255-204-255
	51-102-0		102-255-0		204-102-0		255-255-0
	51-102-51		102-255-51		204-102-51		255-255-51
	51-102-102		102-255-102		204-102-102		255-255-102
	51-102-153		102-255-153		204-102-153		255-255-153
	51-102-204		102-255-204		204-102-204		255-255-204
	51-102-255		102-255-255		204-102-255		255-255-255

Specifying Dimensions

Most Web images should be relatively small to limit file size, which affects loading speed. Figure 1.2 shows a default rule (<HR>) and five images of various sizes. The red rule measures 600 × 15 pixels based on the typical monitor resolution of 640 by 480. From left to right, the button is 25 × 25 pixels, the two-color square is 60 × 60 pixels, the three-color square is 120 × 120 pixels, and the rainbow rectangle is 150 × 200 pixels. With two exceptions, the files are 1 kilobyte in size. Because of the number of colors used, the multicolored square is 4 kilobytes. The rainbow rectangle is 2 kilobytes because of both the size of the figure and the number of colors. You can use the images in this figure to estimate the desired size of your images.

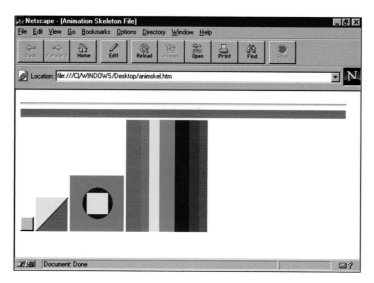

Figure 1.2 A browser window with five images.

Popular art programs offer several common units of measure. A measurement of one inch is equivalent to 2.54 centimeters, 72 points, 6 picas, 25.4 millimeters, or 90 pixels (at 640 × 480 resolution.)

Selecting Graphic Resolution

Some art programs allow you to set graphic resolution for an image. With two-dimensional images, setting a low resolution (for example, less than 100) can result in a small file size with no change in image quality. The final file size depends on the way that the program saves the file and the file format that you select.

Selecting a Color for Transparency

Without GIF89a's transparency feature, all images, including irregularly shaped ones, would either have a rectangular shape or appear on a rectangular background (Figure 1.3). Unless you are willing to match the background color of your Web page with the background color of the image to hide the rectangle, the look of the resulting nontransparent image could be amateurish.

The solution is to draw the image on a background color that you will make transparent either in the art program or in the animation program. If you are creating an image that you will not animate, use your art program's transparency option. But, if you will make the image part of an animation, wait until you are working with your animation program because animation programs do not necessarily recognize transparent colors set in an art program.

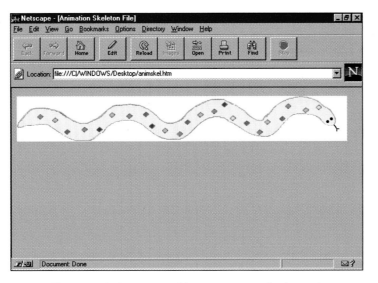

Figure 1.3 An image on a white nontransparent background.

If you will make part of an image transparent, it's very important to carefully choose the color that will become transparent before you draw or paint the first stroke. Choose a color that is in the animation program's color palette (Figure 1.4) but will not be one of the colors used in the image. For example, if you create an black oval sign with white text and you choose white as the transparent color, the text will also be transparent. A better choice is a primary clear color such as red (255-0-0), blue (0-0-255), green (0-255-0), yellow (255-255-0), cyan (0-255-255), or magenta (255-0-255). If you choose a color with a background pattern or dots, you won't know its exact red-green-blue code. Figure 1.5 shows an image with a transparent background.

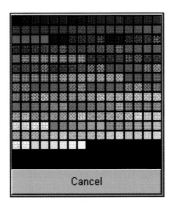

Figure 1.4 The GIF Construction Set's 216-color palette.

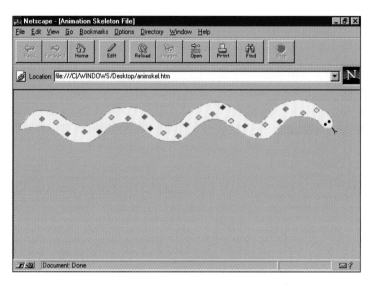

Figure 1.5 An image with a transparent background.

DRAWING OR PAINTING AN IMAGE

The methods that you use to create an image depend heavily on your art program, which has its own unique features and functions. In general, the more feature-laden the program is, the better results you will have. However, even the most inexpensive programs can produce excellent images—especially if you plan and design using the information provided earlier in this chapter.

Of course, you are better off with a certain amount of artistic ability and imagination. But it's amazing what an amateur artist can do with a set of geometric shapes arranged in a particular order as well as a willingness to spend time editing an image zoomed in to the pixel level.

Perhaps the most important tip is to keep your images simple. Why take the extra time to construct, add details to, and edit an image loaded with many colors and details when a plainer image will look just as good and get the same positive reaction from the visitors to your site?

OBTAINING IMAGES FROM OTHER SOURCES

Scanners, screen capture programs, movie frames, and clip art can produce good-looking images, which you can edit to make them unique.

Scanning Images

You can scan images from within most art programs. To use a scanner, you must define it to the art program. Then, start your scanner program by issuing commands from within the art program. Scanned images can be quite large, so consider saving each image as a GIF file before you edit it in your art program's work area. Because saving as a GIF compresses the file and usually decreases the number of colors, you'll have a realistic view of the image before you start editing.

 NOTE   When you scan an image into Adobe Photoshop, Photoshop creates a special 256-color indexed-color table, which will not match the typical 216-color table but may allow you to apply a variety of subtle shadings to the image. In fact, the colors can even be in the same color family (for example, golds and yellows). You can also use indexed color mode on images created in Photoshop. For more information, refer to the *Adobe Photoshop User Guide*.

OBSERVING COPYRIGHT LAWS

When you scan an image or when you use an image or animation downloaded from the Internet, you may be infringing a copyright. The Copyright Act of the United States is a long and complex code that protects creative artists from infringement of their works. This sidebar presents only a few of the important elements of the code.

Note that:

◆   All original and creative pictorial and graphic works of art, including those created on a computer, are copyrightable. Works that are not considered to be original and creative are common property (for example, hardware, rulers, calendars, and so on).

◆   The creator of the original work automatically has a copyright at the time of creation.

◆   The owner of a copyright can distribute or display his or her work as he or she wishes.

◆   In general, copyrighted works created on or after January 1, 1978, are protected for the lifetime of the creator plus 50 years after the creator's death. In general, copyrighted works created before January 1, 1978, are protected for 28 years renewable for an additional 28 or 47 years, with a maximum of 75 years.

◆   To protect his or her work, the creator should place a copyright notice on his or her work at the first publication. Works published before March 1, 1989, must include a copyright notice.

◆   You may be infringing a copyrighted work if that work is copyrighted in a foreign country.

To avoid infringing a copyrighted work, ask yourself this question: If the original and edited versions of a work appear side by side, can an individual tell that the edited version is related in any way to the original? If so, the copier is probably infringing on the original.

Copyright law is very complex—with many provisions and exceptions. For more copyright information, consult your attorney and check these Internet sites:

The United States Copyright Office (**http://lcweb.loc.gov/copyright**), which provides many links to copyright information

The Copyright Act of the United States (**http://www.law.cornell.edu/uscode/17/**), which includes the full text of the act, updated through July 1996

Nolo's Legal Encyclopedia for Copyright Law (**http://www.nolo.com/ChunkPCT/PCT.index.html#3**), which includes links to frequently asked questions (FAQs), articles, information about books, and other copyright resources on the Internet.

Capturing Images

You can electronically capture images displayed on your computer screen by using a screen-capture program. When you capture an image, the program automatically saves it in a file using one of the popular file formats. For example, Collage Capture, the program used to capture Windows-based figures and graphics for this book, supports .GIF, .BMP, .DCX, .JPG, .PCX, .PCT, .TGA, .TIF, .WMF, and .WPG formats.

Some computer systems have built-in screen-capture capabilities.

You can copy the contents of the screen into the Windows Clipboard by pressing the **Print Screen** key. Then choose **Edit: Paste** or press **Ctrl+V** to paste the contents of the Windows Clipboard into the current image window.

You can copy the contents of the screen to a PICT file named Picture **n** (where **n** represents a number higher than that of the previous Picture file) by pressing **Command+Shift+3**.

You can copy the active window, active dialog box, or entire screen by pressing **Alt+Print Screen**. Then choose **Edit: Paste** or press **Ctrl+V** to paste the contents of the clipboard into the current image window.

Using Clip Art

You can either scan clip art or open clip art files in an art program and edit them as you wish. If you use copyright-free images, you won't have to worry about infringing on other people's work.

Using Frames from Movies

Some art programs allow you to import frames from movies or videos onto a computer. After you import a series of frames, you can edit them as you wish and then save them as GIF files. A major advantage of importing movie frames is that they lend themselves to use in GIF animations.

Creating an Animation

At its best, a GIF animation is a very small but recognizable relative of animated films. Both animated films and GIF animations are composed of frames of static images. When run, the frames simulate motion. Theoretically, GIF animations can be as long as an animated film. Realistically, GIF animations should consist of a few frames, to allow for fast movement of data from a server to your visitor's computer.

By definition, a GIF animation is a group of images inserted into a single GIF file. To add a GIF animation to an HTML document, use the <IMG> tag in exactly the same way that you would add any single-image GIF file. When an individual links to the page containing the animation, the page and its contents, including the animation, are downloaded from the server on which it is stored to the user's computer *cache* (that is, an area in which information is stored temporarily or, in the case of Web browsers, permanently—until you delete some or all of its contents). If the browser supports GIF animations, the animation shows movement. Otherwise, the first or last image in the animation appears onscreen.

 NOTE When a GIF animation is stored in your computer's cache, it can continue to play in your Web browser window until you exit the browser program whether or not you are connected to your Internet service provider.

As you learned in the Chapter 1, GIF87a and GIF89a provide all the tools for creating and fine-tuning GIF animations. The combined standards allow you not only to incorporate many images within a single file but also to define a transparent color, define the delay between frames, run the animation a certain number of times, change the position of an individual frame within the animation, and so on.

PLANNING AND DESIGNING AN ANIMATION

This section provides a checklist for planning and designing an animation.

Planning an Animation

The first step in the animation development cycle is determining the content, look, and size of the animation. You should consider the following factors when planning:

- To minimize file size, carefully choose the fewest number of colors, smallest height and width, and lowest resolution. Remember that many, if not most, of the visitors to your site will use computers running at relatively slow processing speeds with modems that transfer data at 14.4 baud. According to many animation experts, an animation file should not be larger than 70 kilobytes. Because animations can be composed of many image files, it can be very easy to reach 70 kilobytes and go well beyond.
- Estimate the number of frames in the animation.
- Unless the images making up the animation will be rectangular, decide on the color that will be transparent.
- Decide whether the animation will look best when running infinitely or a set number of times.
- Decide whether the animation will look better when run fast or slow.

Remember that you can look throughout this book for examples on which you can base your own animations. Also check the "Animation Effects" section at the end of this chapter for tips on creating various types of animations.

Designing an Animation

To design the animation, make a storyboard of each frame as you would a cartoon or short animated film. Draw a rough image of each frame with pencil or pen on paper.

- Demonstrate in each frame how you will show motion. Do you have to actually move elements of the image? Will color changes indicate movement?
- Can you take advantage of features in your art program to create motion effects automatically? For example, can the program rotate, flip, scale, distort, or resize images or selections?
- Can you simplify each frame by reducing the number of colors or removing extraneous elements?
- Can you reuse any of the frames in the animation?
- Can you animate small image files on a larger static background or will you have to use a series of same-size image files?
- Try to make sure that the first and last frames include good static images for display on browsers that do not support GIF animations.

CREATING AN ANIMATION

With your art program, create images, or frames, for the animation. For information on using the art programs featured in this book, refer to:

- Chapter 3 "Working with Microsoft Image Composer and Microsoft GIF Animator"
- Chapter 4 "Working with Paint Shop Pro"
- Chapter 6 "Working with Adobe Photoshop"
- Chapter 7 "Working with Adobe Illustrator"
- Chapter 8 "Working with CorelDRAW"

Working on the First Frame

The first frame of an animation is the most important, because it is the basis for the remaining frames. So, use your checklist and storyboard to select the colors and dimensions. If you have any questions about image creation basics, refer to Chapter 1.

NOTE As you will learn in the "Animating Part of an Image" section later in the chapter, you don't always have to work with the same dimensions throughout an animation. Sometimes, you can reduce the size of a file by working with a small moving area on a larger static background. When you produce this type of animation, the first frame should include the background, which means that that frame will be wider, higher, or both.

After you complete the first frame, save the file:

- Select a name that is a memory jogger. If you create many animations, you want to be able to identify a specific file so that you can find it a few weeks or months after you create it.
- Use an eight-character, or less, name to allow for animation programs that do not support long file names.
- Use identical characters at the start of the file name to ensure that all the files in the animation will be located in the same location in the folder in which it will be stored.
- At the end of the file name, make room for two digits, starting with *01* (for example, **hzrule01** or **smile01**), to allow for a maximum of 99 total frames. Obviously, most animations will not and should not be composed of 99 frames, but one digit would limit you to nine frames, which is inadequate for most animations. However, if you know that an animation will be composed of nine frames or less, you can ignore this suggestion

SHORTCUT If your animation will be composed of 26 or fewer frames, consider file names that end with letters of the alphabet (for example, **redcirca**, **redcircb**, and so on).

- If you can save the file in the GIF file format, do so. Then, you will see whether saving it as a GIF file has changed its appearance in any way. If you are prompted to interlace the file, choose **No**, or clear an Interlace checkbox.

Adding Frames

Most animations build on the first frame. The remaining frames usually use the same dimensions, color palette, and so on. So, after creating the first frame, the easiest way to start on the next is to choose **File: Save As** and make a copy of the first frame using the next filename in the series (for example, **hzrule02**).

In the new file, incorporate the changes that will show a little movement. Save the file and again choose **File: Save As** to make a copy of the file, giving the copy the next name in the series (for example, **hzrule03**).

SHORTCUT   If you think that there's a possibility that you will need to add intermediate files to smooth out the action, number the original files, leaving a gap. For example, you can use the end numbers 02, 04, 06, and so on. Even if you don't allow for in-between files, you can always renumber them later.

Create the remaining frames, continuing to edit for motion and saving using sequential file names. If you can display all the images in the art program's work area, do so. Arrange the frames in the order in which they will be animated and view them carefully, looking for drawing or painting errors and deciding whether you need to add or remove frames to ensure the most appropriate motion from frame to frame. After editing, save as needed.

MANUFACTURING THE GIF ANIMATION

With your GIF animation program, create the animation. You can preview the animation and individual frames before or after you select looping, timing, transparency, and other options. Expect to preview and change the options several times.

When you preview an animation and its frames:

- Judge the quality of movement. Jerky movement might mean that you'll have to insert in-between frames. If an animation moves smoothly and slowly, you may have to increase the speed or remove frames.

- Judge the speed of the animation. A fast speed will not allow visitors to see every detail of an animation. A slow speed can drag the animation. Note that speeding up an animation will not correct jerky movement and may even emphasize flaws in the images.

- If the animation is composed of irregularly shaped images, can you see a rectangular area behind any of the frames? This means that you should select a transparent color.

- Look for flickering in the animation. This might indicate an unplanned difference between frames. Even a single missing or extra pixel in one frame can cause an unwanted flicker. However, sometimes a flicker is a good effect. For example, if you want your animation to simulate an old movie, built-in flicker and other flaws can work well.

- Look for mistakes in individual frames. If you find color outside the image itself, you may have to edit a frame within the art program.

When an animation looks just right, save it. If you want the animation and its component files stored together in the same folder, remove the digits from the end of the file name but keep the first few characters. It's a good idea to keep both the frame and animation files for future editing.

For information on using the GIF animation programs featured in this book, refer to:

- Chapter 3 "Working with Microsoft Image Composer and Microsoft GIF Animator"
- Chapter 5 "Working with GIF Construction Set"
- Chapter 9 "Working with GIFBuilder"

INSERTING AN ANIMATION IN AN HTML DOCUMENT

To insert a GIF animation in an HTML document, use the <IMG> tag just as you would to insert a single static image. For example, the small HTML document used to test animations for this book follows:

```
<!DOCTYPE HTML PUBLIC "-//W3C//DTD HTML 3.2//EN">
<HTML>
<HEAD>
<TITLE>Animation Skeleton File</TITLE>
</HEAD>
<BODY BGCOLOR="silver">
<IMG SRC="rotball.gif">
</BODY>
</HTML>
```

The <IMG SRC="rotball.gif"> line inserts the file **rotball.gif** in the HTML document. If you look at this document in a browser window, the animation will be in the upper-left corner of the screen.

The <BODY BGCOLOR="silver"> line defines the body of the HTML document and sets the background color to silver. A silver background allows visual checking for transparency.

For more information about HTML, see *HTML in Plain English*, a reference handbook also by Sandra E. Eddy and published by MIS:Press.

TESTING AN ANIMATION

You don't have to wait to complete an animation before testing individual frames. In fact, it's better to test early—before you have created a complete set of frames. For example, if you want to evaluate your choice of colors or the overall look of the first image in an animation, view it using at least two Web browsers.

Running an animation from within a Web browser gives you a preview of what the visitors to your page will see. You can ensure that the animation runs smoothly, looks good, and doesn't reveal any surprises. At minimum, test your animation using Netscape Navigator and Microsoft Internet Explorer, the most popular browsers. If you can run the animation on two or more computers, you'll be able to see the effects of different monitors and video cards.

If the animation fails, you may have to return all the way to the art program. But, considering the number of individuals who might view your animation, it's better to aim for perfection than compromise on quality.

GIF ANIMATION PROGRAMS

Whatever your computer platform, you can find a program with which you can animate GIF files. Table 2.1 lists selected programs. Each entry in the table includes the home page URL of the developer and the platform.

Table 2.1 GIF Animation Programs

Program	Home Page	Platform(s)/Comments
Animagic GIF Animator	http://www.rtlsoft.com/animagic/	Windows
Cel Assembler	http://www.gamani.com/tools/	Windows
Formula Graphics	http://www.harrow.com.au/formula/	Windows
GIF Animator	http://www.microsoft.com/imagecomposer/gifanimator/gifanin.htm	Windows
GIFBuilder	http://www.pascal.com/mirrors/gifbuilder/	Macintosh
GIF Construction Set	http://www.mindworkshop.com/alchemy/gifcon.html	Windows
GIF Converter	http://www.kamit.com/gifconverter.html	Macintosh
Gif.glf.giF	http://www.peda.com/ggg	Windows, Macintosh
GIFmation	http://nergal.boxtopsoft.com/GIFmation/	Macintosh
GIFMerge	http://www.iis.ee.ethz.ch/~Kiwi/GIFMerge/	Sun, SGI, UNIX, OS/2, Atari, DOS, Windows
GIF Wizard	http://www.raspberryhill.com/gifwizard.html	Windows, Macintosh
gifx	http://www.interdim.com/	Windows, Macintosh
Giffy Animation Builder	http://www.web-ready.com/cgiffy.html	Windows

Program	Home Page	Platform(s)/Comments
Image Magick	**http://www.wizards.dupont.com/cristy/ ImageMagick.html**	UNIX, Linux, Windows, Macintosh, VMS
MainActor	**http://www.mainconcept.de/products/index.html**	Windows, Amiga, OS/2
Micrografx Simply 3D	**http://www.micrografx.com/products/ products.html**	Windows
MultiGIF	**http://www.peritas.com/~abw/code/multigif.html**	Many platforms
Net Animator™	**http://www.hypno.net/web/netanim.html**	Macintosh, Windows (11/97)
Smart Dubbing	**http://www.xs4all.nl/~polder**	Macintosh
Ulead (PhotoImpact) GIF Animator	**http://www.ulead.com/products/ga_main.htm**	Windows
VideoCraft GIF Animator	**http://www.andatech.com/vidcraft/index.html**	Windows
Web Image	**http://www.group42.com/webimage.htm**	Windows
WebPaint	**http://www.barentsnett.no/webpaint/english.html**	Windows
WebPainter	**http://www.totallyhip.com/**	Macintosh, Windows
WhirlGIF	**http://www.msg.net/utility/whirlgif/**	Many platforms
WebImage	**http://www.group42.com/webimage.htm**	Windows
WWW Gif Animator	**http://stud1.tuwien.ac.at/~e8925005/**	Windows

ANIMATION EFFECTS

This final section of the chapter discusses and illustrates commonly used animation techniques—including the pitfalls and shortcuts.

Rotating an Object

To complete an animation of a rotating object, you will rotate it 360 degrees around a center point. Based on a 360-degree rotation, the last frame in the rotation should look the same as the first frame. This means that you can eliminate the last frame altogether. Depending on how smooth you want the animation to run, the number of degrees in each step of the rotation can vary widely. The number of degrees in each step should divide evenly into 360 (for example, 10, 12, 24, 30, 36, and so on). Most art programs enable you to rotate an object a set number of degrees. Unfortunately, many art programs rotate unevenly. The center of the object does not stay in the exact center of the image window. So, you may have to move some objects until they are centered. If the art program shows x and y coordinates of particular locations onscreen, you can match coordinate values for every frame. Otherwise, you might have to "eyeball" it. Both the rotating beach ball in Chapter 3 and the cool faucet in Chapter 6 demonstrate rotation.

Flipping an Object

Most art programs allow you to flip objects from side to side or from top to bottom and back again. To produce the best looking flip, you may have to create one or more intermediate frames to show the transition from one side of the flip to the other. Fortunately, you can reuse these in-between frames when flipping the object back to its starting position. The following frames are from the **padrule.gif** animation. All but the first and middle frames are used twice. When you look at this animation it appears to revolve.

Revolving an Object

Other than finding an art program that revolves objects (usually three-dimensional) around a vertically or horizontally aligned axis, there are two ways to make an object revolve. One is to flip the object either top to bottom or left to right. Then, add in-between objects as described in the previous section.

The other method is time-consuming and often requires meticulous pixel-by-pixel work. Here you create a static background image and then add a foreground image that you will move in stages across or between the top and bottom of the background image, saving a new frame after each movement. As you move the foreground image, erase any pixels that are beyond the boundaries of the background image. Art programs such as Adobe Photoshop and Adobe Illustrator, which allow you to work with layers, are ideal for revolving objects. You can edit an image on one layer without disturbing other layers. The following graphics are frames from the **pencil.gif** animation. The time delay for the blank pencil's display should be three times longer than for other frames. This simulates three movements of the pencil before the text is revealed again.

Building on Text

If you want to build a word or phrase character by character, start with the complete word or phrase, save the file, remove a character, save the file using the last file name in the series, remove the next character, save the file, and so on. Save the last "characterless" file using the first file name in the series. You can also reverse the procedure in order to remove a word or phrase one character at a time. You'll find two versions of the example file, **newpappr.gif** and **newmappr.gif**, on the CD-ROM disk.

For a different effect, you can apply a thin layer of paint over the character that you are removing and save two or three versions of the file as the letter gradually fades away or appears.

Changing Colors

A very easy animation method is to change the background color or pattern of an image while keeping the foreground the same. Every time you change the background, save a new file.

You can also change both the background and the foreground. For example, if you are using text in the foreground, you can change its color or size, gradually fade it into the background, or even change the font for an interesting animation.

You can also use the color-changing effect in a black-and-white animation. In one frame, insert black text on a white background; in the second frame, change the black text to white and the background to black.

The example animation, **fluornew.gif**, is on the CD-ROM disk.

 If you intend to use many colors in this type of animation and if the images are not rectangles, be sure to reserve a color for transparency. Then, do not use that color in the animation.

Flickering Images

Flickering images are like an exaggerated version of a clear night sky. Dots of colors (or white simulated stars) appear randomly in each frame of an animation. Creating this animation involves zooming in and working at the pixel level. Bright colors or white work best in this effect. The example animation, **colordot.gif**, is on the CD-ROM disk.

In a related animation, you can animate fireworks. On a black or dark blue background, create a fireworks image. For the first frame, place a dot of color. In subsequent frames, drag the dot in an arc toward the top of the frame. At the top of the arc, start adding downward arcs to the dot. With the next frames, increase the length of each arc. Finally, gradually erase portions all the arcs, until the background is empty. You can copy and paste copies of the fireworks image to other parts of the sky. To get the best effect, change the color of each copied image.

Fading In

You can simulate a fade-in effect by creating the foreground of the first frame with a setting somewhere between opacity and transparency. The light application of paint will allow you to see some, but not all, of the background through the foreground image. Save the frame, increase the level of opacity, and paint the image with a new layer of paint set at a higher opacity. Continue to create new frames, increasing the opacity each time. You can also reverse the process by animating the files from the last to the first.

In this example, the telltale yellow circle fades in, followed by the eyes and smile.

If you select colors carefully, you can change colors of the foreground image from light to dark. However, if you plan on using white as the transparent color, fading will result in a white halo around the circumference of the yellow circle. To resolve the problem, you'll have to edit all the pixels between the circle and the background.

Fading Out

To produce fade-out animation, use the **Spray Paint** tool and the color that will be transparent. In the first frame, start with a sharp image. In the next frame, spray the center of the image, using a big brush, and save the file. Repeat in subsequent files until the image completely disappears. If needed, paint or fill the last image to make sure that all traces of non-transparent paint have been removed. This is a good example for displaying all the frames on the computer screen so that you can determine whether to delete in-between images that don't fade enough.

 NOTE Adobe Photoshop enables you to fade an object automatically using options in the Airbrush Options palette. To fade out, check the **Fade** check box, type the number of steps before a complete fade-out, and then either select **Transparent** or **Background**.

Animating Rigid and Flexible Objects

Rigid objects do not change shape when they bounce off a frame border. However, flexible objects flatten slightly under the same circumstances. To flatten an object, select a scaling command and move both the top and the bottom (if the object will bounce off the top or bottom of the frame) or the left and the right (if the bounce is off the left or right side). The bouncing ball, *bounball.gif*, in Chapter 6 shows how a flexible object bounces.

If you flatten an object too much, it will look as though it is revolving.

Showing Speed

One way of indicating speed in an object is to use a smudge or smear tool to drag color beyond the borders of the object away from the direction in which the object is moving. The longer the smear, the faster the object appears to be speeding. You can also blur the entire image to indicate speed.

Smearing an object demonstrates the importance of selecting a transparent color that will not be a part of any frame. For example, if white is your transparent color and white is part of the frame that you want to smear, the smeared area may show a large smudge of white when you run the animation. When you plan a "speed" animation, be extremely careful in choosing your transparent color. Smearing can also introduce a color that is not part of the 216-color palette, which may produce strange-looking results.

If an object is rectangular, you can skew it slightly so that the top front of the object is slightly ahead of the bottom front. This makes the object appear to lean into its speed—just as many runners lean forward as they accelerate. The more forward action you want to indicate, the more you should skew.

You can also skew an object with the bottom front of the object slightly ahead to exaggerate the flattening caused by speed. If you actually flatten the image and blur it, the image will appear to move even more rapidly.

Dragging Objects to Animate

You can drag objects around a frame to indicate movement. Perhaps the easiest way to do this is to create an object and either copy or cut it to the Clipboard. Then, paste the object, and drag it to show movement. If you cut an object and your art program leaves a gap filled with the background color, you can either change the background color to match that of the surrounding area or fill the gaps using a fill tool or paintbrush.

It's important to display every frame in the work area while you are dragging to be able to compare the movement in a frame and its successor frame.

The apple tree animation in Chapter 3 is an example of dragging to animate. It was created in Microsoft Image Composer, which is ideal for this type of animation because its compositions are made up of individual sprites. Each apple in the animation is a separate sprite, which is dragged in stages down toward the bottom of the frame.

Animating Part of an Image

When an animation is going to be large and stretch the limits of file size and loading speed, consider animating part of the image instead of the entire thing. For example, you can rotate a small gear within a large rectangle holding the title of a manufacturing company, or you can animate smoke rising from the chimney of a static house.

When you create this type of animation, the first frame must include the static part of the image. It can also include the first image in the animation, or you can start the animation in the second frame.

A major consideration in producing a "partial" animation is placing it against the static background. Unless the "partial" animation is in the upper-left corner of the frame, you must offset it by a certain number of pixels vertically, horizontally, or both, in your animation program.

For example, you can animate a 600×7 rule by accumulating small diamonds along its length. You can either build the animation in the usual way by creating a series of files in which you insert a new diamond next to the previously inserted diamond until you reach the end of the rule or use the rule as a static background and repeatedly insert a second file containing the diamond, offsetting it by a higher horizontal value each time you insert it. In our example, the diamond file is inserted 121 times and is offset by 5 pixels horizontally (that is, 0, 5, 10, 15, and so on, with the last file offset by 600). Because the diamond is the same height as the rule, there is no need to offset vertically. Although building the animation is time-consuming, it's much easier than creating 121 separate rules with dots. You'll find the example file, **bdotrule.gif**, on the CD-ROM disk.

Rotoscoping an Animation

Max Fleischer was the co-founder of the Fleischer Studios, the home of Betty Boop, Popeye the Sailor, and many other characters. Not only was Fleischer a well-known early cartoonist but he also developed timesaving animation techniques. Perhaps his most famous invention was rotoscoping, which remains a valuable technique today. Basically, rotoscoping starts with a live-action film, which is projected, one frame at a time, onto a cartoonist's drawing table. The cartoonist traces an image from a live-action frame, and saves it as an original frame. He or she continues this process until all the desired frames are "traced over." For example, the following horses were rotoscoped from a series of 25 black-and-white photographs taken by Edweard Muybridge, a pioneer in animal and human motion studies. Each photograph was opened in Adobe Photoshop, painted in two colors, scaled down, placed in a white square 1.5 × 1.5 inches, and saved.

Walking a Character

To be effective in animating people and animals, you must master the art of showing actions such as walking and running. If you are not a professional artist, the easiest way to do this is by rotoscoping and editing heavily to avoid copyright infringement. However, if you study walking and running movements as well as books on animation, you may be able to translate these movements to your characters. You can "walk" all characters—human and animal—in the same way.

To show running, simply lengthen the stride and speed up the frames.

Showing Facial Emotion

Showing emotion in GIF animations is very difficult for many artists—both professional and amateur—because one facial expression, for example, can show a variety of emotions. Think of the number of different smiles that you can see in a single day. Add to that the many degrees of sadness, anger, greed, and so on, as well as efforts to hide emotions. To indicate powerful emotions, the best route is to exaggerate.

You can animate a range of emotions, from start to finish:

and

Working with Microsoft Image Composer and Microsoft GIF Animator

3

With Microsoft Image Composer, you can create compositions, which are images made up of sprites. Sprites, which are Image Composer's smallest image objects, are composed of transparent and nontransparent pixels. You can make compositions from several sources: you can create sprites from scratch in Image Composer, import images from other art programs or libraries of images, or scan images into Image Composer. Image Composer is a superior art-creation and -editing program. Because it is a Windows-based program, Image Composer allows you to copy, move, and paste sprites, and undo your actions using familiar buttons and Edit menu commands. In addition, the user interface will also be familiar to those who run a Windows PC. Image Composer's extensive help system also includes a tutorial.

Image Composer reads from and writes to the following commonly used drawing file types: TIFF (.TIF), CompuServe GIF (.GIF), Targa (.TGA), JPEG (.JPG), Windows BMP (.BMP), Adobe Photoshop (.PSD), and Microsoft Image Composer (.MIC); Image Composer reads from but does not write to the Altamira Composer (.ACC) file type. Image Composer also supports *plug-ins* (programs, utilities, or libraries that can add features to the current program), such as Impressionist, Kai's Power Tools, and Adobe Photoshop filters.

STARTING IMAGE COMPOSER

To start Microsoft Image Composer, follow these steps:

1. Click on the **Start** button and select **Programs**. Windows opens the Programs menu.
2. Move the mouse pointer over Microsoft Image Composer. Windows opens a submenu.
3. Click on **Image Composer**. The Image Composer window (Figure 3.1) opens with the default Arrange tool palette at the bottom.

SHORTCUT   If you have created a shortcut icon on your desktop for Image Composer, double-click on it to start the program.

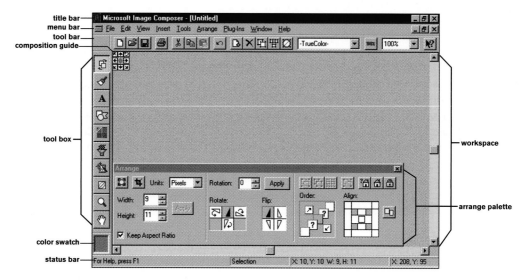

Figure 3.1 The Image Composer window with the default Arrange tool palette and a composition.

THE IMAGE COMPOSER WINDOW

The Image Composer window contains a variety of elements; many are familiar to Windows users, but some require more explanation.

The Title Bar and Menu Bar

The Image Composer title bar and menu bar are standard Windows elements. The title bar includes the name of the program and the current saved file. The menu bar contains menus from which you select commands with which you can perform actions. When you open a menu and highlight a command, Image Composer displays a short description of the command in the status bar at the bottom of the window. Image Composer also contains *context menus,* which contain commands associated with objects on the desktop. To use a context menu, right-click on an object to open the menu, move the mouse pointer to the desired command, and left-click to select the command.

The Toolbar

Below the menu bar is the toolbar, which contains some standard Windows buttons and some buttons and drop-down list boxes that are unique to Image Composer.

 New–Click on this button to start a new composition. This is equivalent to choosing **File: New** or pressing **Ctrl+N**.

Open—Click on this button to open an existing composition file. This is equivalent to choosing **File: Open** or pressing **Ctrl+O**.

Save—Click on this button to save the current composition. This is equivalent to choosing **File: Save** or pressing **Ctrl+S**) or choosing **File: Save As**.

Print—Click on this button to print the current composition file. This is equivalent to choosing **File: Print** or pressing **Ctrl+P**.

Cut—Click on this button to remove the selected sprite or composition and place it in the Windows Clipboard. This is equivalent to choosing **Edit: Cut**, right-clicking and selecting **Cut** from the context menu, or pressing **Ctrl+X**. If this button is dimmed, you have not selected an object.

Copy—Click on this button to copy the selected sprite or composition into the Windows Clipboard. This is equivalent to choosing **Edit: Copy**, right-clicking and selecting **Copy** from the context menu, or pressing **Ctrl+C**. If this button is dimmed, you have not selected an object.

Paste—Click on this button to paste the contents of the Windows Clipboard at the current location in the composition. This is equivalent to choosing **Edit: Paste** or pressing **Ctrl+V**. If this button is dimmed, the Windows Clipboard is empty.

Undo—Click on this button to undo the most recent action. This is equivalent to choosing **Edit: Undo** or pressing **Ctrl+Z**. If this button is dimmed, you have not performed an action or you can't undo the action.

Insert Image File—Click on this button to insert a file at the current location in the composition. This is equivalent to choosing **Insert: From File**.

Delete—Click on this button to remove the selected sprite or composition permanently. This is equivalent to choosing **Edit: Delete** or pressing the **Del** key. If this button is dimmed, you have not selected an object.

Duplicate—Click on this button to add a duplicate of the selected sprite to the composition without placing it in the Windows Clipboard first. This is equivalent to choosing **Edit: Duplicate** or pressing **Ctrl+D**. If this button is dimmed, you have not selected an object.

Select All—Click on this button to select all the sprites. This is equivalent to choosing **Edit: Select All** or pressing **Ctrl+A**.

Clear Selection—Click on this button to "deselect" all the selected sprites. This is equivalent to choosing **Edit: Clear Selection** or pressing **Ctrl+T**.

| -TrueColor- ▼ |

Color Format—Open this drop-down list box to change the color format for the contents of the current window. You can choose **TrueColor** (the default), **Balanced Ramp**, **Gray Ramp**, or **Black and White**. For more information about Image Composer default and custom color palettes, refer to "The Color Swatch" section later in this chapter.

Actual Size—Click on this button to display the current composition at its actual size. This is equivalent to choosing **View: Actual Size** or right-clicking on the background of the composition and choosing **Actual Size**. You will learn more about zooming and its effects in the "Zooming the Composition Guide" later in this chapter.

| 100% ▼ |

Zoom Percent—Open this drop-down list box to change the size of the current composition onscreen. (This does not change the actual dimensions of the composition.) You can select from 10% to 1000% of the actual size. You will learn more about zooming and its effects in the "Zooming the Composition Guide" later in this chapter.

Help–Click on this button and then click on an object onscreen to display context-sensitive help about that object or the help window. This is equivalent to pressing **Shift+F1**. You can open the help window by choosing **Help: Microsoft Image Composer Help Topics** or by pressing **F1**. To "deselect" context-sensitive help, either click on the **Help** button again or press **Esc**.

Learning More About Toolbars

Image Composer button bars, such as the toolbar and the toolbox (described in the following section), have certain common characteristics.

◆ When you move the mouse pointer over a toolbar or toolbox button, Image Composer displays a ToolTip, a small yellow box that states the name of the button and, in the status bar at the bottom of the window, displays a brief explanation of the button.

◆ You can change the location or dimensions of the toolbar or toolbox by pointing to an area of the toolbar above, below, or next to a button or drop-down list box and dragging.

◆ You can move the toolbar to the left side, bottom, or middle of the window; and you can move the toolbox anywhere in the window. If you move the toolbar or toolbox away from the sides of the window, it floats.

◆ You can drag a floating toolbar around by its title bar.

◆ You can change the size of a floating toolbar by pointing to an edge of the toolbar and, when the mouse pointer changes to a double-pointed arrow, dragging the edge and releasing the mouse button when the toolbar is the desired size.

The Elements of the Floating Toolbar

Occasionally, when you "float" a toolbar, some buttons replace others (Figure 3.2).

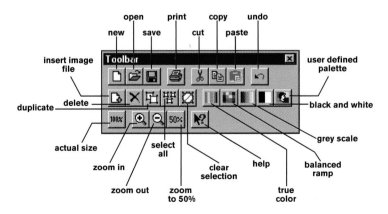

Figure 3.2 Image Composer's floating toolbar replaces drop-down list boxes with buttons.

In the Image Composer floating toolbar, the following buttons replace the drop-down list boxes in the default fixed toolbar.

True Color–Click on this button (the default) to change the color format for the contents of the current window to the True Color palette, which uses the red, green, and blue colors from your video card.

Balanced Ramp–Click on this button to change the color format for the contents of the current window to the Balanced Ramp palette, which is a default custom color palette.

Gray Scale–Click on this button to change the color format for the contents of the current window to the Grayscale palette, which is a palette made up of white, various grays, and black.

Black and White–Click on this button to change the color format for the contents of the current window to the Black and White palette.

User Defined Palette–Click on this button to change the color format for the contents of the current window to a custom user-defined palette.

> **NOTE** For more information about Image Composer default and custom color palettes, refer to "The Color Swatch" section later in this chapter.

Zoom In–Click on this button, choose **View: Zoom In**, right-click on the background of the composition and choose **Zoom In**, or press the plus sign (**+**) on the numeric keypad to magnify or zoom in on the composition. Zooming in allows you to see the details of a composition, but sometimes not the entire composition.

Zoom Out–Click on this button, choose **View: Zoom Out**, right-click on the background of the composition and choose **Zoom Out**, or press the minus sign (**-**) on the numeric keypad to reduce the viewing size or zoom out on the composition. Zooming out allows you to see all or most of a composition, but not the details.

Zoom to 50%–Click on this button to reduce the viewing size of the composition to half its actual size. Zooming out allows you to see all or most of a composition, but not the details.

> **NOTE** You will learn more about zooming and its effects in the "Zooming the Composition Guide" section later in this chapter.

Hiding and Displaying the Toolbar

Sometimes, particularly when working on a large or magnified picture, it's easier to edit or draw in a work area temporarily cleared of toolbars. To hide or display the toolbar, choose **View: Toolbars**. In the Toolbars dialog box (Figure 3.3), clear (to hide) or check (to display) the Toolbar check box and click on **OK**.

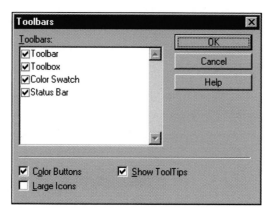

Figure 3.3 The Toolbars dialog box with its default settings.

The Toolbox

The Image Composer toolbox is a toolbar that, by default, is placed on the left side of the window. The toolbox contains ten buttons, eight of which open palettes with which you can create and edit sprites and compositions. The other two buttons, **Zoom** and **Pan**, allow you to zoom in on the composition and move it around the window.

 Arrange–Click on this button, choose **Tools: Arrange**, right-click and select one of the commands preceded by *Bring* or *Send*, or press **Alt+1** to display the Arrange palette, the default palette. Use the Arrange tools to change the size or appearance of the selected sprite or to change its order in a group of sprites. For more information about using the Arrange palette, see the "Manipulating Sprites–Example 2" section later in this chapter.

 Paint–Click on this button, choose **Tools: Paint**, or press **Alt+2** to display the Paint palette, with which you can change the size or type of the tool with which you "paint" a sprite or group of sprites. For more information about using the Paint palette, see the "Applying Colors–Example 3" section later in this chapter.

 Text–Click on this button, choose **Tools: Text**, or press **Alt+3** to display the Text palette, with which you can specify characters of and insert a text sprite into a composition. For more information about using the Text palette, see "Adding Text–Example 4" section later in this chapter.

 Shapes–Click on this button, choose **Tools: Shapes**, or press **Alt+4** to display the Shapes palette, with which you can insert geometric shapes into a composition and specify the characteristics for *splines*, open-ended or closed-ended curves that define sprites. For more information about using the Shapes palette, see the "Creating a Sprite–Example 1" section later in this chapter.

 Patterns and Fills–Click on this button, choose **Tools: Patterns and Fills**, or press **Alt+5** to display the Patterns and Fills palette, with which you can enhance sprites with color and patterns. For more information about using the Patterns and Fills palette, see "Applying Patterns and Fills" later in this chapter.

Warps and Filters–Click on this button, choose **Tools: Warps and Filters**, or press **Alt+6** to display the Warps and Filters palette, with which you can change the shape of sprites. For more information about using the Warps and Filters palette, see "Applying Warps and Filters" later in this chapter.

 Art Effects–Click on this button, choose **Tools: Art Effects**, or press **Alt+7** to display the Art Effects palette, with which you can apply fine art effects to sprites. For more information about using the Art Effects palette, see "Applying Art Effects" later in this chapter.

 Color Tuning–Click on this button, choose **Tools: Color Tuning**, or press **Alt+8** to display the Color Tuning palette, with which you can adjust color attributes of sprites. For more information about using the Color Tuning palette, see the "Tuning the Colors" section later in this chapter.

 Zoom–Click on this button, choose **Tools: Zoom**, or press **Alt+9** to be able to use the mouse pointer to zoom in on the composition. When you click on the **Zoom** button, the mouse pointer looks like a magnifying glass. To view a larger version, move the magnifying-glass mouse pointer to the composition. For more information about zooming, see "Zooming the Composition Guide" later in this chapter.

 Pan–Click on this button, choose **Tools: Pan**, or press **Alt+0** to be able to drag the *Composition Guide*, the box in which the composition is located, around the window. For more information about panning, see "Panning the Composition Guide" later in this chapter.

Hiding and Displaying the Toolbox

You can hide or display the toolbox by choosing **View: Toolbars**. Then, in the Toolbars dialog box (see Figure 3.3), clear (to hide) or check (to display) the Toolbox check box. Finally, click on **OK**.

You can control the appearance of the toolbox onscreen in two ways: by using a toggle command or by changing the setting of an option. To temporarily hide the currently selected palette, press **F2** or choose **View: Toggle Palette View**. To display it again, either press **F2** or choose **View: Toggle Palette View** again.

To hide the currently selected palette whenever you move the mouse pointer away from the palette, follow these steps:

1. Choose **Tools: Options**.
2. In the Options dialog box, click on the **Tool Palettes** tab.
3. In the Tool Palettes section of the dialog box (Figure 3.4), click on the AutoHide Tool Palette check box.
4. Click on **OK**.

To reveal a hidden palette, either click on its toolbox button, or move the mouse pointer to the status bar at the bottom of the window. To hide it again, move the mouse pointer away from the palette.

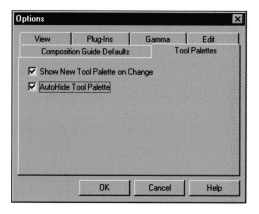

Figure 3.4 The Tool Palettes section of the Options dialog box with a checked AutoHide Tool Palette check box.

The Workspace

The Image Composer workspace is the entire area below the toolbar, to the right of the tool-box, and above the status bar at the bottom of the window. The workspace includes the Composition Guide, which by default is located in the upper-left corner, and a vertical and horizontal scroll bar.

You can see only a small part of the workspace on your computer screen; the workspace extends to the right and below the window for a space that is limited only by your computer's hard drive capacity. You can use the workspace to hold sprites that you don't plan—at least for now—to include in the current composition or sprites on which you have tested effects, colors, and so on. Simply drag these sprites onto the gray area of the workspace to move them out of the composition. In the unlikely event that you place so many sprites on the workspace that you run out of hard drive space, you will have found the limits of the workspace.

Image Composer allows you to open more than one window in the workspace. Simply choose **Window: New Window** to open a new window. Then, select **Window: Cascade** to display one window behind the other with both title bars showing. Or, select **Window: Tile** to display both windows, one above the other. To close a window, click on the **Close** button (the *X* in the upper right corner of the window). To maximize the remaining window, click on the **Maximize** button to the left of the **Close** button. Another way to maximize the remaining window, to fill in the empty space left by a closed window, is to choose **Window: Tile**.

The most important reason for opening more than one window at a time is to view and work on your composition in two different ways. For example, you can show it at its actual size in one window and magnify or zoom in on it in another window. When you change the composition in one window, it automatically changes in the other. For more information about zooming, refer to "Zooming the Composition Guide" later in this chapter.

SHORTCUT If you work with more than one window at a time, consider providing more space in which to work by automatically hiding the palettes, as described at the end of a previous section, "Hiding and Displaying the Toolbox."

The Composition Guide

The Composition Guide is the area in the workspace that contains the current composition. By default, the Composition Guide is a 30 × 30-pixel white rectangle in the upper-left corner of the workspace.

When you print in Image Composer, only the contents of the Composition Guide are printed. However, when you save an Image Composer composition, you not only save the contents of the Composition Guide but also the sprites that are located outside the Composition Guide in the workspace.

SHORTCUT Because of the immense size of the workspace, when you zoom in on the Composition Guide, you may no longer see it onscreen. To display the Composition Guide in the upper-left corner of the window, either choose **View: Go To Composition Guide** or press the **Home** key. To center the Composition Guide in the window, either choose **View: Center on Selection** or press **F8**.

Changing the Dimensions of the Composition Guide

You will not always create 30 × 30-pixel compositions, so Image Composer enables you to change Composition Guide dimensions temporarily (for the current composition) or permanently (for all compositions until you change the default dimensions again).

To temporarily change the dimensions of the Composition Guide, follow these steps:

1. Choose **File: Composition Properties**, or right-click on the background of a composition and select Properties from the context menu.
2. In the Composition Properties dialog box (Figure 3.5), change the values in the Width and/or Height text boxes to the new dimensions.
3. Click on **OK** to change the dimensions and close the dialog box, or click on **Apply** to change the dimensions but keep the dialog box open for additional changes.

To permanently change the dimensions of the Composition Guide, follow these steps:

1. Choose **Tools: Options**. Image Composer displays the Composition Guide Defaults section of the Options dialog box (Figure 3.6).
2. Change the width by either typing values or clicking on the up or down button to select a value in the Width text/option box.
3. Change the height by either typing values or clicking on the up or down button to select a value in the Height text/option box.
4. Click on **OK** to apply the changes and close the dialog box.

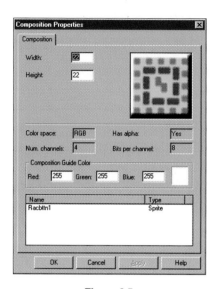

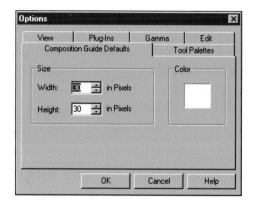

Figure 3.5
The Composition Properties dialog box showing
a toolbar button composition and its dimensions.

Figure 3.6
The Composition Guide Defaults section of the
Options dialog box with its starting values.

The Color Swatch

 The Color Swatch, which is located below the toolbox, shows the current *foreground color,* the color that you can apply to a selected sprite (that is, the color of the image). You can change the foreground color using one of two sets of color criteria: RGB or HSV.

 The color of the Composition Guide, which is white by default, is the current *background color,* the color on which the sprites in a composition are arranged. To learn about changing the background color, see the "Changing the Background Color" section, later in this chapter. You will learn how to apply effects that use the foreground color, the background color, or both.

About RGB Colors

RGB (red-green-blue) colors combine red, green, and blue values from your video card. Colors range from black (with a RGB value of 0-0-0) to white (255-255-255) and include many colors between. RGB colors are the basis for Web color palettes.

Colors vary according to the graphics board and software installed in a computer, so it's best to view all colors and see how they work together before making a final color choice. Regardless of your color choices, there is a very good chance that some browser will interpret your colors in a very strange way.

About HSV Colors

HSV (hue-saturation-value) composes a color with hue, saturation, and value.

◆ *Hue* is what we normally think of as the color. Image Composer hues go through the colors of the rainbow: red, orange, yellow, green, blue, indigo, violet, and back to red again. (Think of a circle of rainbow colors starting and ending at red.) Valid values range from 0 to 359.

◆ *Saturation* is the lesser or greater amounts of gray in a color. Valid values range from 0 (that is, white) to 100 (the most pure value of the hue).

◆ *Value* is the amount of lightness and darkness in a color. Valid values range from 0 (that is, black) to 100 (the most pure value of the hue).

Changing the Color Swatch Color

To change the color of the Color Swatch, follow these steps:

1. Click on the Color Swatch or choose **Tools: Color Picker**. Image Composer opens the True Color section of the Color Picker dialog box (Figures 3.7 and 3.8).

2. Click on the RGB or HSV option button to work with red-blue-green or hue-saturation-value color settings. RGB is preferable for Web graphics.

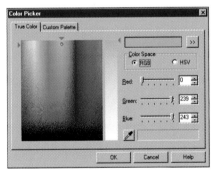

Figure 3.7
The True Color section of the Color Picker dialog box with the RGB option button selected.

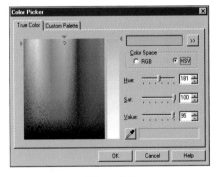

Figure 3.8
The True Color section of the Color Picker dialog box with the HSV option button selected.

3. To choose an RGB color:

◆ Slide any combination of sliders next to Red, Green, or Blue.
◆ Type a value between 0 and 255 in the Red, Green, and/or Blue text/option box.
◆ Click on the up or down button in the Red, Green, and/or Blue text/option box.
◆ Move the arrows around the Color Ramp Showing Hue/Blackness box.

◆ Slide the arrow between the top and bottom of the Color Ramp Showing Hue/Whiteness box.

4. To choose an HSV color:

◆ Slide any combination of sliders next to Hue, Sat, or Value.
◆ Type a value between 0 and 255 in the Hue, Sat, and/or Value text/option box.
◆ Click on the up or down button in the Hue, Sat, and/or Value text/option box.
◆ Move the arrows around the Color Ramp Showing Hue/Blackness box.
◆ Slide the arrow between the top and bottom of the Color Ramp Showing Hue/Whiteness box.

5. To choose a color using the **Pick a Color** button, click on the button, and click on a color on your desktop.

6. Click on **OK** to change the Color Picker color and close the dialog box.

SHORTCUT To open a small Color Picker palette from which you can choose, point to the Color Swatch and press and hold down the right mouse button. Move the mouse pointer around the palette until the Color Swatch is the desired color. Then release the mouse button.

To hide the Color Swatch, click **Toolbars** on the View menu. Then click to clear the Color Swatch option, and click **OK**.

Changing the Color of the Composition Guide

By default, the Composition Guide is white, which is also the background color of a composition. When you apply certain effects to sprites, Image Composer applies the background color. You can change the Composition Guide color—if you prefer to work with a different color in the background or if you plan to apply effects using particular foreground and background colors. You can change the background color temporarily (for the current composition) or permanently (for all compositions until you change the permanent background color again).

When you temporarily change the Composition Guide color, you open the Composition Properties dialog box. Then you can choose a color by typing RGB (red-green-blue) codes in the text boxes or by opening the Color Picker dialog box in which you can set the hue, saturation, and/or value.

To temporarily change the color of the Composition Guide, follow these steps:

1. Choose **File: Composition Properties**.

2. In the Composition Properties dialog box (see Figure 3.5), change the values in the Composition Guide Color text boxes.

3. Then, click on **OK**.

To permanently change the color of the Composition Guide, follow these steps:

1. Choose **Tools: Options**. Image Composer displays the Composition Guide Defaults section of the Options dialog box (see Figure 3.6).

2. Click on the white box in the Color section.

3. In the Color Picker dialog box, select a new color. For more information about using the Color Picker dialog box, see the section "Changing the Color Swatch Color" earlier in this chapter.

4. Click on **OK** to close the dialog box.

The Status Bar

A status bar (Figure 3.9), which displays Image Composer information, appears at the bottom of the window.

Figure 3.9 The Image Composer status bar.

- ◆ If you have selected a menu command, the status bar contains a short description. The default description tells you how to get help.
- ◆ The status bar displays the current mode: **Selection** (the default), **Zoom**, or **Pan**.
- ◆ If you have selected a sprite, the status bar displays the current *X-Y* coordinates and the width and height of the selected sprite. On the right side of the status bar are the current *X-Y* coordinates of the mouse pointer.
- ◆ To hide the status bar, choose **View: Toolbars**. Then, click to clear the Status Bar option and click **OK**.

Zooming the Composition Guide

When you view a composition at its actual size, you may not be able to work on its details, or, conversely, you may not be able to see it completely—especially if it extends beyond the limits of your computer screen. Image Composer allows you to zoom in (that is, see the details as small as a pixel, depending on the percentage you have zoomed in) or zoom out (that is, see a greater part of a large composition). You can zoom in up to 1000% of the actual size; you can zoom out to 10% of the actual size.

You can zoom in using several methods described below.

◆ Click on the **Zoom** tool, choose **Tools: Zoom**, or press **Alt+9**. Then, move the magnifying-glass mouse pointer to the composition, and click repeatedly until the composition looks as large as you want.

◆ Choose **View: Zoom In** or press the plus sign (**+**) on the numeric keypad repeatedly until the composition looks as large as you want.

◆ If you have "floated" the toolbar, click on the **Zoom In** button, and click repeatedly until the composition looks as large as you want.

You can zoom out using several methods described below.

◆ If you have "floated" the toolbar, click on the **Zoom Out** button, and click repeatedly until the composition looks as small as you want.

◆ Choose **View: Zoom Out** or press the minus sign (**-**) on the numeric keypad repeatedly until the composition looks as small as you want.

◆ To return to the actual size of the composition, either click on the **Actual Size** button or choose **View: Actual Size**.

SHORTCUT If you can see one or more borders of a composition in a window, you can center it in the window. To do so, press **F8** or choose **View: Center on Selection**.

Figure 3.10 shows three windows containing images of the Statue of Liberty. Liberty: 1 shows the image at its actual size, Liberty: 2 shows the zoomed-in torch, and Liberty: 3 is zoomed-out and selected.

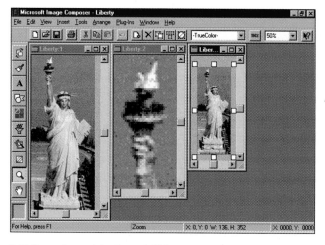

Figure 3.10 Three views of the Statue of Liberty: actual, zoomed in, and zoomed out.

Panning the Composition Guide

 The Composition Guide does not always have to be in the upper-left corner of its window. You can move the Composition Guide around the workspace by clicking on the **Pan** button, choosing **Tools: Pan**, or pressing **Alt+0**. When the mouse pointer changes to a hand, simply drag the Composition Guide to the desired location—even beyond the boundaries of the window.

SHORTCUT If you drag the Composition Guide off the window, you can press **Home** (or choose **View: Go to Composition Guide**) to move it to the upper right corner or press **F8** (or choose **View: Center on Selection**) to center it in the window. You can also use the vertical and horizontal scroll bars to find the Composition Guide, but that method is not particularly efficient.

CREATING A SPRITE—EXAMPLE 1

To create a sprite from scratch, click on the **Shapes** button, choose **Tools: Shapes**, or press **Alt+4** to open the Shapes palette with which you can draw rectangles, ovals, splines, and polygons. You can also use the Shapes palette to define attributes for geometric shapes, to apply the color of a sprite to another sprite, and to edit splines and polygons.

◆ Use the **Rectangle** tool to draw rectangles and squares. To draw a rectangle, click on the **Rectangle** tool, move the mouse pointer to a starting point, drag the mouse pointer to the opposite corner of the rectangle, and release the mouse button. To draw a square, click on the **Rectangle** tool, hold down the **Shift** key, move the mouse pointer to a starting point, drag the mouse pointer to the opposite corner of the square, and release the mouse button and **Shift** key. When you have completed the sprite, click on the **Render** button or a drawing tool button.

◆ Use the **Oval** tool to draw ovals and circles. To draw an oval, click on the **Oval** tool, move the mouse pointer to a starting point, and drag the mouse pointer to the opposite side of the oval. Image Composer surrounds the oval with a rectangular *bounding box*, which indicates the dimensions of the oval. When you release the mouse button, an oval sprite replaces the bounding box. To draw a circle, click on the **Oval** tool, hold down the **Shift** key, move the mouse pointer to a starting point, drag the mouse pointer to the opposite corner of the circle, and release the mouse button and **Shift** key. When you have completed the sprite, click on the **Render** button or a drawing tool button.

◆ Use the **Spline** tool to draw free-form shapes composed of curves. Splines can be open-ended (a curved line), closed (the starting point meets the ending point), or filled (a closed shape that is filled with color). To draw a spline, click on the **Spline** tool, click the mouse pointer at a starting point, and click to add points to the spline.

When you have completed the sprite, click on the **Render** button or a drawing tool button.

> **NOTE** If the Close check box is checked, splines and polygons will be closed. If the Close check box is cleared, splines and polygons will be open-ended. If the Fill check box is checked, closed splines and polygons will be filled. You cannot fill open-ended splines and polygons.

◆ Use the **Polygon** tool to draw free-form shapes composed of lines. Polygons can be open-ended (a series of lines), closed (the starting point meets the ending point), or filled (a closed shape that is filled with color). To draw a polygon, click on the **Polygon** tool, click the mouse pointer at a starting point, and click to add points to the polygon. When you have completed the sprite, click on the **Render** button or a drawing tool button.

To create a sprite, follow these steps:

1. Start Image Composer.
2. Change the dimensions of the Composition Guide, if needed. Choose **File: Composition** and enter the new values in the Width and/or Height text boxes.
3. If you want to work on a magnified version of the composition, zoom in. Choose **View: Zoom** In or press the plus sign (+) on the numeric keypad.
4. Press the **Home** key to display the Composition Guide in the upper-left corner of the workspace.

> **SHORTCUT** If you want to work with a clear workspace, either close the palette at the bottom of the window or "autohide" it by choosing **Tools: Options**, clicking on the **Tool Palettes** tab, checking the AutoHide Tool Palette, and clicking on **OK**.

5. Click on the Color Swatch, and change the color that you will use to fill the sprite (that is, the foreground color of the sprite).
6. If you need to change the color of the Composition Guide (that is, the background color of the sprite), choose **File: Composition Properties**. In the Composition Guide Color section, either type the RGB color values in the Red, Green, and Blue text boxes, or click on the white box at the right side of the section and select options in the Color Picker dialog box. For more information, see the section "Changing the Color of the Composition Guide" earlier in this chapter.

7. Click on the **Shapes** tool, choose **Tools: Shapes**, or press **Alt+4** to open the Shapes palette (Figure 3.11).

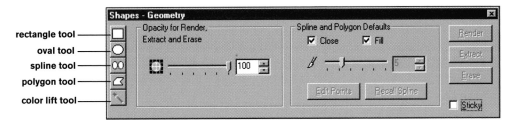

Figure 3.11 The Shapes palette.

8. Click on a tool and draw the sprite. You can change its dimensions by dragging its edges.

9. Click on the **Render** button to complete the drawing and fill it with the foreground color.

10. Draw additional sprites by following steps 5 through 8.

11. Save your work using the default Image Composer file format.

 WARNING

The Image Composer file format (MIC) allows you to keep the sprites as individual objects to be manipulated for an animation. If you save the composition as a GIF file, Image Composer flattens the composition; that is, it incorporates all the sprites into the file. From this point on, you can no longer manipulate individual sprites. It's a good idea to save your compositions as MIC files. Then, immediately before animating a set of files, open each MIC file in a set and save it as a GIF file. (Choose **File: Save As**, select the CompuServe GIF file type, and click on the **Save** button.)

BUILDING A COMPOSITION

After creating a few sprites and saving the file, you can create the composition. To do so, simply move sprites around the Composition Guide. At any time, you can create new sprites and add them to the composition. Or, you can delete a sprite. If you move a sprite off the Composition Guide, it is no longer part of the composition. However, when you save the file, remember that all the sprites in the Composition Guide and in the workspace are saved.

 Selecting a sprite—To select a sprite, click on it. A selected sprite is surrounded by a bounding box with handles at the corners and sides. Each handle indicates the action that will be taken using that particular handle.

Selecting several contiguous sprites—To select several sprites adjacent to each other, click on a sprite at one end of the range, hold down the **Shift** key, and click on the sprite at the other end of the range. Image Composer selects all the sprites in the range.

Selecting several noncontiguous sprites—To select several sprites that are not necessarily adjacent to each other, click on a sprite, hold down the **Ctrl** key, and continue to click on sprites.

Selecting all the sprites–To select all the sprites in the Composition Guide, click on the **Select All** button, choose **Edit: Select All**, or press **Ctrl+A**.

 "Unselecting" all the selected sprites–To "unselect" all the selected sprites, click on the **Clear Selection** button, choose **Edit: Clear Selection**, press **Ctrl+T**, or click on the work-space or on the background of the Composition Guide.

Moving a sprite–To move a sprite, move the mouse pointer to the sprite, hold down the left mouse button, drag the sprite to a new location on the Composition Guide or in the workspace, and release the mouse button.

Duplicating a sprite–To make a copy of a sprite, select it and choose **Edit: Duplicate** or press **Ctrl+D**.

 Copying a sprite–To copy a sprite to the Windows Clipboard, select it, and then click on the **Copy** button, choose **Edit: Copy**, right-click and select **Copy**, or press **Ctrl+C**.

 Pasting a sprite–To paste a sprite, click on the **Paste** button, choose **Edit: Paste**, right-click and select **Paste**, or press **Ctrl+V**. Then, move the sprite to an appropriate place in the com-position.

Figure 3.12 shows an apple tree composed of a rectangular trunk, an oval treetop, many copied circular apples, and a rectangular lawn.

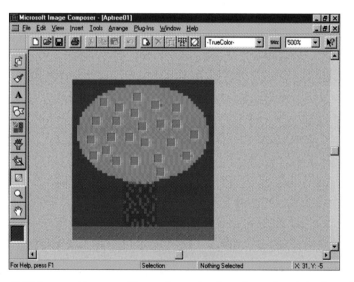

Figure 3.12 A zoomed-in composition made up of rectangular, oval, and circular sprites.

To move a composition made up of many sprites, don't move one sprite at a time—particularly if you have spent a great deal of time placing the sprites. To move an entire composition, select all the sprites by clicking on the **Select All** button, choosing **Edit: Select All**, or pressing **Ctrl+A**. Then, group the selected sprites and groups that you have already grouped by choosing **Arrange: Group**, pressing **Ctrl+G**, or opening the Arrange palette and clicking on the **Group** button. Image Composer surrounds the grouped composition with a bounding box. Drag the composition to its new location. Finally, ungroup the composition (if needed) into its individual sprites and prior groups by choosing **Arrange: Ungroup**, pressing **Ctrl+U**, or opening the Arrange palette and clicking on the **Ungroup** button.

Creating Compositions for Animation

If an Image Composer composition is ungrouped, you can move each one of the sprites. As you have learned, slight changes (that is, moved sprites) from one composition to another can simulate motion. To animate the apple tree created in the previous section, simply drag some apple sprites from the tree to the ground, periodically saving the results in a new file. To indicate a slower fall, drag an apple sprite a short distance down; to indicate a speedier fall, drag the sprite down a slightly longer distance.

ABOUT THIS ANIMATION—APPLE TREE

appltree.gif 12K 55 × 60 Level: Easy

The apple tree animation shows apples falling off a small tree onto the ground.

- This animation is composed of 13 GIFs.
- The tree trunk and ground are rectangles, and the leaves are an oval, drawn using the tools in the Shapes palette.
- The green leaves are painted in two colors (0,192,104 and 0,192,0) that are not part of the 216-color palette. This results in a mottled color that simulates the texture of leaves.
- Apples are small circles copied and pasted from one original sprite.
- The background (not shown in the following illustrations) is blue (0,0,255), which was selected because it is not used in any part of the picture.
- The first file (**aptree01.gif**) is an apple tree filled with apples, and the last file (**aptree13.gif**) shows the tree with one apple and the rest on the ground.
- To start the animation, drag two or three random apples straight down toward the ground, and save a file (aptree02.gif).
- After you have dragged an apple, don't stop its movement in subsequent files (**aptree03.gif–aptree13.gif**). Continue dragging until the apple rests on the ground.
- Many browsers do not recognize animations. For browsers that show the first file in an animation, the tree filled with apples works well. However, for browsers that show the last file in an animation, apples on the ground is a less effective graphic.

◆ Carefully consider whether it's a good idea to loop this animation.

◆ Consider setting this animation to a slower speed.

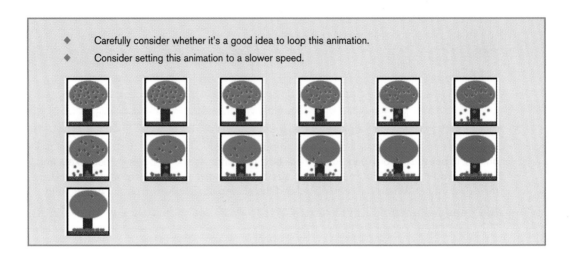

MANIPULATING SPRITES—EXAMPLE 2

On the Arrange palette (Figure 3.13), Image Composer has a comprehensive set of tools to manipulate sprites: resize, crop, rotate, flip, align, or flatten the sprite; change its order compared to other sprites in the composition; group selected sprites; or ungroup or explode a group. After selecting one or more sprites or groups for manipulation, click on the **Arrange** tool, choose **Tools: Arrange** or press **Alt+1** to open the Arrange palette.

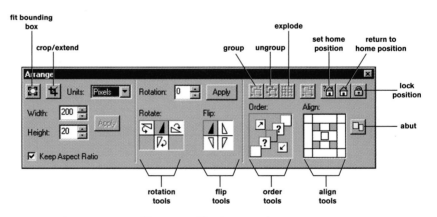

Figure 3.13 The Arrange palette.

You can perform the following actions on a selected sprite, several selected sprites, or a group.

NOTE — Image Composer sometimes displays a Hint message box that prompts you for your next action. Read the hint, click on OK, and take the action.

Move the sides of the bounding box closer–Click on the **Fit Bounding Box** button to move the sides of the bounding boxes surrounding one or more selected sprite to tighten the fit against nontransparent pixels.

 Crop or extend it–Click on the **Crop/Extend** button to change the size of the bounding box for the selected sprite while not changing the sprite's scale. Moving the bounding box into the sprite crops it. Moving the bounding box away from the sprite extends the bounding box.

Change its size by a percentage or pixels–To scale the selected sprite, enter or select new dimensions from the Width and/or Height text/option boxes. To keep the sprite in its original proportions, check the Keep Aspect Ratio check box. To change its size by pixels, select **Pixels** from the Units drop-down list box; to change its size by a percentage, select **Percent** from the Units drop-down list box. When you have completed the scaling operation, click on the **Apply** button.

Rotate it by a specified angle–To rotate the selected sprite by a particular number of degrees, from +359 to -359, type or select a value in the Rotation text/option box. When you have entered the desired value, click on the **Apply** button to complete the rotation.

 SHORTCUT You can rotate the selected sprite by dragging it by the handle in the upper-right corner of the bounding box. While you drag the handle, look at the right side of the status bar to see how many degrees you have rotated the sprite. When you have completed the rotation, release the left mouse button. To undo the rotation, either click on the **Undo** button, choose **Edit: Undo**, or press **Ctrl+Z** before you perform your next action or command.

 Rotate it 90 degrees to the right–Click on the **Rotate Right 90** button or choose **Arrange: Rotate: Right 90** to rotate the sprite 90 degrees to the right. To rotate it to its prior position, see the next entry.

 Rotate it 90 degrees to the left–Click on the **Rotate Left 90** button or choose **Arrange: Rotate: Left 90** to rotate the sprite 90 degrees to the left. To rotate it to its prior position, see the previous entry.

 Rotate it 180 degrees to the right–Click on the **Rotate 180** button or choose **Arrange: Rotate: 180** to rotate the sprite 180 degrees to the right. To rotate it to its prior position, repeat the command.

 Flip it from top to bottom–Click on the **Flip Vertically** button or choose **Arrange: Flip: Vertical** to flip the sprite from top to bottom. To flip it to its prior position, repeat the command.

 Flip it from left to right–Click on the **Flip Horizontally** button or choose **Arrange: Flip: Horizontal** to flip the sprite from the left to the right. To flip it to its prior position, repeat the command.

 Flip it from top to bottom and from left to right–Click on the **Flip Both** button or choose **Arrange: Flip: Both** to flip the sprite vertically and horizontally. To flip it to its prior position, repeat the command.

 Group selected sprites into one sprite–Click on the **Group** button, choose **Arrange: Group**, or press **Ctrl+G** to group all the selected sprites into one sprite, which you can edit, size, or move in its entirety. To "ungroup" the sprite into its individual sprites, see the next entry.

 "Ungroup" a grouped sprite–Click on the **Ungroup** button, choose **Arrange: Ungroup**, or press **Ctrl+U** to "ungroup" the grouped sprite into its individual sprites and grouped sprites that were part of the group.

"Ungroup" all grouped sprites–Click on the **Explode** button, choose **Arrange: Explode Group**, or press **Ctrl+E** to "ungroup" all grouped sprites into their individual sprites.

Make a single sprite out of all the selected sprites–Click on the **Flatten Selection** button, choose **Arrange: Flatten Selection**, or press **Ctrl+F** to make a single sprite out of all the selected sprites. To undo the flatten operation, either click on the **Undo** button, choose **Edit: Undo**, or press **Ctrl+Z** before you perform your next action or command.

WARNING After you have flattened a selection, you cannot separate the new sprite into the sprites with which it was made.

Store the location of its current position–Choose **Arrange: Set Home Position**, press **Alt+Home**, or click on the **Set Home Position** button to store its current position, so that you can have Image Composer return the sprite to that position if it is moved. (See the next entry.)

Move it to the stored position–Choose **Arrange: Return to Home Position**, press **Ctrl+Home**, or click on the **Return to Home Position** button to move the sprite back to its stored position. (See the previous entry.)

Lock it in its current position–Choose **Arrange: Lock Position**, press **Ctrl+L**, or click on the **Lock Position** button to lock the sprite in its current position. However, you can still manipulate a locked sprite; you just can't move it. When you select a locked sprite, Image Composer adds a lock to the mouse pointer. To unlock a sprite, issue the command again.

Move it to the front of all other sprites–Click on the **To Front** button or choose **Arrange: Bring to Front** to move the sprite to the top of the stack of sprites in the composition.

Move it to the back of all other sprites–Choose **Arrange: Send to Back** or click on the **To Back** button to move the sprite to the bottom of the stack of sprites in the composition.

Move it toward the front of all other sprites–Choose **Arrange: Bring Forward** or click on the **Bring Forward** button to move the sprite up one in the stack.

Move it toward the back of all other sprites–Choose **Arrange: Send Backward** or click on the **Send Backward** button to move the sprite back one in the stack.

Move it in front of a specific sprite–Click on the **Before** button to move the selected sprite in front of a clicked-on sprite.

Move it in back of a specific sprite–Click on the **Behind** button to move the selected sprite behind a clicked-on sprite.

SHORTCUT To find the location of a particular sprite in a stack of sprites, repeatedly press the Tab key until the sprite is selected.

Align it with another sprite–Click on part of the Align box to align the selected sprite with other specified sprites in the Composition Guide. You can align the sprite with the tops, bottoms, left or right sides, upper-left or -right corners, or lower-left or -right corners, or center it vertically or horizontally.

Place the selected sprite side-by-side with another sprite–Click on the **Abut** button to move the selected sprite immediately next to a clicked-on sprite.

One of the most common animations is the rotation of one or more objects. Using the Image Composer Rotation text/option box, you can rotate a sprite by a set number of degrees. So, if you want to limit an animation to nine pictures spread over a complete 360-degree rotation, you must increment each rotation by 40 degrees. Or, to show a smoother motion, rotate more slowly and create more files (for example, rotate each sprite by 12 degrees in 30 files).

ABOUT THIS ANIMATION—ROTATING BEACH BALL

rotball.gif 8K 30 × 30 Level: Medium

The rotating beach ball is a small four-color circle that rotates 360 degrees.

◆   This animation is composed of 24 GIFs.

◆   The file started as a red circle. Using the Paintbrush tool from the Paint palette and zooming 400%, the other three primary colors were painted onto the circle.

◆   The animation was created by rotating the ball 15 degrees and saving the file using a new name (*rotbal02–rotbal24*).

◆   Many browsers do not recognize animations. For these browsers, repeat the first file (*rotbal01*) at the end of the animation.

◆   This animation should be looped.

◆   This animation works at any speed.

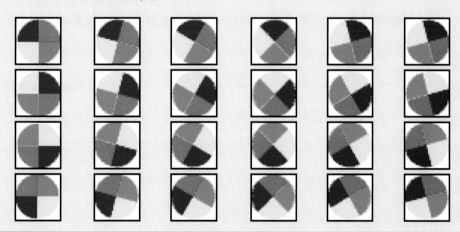

APPLYING COLORS—EXAMPLE 3

Use the tools in the Paint palette (Figure 3.14) to change the colors of or apply paint effects to a sprite. Using a Paint palette tool, you can smooth out the color of an imported BMP file or even "paint" different colors on a sprite to make it look three-dimensional. To open the Paint palette, click on the **Paint** button, choose **Tools: Paint**, or press **Alt+2.**

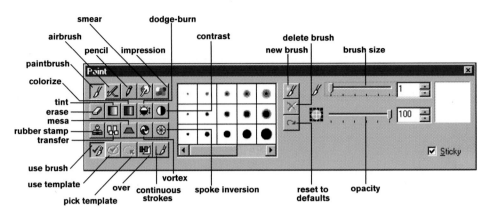

Figure 3.14 The Paint palette.

Use the following tools to "paint" a sprite or composition.

 Paintbrush—Use this tool to paint on a sprite with the current foreground color. Set the width of the paintbrush stroke by clicking within a box to the right of the tools, sliding the slider, or typing or selecting a numeric value in the Brush Size text/option box. You can slide the Opacity slider, type, or select a value from 0% to 100% to adjust the opacity of the applied color, which by default is 100%.

 SHORTCUT

When the Paint palette is onscreen, you can open a small Color Picker palette. To do so, point to any area on the workspace and right-click. To choose a new foreground color, move the mouse pointer around the palette until the Color Swatch is the desired color, and click the left mouse button.

 Airbrush—Use this tool to apply an airbrush effect to the sprite with the current foreground color. The longer you hold down the mouse button, the more color is sprayed. Set the width of the airbrush effect by clicking within a box to the right of the tools, sliding the slider, or typing or selecting a numeric value in the Brush Size text/option box. You can slide the Opacity slider, type, or select a value from 0% to 100% to adjust the opacity of the applied color, which by default is 100%.

 Pencil—Use this tool to draw on a sprite with the current foreground color. Set the width of the pencil point by clicking within a box to the right of the tools, sliding the slider, or typing or selecting a numeric value in the Brush Size text/option box. The wider the point, the more the pencil stroke looks like an airbrush effect. You can slide the Opacity slider, type, or select a value from 0% to 100% to adjust the opacity of the applied color, which by default is 100%.

 Smear—Use this tool to smear the colors on the sprite. Set the width of the smear by clicking within a box to the right of the tools, sliding the slider, or typing or selecting a numeric value in the Brush Size text/option box. You can slide the Opacity slider, type, or select a value from 0% to 100% to adjust the opacity of the applied color, which by default is 100%. Note that the Smear tool will change colors to values not within the 216-color palette.

Impression–Use this tool to smudge the colors on the sprite. The **Impression** tool affects a larger area than the **Smear** tool does. Set the width of the smudge by clicking within a box to the right of the tools, sliding the slider, or typing or selecting a numeric value in the Brush Size text/option box. You can slide the Opacity slider, type, or select a value from 0% to 100% to adjust the opacity of the applied color, which by default is 100%.

 Erase–Use this tool to make the color of the erased pixels transparent. Set the width of the eraser by clicking within a box to the right of the tools, sliding the slider, or typing or selecting a numeric value in the Brush Size text/option box. You can slide the Opacity slider, type, or select a value from 0% to 100% to adjust the opacity of the applied color, which by default is 100%. The only way to add color to the transparent portions of a sprite is to click on the **Over** button and a drawing tool and start drawing.

 Tint–Use this tool to apply a light coat of the current color to the sprite using the last tool selected. Set the width of the stroke by clicking within a box to the right of the tools, sliding the slider, or typing or selecting a numeric value in the Brush Size text/option box. You can slide the Opacity slider, type, or select a value from 0% to 100% to adjust the opacity of the applied color, which by default is 50%.

 Colorize–Use this tool to apply the current color to the sprite without changing the dark and light values already applied. Set the width of the stroke by clicking within a box to the right of the tools, sliding the slider, or typing or selecting a numeric value in the Brush Size text/option box. You can slide the Opacity slider, type, or select a value from 0% to 100% to adjust the opacity of the applied color, which by default is 100%.

 Dodge-Burn–Use this tool to lighten or darken an area of the sprite. Set the width of the tool by clicking within a box to the right of the tools, sliding the slider, or typing or selecting a numeric value in the Brush Size text/option box. You can slide the Dodge/Burn slider, type, or select a value from -100% (the darkest) to 100% (the lightest) to adjust the lightness or darkness, which by default is 0%.

 Contrast–Use this tool to change the contrast of an area of the sprite. Set the width of the tool by clicking within a box to the right of the tools, sliding the slider, or typing or selecting a numeric value in the Brush Size text/option box. You can slide the Step Contrast slider, type, or select a value from -100% (the least intense) to 100% (the most intense) to adjust the lightness or darkness, which by default is 0%.

 Rubber Stamp–Use this tool to copy an area of a sprite to another area of the sprite or to a different sprite. To use the **Rubber Stamp** tool, click on its button, click on the area to be copied, and click at the location in which you want to place the copy. Set the width of the area copied by clicking within a box to the right of the tools, sliding the slider, or typing or selecting a numeric value in the Brush Size text/option box. You can slide the Opacity slider, type, or select a value from 0% to 100% to adjust the opacity of the stamped area, which by default is 100%.

 Transfer–Use this tool to copy the colors and effects in an area of a sprite to another area of the sprite or to a different sprite. To use the **Transfer** tool, click on its button, click on the area to be copied, and click at the location in which you want to place the copy. Set the width of the area copied by clicking within a box to the right of the tools, sliding the slider, or typing or selecting a numeric value in the Brush Size text/option box. You can slide the Opacity slider, type, or select a value from 0% to 100% to adjust the opacity of the stamped area, which by default is 100%.

Mesa–Use this tool to change the direction of pixels in the sprite. The best way to learn about this tool is to experiment with it. Set the width of the tool by clicking within a box to the right of the tools, sliding the slider, or typing or selecting a numeric value in the Brush Size text/option box. Set the Radius Factor, the amount of change, from 0% to 100%. The default is 77%.

 Vortex–Use this tool to apply a "whirl" pattern to pixels in the sprite. The best way to learn about this tool is to experiment with it. Set the width of the tool by clicking within a box to the right of the tools, sliding the slider, or typing or selecting a numeric value in the Brush Size text/option box. Set the Angle, the amount of change, from 180% to -180%. The default is 45%.

 Spoke Inversion–Use this tool to apply a disk-like pattern to an area in the sprite. The best way to learn about this tool is to experiment with it. Set the width of the tool by clicking within a box to the right of the tools, sliding the slider, or typing or selecting a numeric value in the Brush Size text/option box. Set the Value, the amount of change, from 1 to 100, the default.

 Use Brush–Use this tool to indicate that you will use a brush tool rather than a template to apply an art effect. Set the width of the paintbrush stroke by clicking within a box to the right of the tools, sliding the slider, or typing or selecting a numeric value in the Brush Size text/option box. You can slide the Opacity slider, type, or select a value from 0% to 100% to adjust the opacity of the applied color, which by default is 100%.

 Use Template–Use this tool to use a template rather than a brush tool to change a sprite. To use a template, pick a template (see the **Pick Template** tool), click on a paint tool, and click on **Use Template**. Then apply the effects.

 Pick Template–Use this tool to choose a sprite to use as a template for applying paint effects. To pick a template, click on the **Pick Template** tool, and click on the sprite to be used as a template. After you choose a template, it remains in effect until you choose another template.

 Over–Use this tool to apply paint effects to transparent areas of a sprite. By default, you cannot apply effects to transparent areas. If you click on the **Over** tool, you can change transparent areas (analogous to overtyping, rather than inserting, text in a word processor).

 Continuous Strokes–Use this tool to apply a continuous flow of paint and the appearance of layers of paint to a sprite. Otherwise, the effect is a single application of paint with no buildup of layers. When you choose certain tools (that is, **Airbrush**, **Smear**, **Impression**, **Tint**, **Colorize**, **Dodge-Burn**, **Contrast**, **Rubber Stamp**, **Transfer**, **Mesa**, **Vortex**, and **Spoke Inversion**), Continuous Strokes is automatically selected.

ABOUT THIS ANIMATION—HAPPY DOG

wagdog.gif 8K 60 × 61 Level: Difficult

The happy dog animation shows a sitting dog with a wagging tail.

- ◆ This animation is composed of six GIFs—most used twice, to wag from left to right and then right to left.
- ◆ The dog body file and a separate tail file were created in Windows Paint.
- ◆ Because the original Windows Paint color was mottled, it was necessary to paint the dog body in Image Composer using the **Paintbrush** tool. After zooming in 400%, paint with a light solid yellow color (RGB = 255, 255, 204), which is part of the 216-color palette.
- ◆ The tail file was opened in Image Composer and the tail was painted light yellow. Several files (**tail01–tail06**) were saved after rotating by 10 degrees each.
- ◆ Because of color changes during rotation, each rotated tail file was zoomed to 400–500% and was touched up using the **Paintbrush** and **Eraser** tools.
- ◆ After touching up, a counterpart file was created for each tail file. Each new file was created by flipping the tail horizontally and saving it under a different name. In the animation, two of these files showed the wagging to the left of the dog body.
- ◆ Before combining the dog body and each tail, the background of the dog body file was made transparent. Otherwise, an added tail would not be visible when placed behind the dog body. To differentiate between a white background and transparent pixels, which also appear to be white, the background was temporarily painted with a pale color. Then, the background was erased with the **Eraser** tool, resulting in a white transparent background.
- ◆ To add a detail (such as a tail) to a main file (such as the dog body), open the main file, zoom it about 200%, choose **Insert: From File**, and choose a detail file. Image Composer places the detail file on top of the main file. Simply move the detail file to the appropriate location on the main file. Then, open the Arrange palette, and click on **Send Backward** to move the tail behind the dog body.
- ◆ To show the dog panting, zoom the picture to about 400% and use the **Paintbrush** tool to paint a longer tongue in every other file making up the animation.
- ◆ This animation should be looped and can be set to any speed.

TUNING THE COLORS

Use the tools in the Color Tuning palette (Figures 3.15, 3.16, and 3.17) to edit the color of a sprite. To open the Color Tuning palette, click on the **Color Tuning** button, choose **Tools: Color Tuning**, or press **Alt+8.** In all three sections of the palette, click on **Apply** to apply the new settings, and click on **Reset** to revert to the original settings.

The Color Shifting section of the Color Tuning palette contains tools with which you can adjust the color (all the colors, the red, the green, or the blue) and other color-related values of the selected sprite.

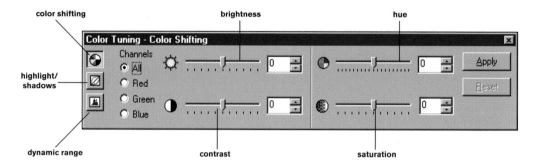

Figure 3.15 The Color Shifting section of the Color Tuning palette.

Slide the Brightness slider or type or select a value in the Brightness text/option box to adjust the brightness of the selected sprite. Valid values range from -100 (the darkest) to 100 (the brightest).

Slide the Contrast slider or type or select a value in the Contrast text/option box to adjust the contrast, the difference between the lightest and darkest color, of the selected sprite. Valid values range from -100 to 100.

Slide the Hue slider or type or select a value in the Hue text/option box to change the color of the selected sprite. Valid values range from -100 to 100.

Slide the Saturation slider or type or select a value in the Saturation text/option box to adjust the saturation of the selected sprite. Valid values range from -100 (the most gray) to 100 (the least gray).

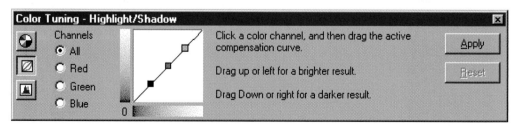

Figure 3.16 The Highlight/Shadow section of the Color Tuning palette.

The Color Shifting section of the Color Tuning palette contains tools with which you can adjust the intensity of shadows, midtones, and highlights of the color (all the colors, the red, the green, or the blue).

In the chart, drag the Shadow handle (the darkest square), the Highlight handle (the lightest square), and/or the Midtone handle to change the shadows, highlights, midtones, respectively. Drag toward the upper-left corner of the chart to brighten the selected sprite element. Drag toward the lower-right corner to darken the selected element.

Figure 3.17 The Dynamic Range section of the Color Tuning palette.

The Dynamic Range section of the Color Tuning palette contains tools with which you can adjust the intensity of all the colors in the sprite. The horizontal axis of the histogram shows the range of intensity for any sprite, ranging from the lowest (at the left) to the highest (at the right). The vertical lines categorize the number of pixels, by intensity, for the selected sprite, and the two long vertical bars represent the lowest and highest intensities in the selected sprite.

ADDING TEXT—EXAMPLE 4

 Use the Text palette (Figure 3.18) to add a text sprite in the current foreground color to the workspace. To open the Text palette, click on the **Text** button, choose **Tools: Text**, or press **Alt+3.**

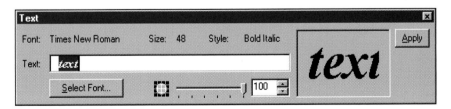

Figure 3.18 The Text palette.

Before or after you enter text, you can change the font (using fonts installed on your computer), point size, or style. Simply click on the **Select Font** button to open the Font dialog box (Figure 3.19).

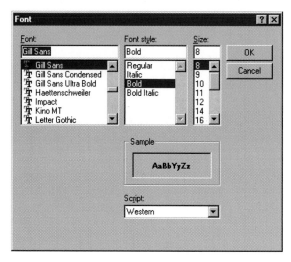

Figure 3.19 The Font dialog box with which you can adjust the font, font style, or size of text in a composition.

 After you have added a text sprite to a composition, you cannot edit it. The only way to change the text is to delete the text sprite and add a new one.

ABOUT THIS ANIMATION—FLASHING NEW SIGN

newsign.gif 1K 38 × 16 Level: Easy

The flashing NEW animation is an icon whose text flashes on and off, signaling a new item on a Web page.

♦   This animation is composed of two GIFs–both inserted more than once.

♦   The background of the icon is a red rectangle painted (**Paintbrush** tool) with yellow. The pattern of the left and right sides of each GIF changes to show movement. Some areas on the left and right sides have been made transparent (**Eraser** tool).

♦   The text is the Gill Sans sans serif font with a point size of 8 and a bold style.

♦   The first and fifth frames in the animation have text, especially planned for browsers that do not support animation. The second, third, and fourth frames are blank.

♦   This animation works better when looped.

♦   Consider setting this animation to a very slow speed (for example, 80 or 90).

APPLYING PATTERNS AND FILLS

Use the Patterns and Fills palette (Figures 3.20, 3.21, 3.22, 3.23, and 3.24) to change a sprite—the color or pattern of its interior or its shape or look. To open the Pattern and Fills palette, click on the **Patterns and Fills** button, choose **Tools: Patterns and Fills**, or press **Alt+5.** Click on the **Apply** button to change the selected sprite.

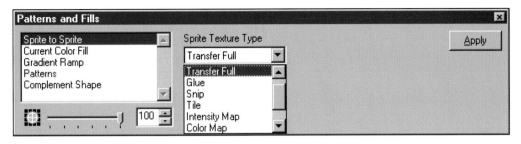

Figure 3.20
The Patterns and Fills palette with Sprite to Sprite selected and the Sprite Texture Type drop-down list box open.

The Sprite to Sprite section uses the attributes of the source sprite to change the characteristics of the destination sprite.

◆ Select **Transfer Shape**, **Transfer Full**, or **Glue** to replace the destination sprites pixels with the source sprite's pixels where the two sprites overlap.

◆ Select **Snip** to remove the destination sprite's pixels where the two sprites overlap.

◆ Select **Tile** to copy the source sprite's nontransparent pixels to the destination sprite using a shape defined by the settings of the Intertile X and Intertile Y text/option boxes.

◆ Select a Map option (**Intensity Map**, **Color Map**, **Transparency Map**, or **Saturation Map**) to copy a color attribute from the source sprite to the destination sprite.

Figure 3.21 The Patterns and Fills palette with Current Color Fill selected.

To use the Current Color Fill section of the Patterns and Fills palette, click on a sprite and click on the **Apply** button. The color of the selected sprite changes to the current foreground color.

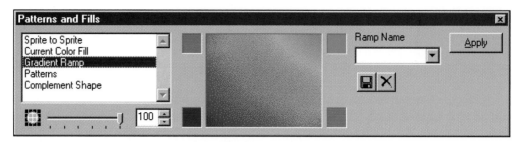

Figure 3.22 The Patterns and Fills palette with Gradient Ramp selected.

To use the Gradient Ramp section of the Patterns and Fills palette, select a ramp (which gradually changes from one color to another, sometimes going through four colors) from the Ramp Name text/drop-down list box and click on the **Apply** button.

NOTE You can design and name your own ramp. Click on one of the four boxes surrounding the box in which the current ramp is displayed. In the Color Picker dialog box, select a new color, and click on **OK**. Then, type the name of the new ramp in the Ramp Name text/drop-down list box. To save the new ramp, click on the **Save** button. To delete a selected ramp, click on the **Delete** button. Image Composer deletes the ramp without any prompts.

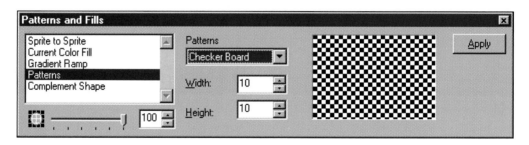

Figure 3.23 The Patterns and Fills palette with Patterns selected.

To use the Patterns section of the Patterns and Fills palette, select a pattern from the Patterns drop-down list box, choosing associated options, and click on the **Apply** button.

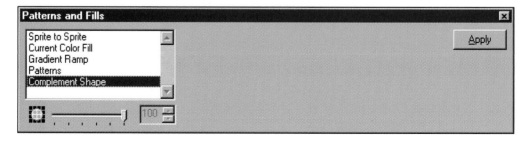

Figure 3.24 The Patterns and Fills palette with Complement Shape selected.

In the Complement Shape section of the Patterns and Fills palette, you can reverse the opaque/transparent pixels of a selected sprite. Any opaque pixels are changed to transparent, and any transparent pixels are changed to opaque.

APPLYING WARPS AND FILTERS

Use the Warps and Filters palette (Figures 3.25, 3.26, 3.27, 3.28, and 3.29) to change the appearance of a sprite. Using the many effects available with this palette, you can modify color, change the edges or interior, or distort the dimensions. To open the Warps and Filters palette, click on the **Warps and Filters** button, choose **Tools: Warps and Filters**, or press **Alt+6.** Click on the **Apply** button to change the selected sprite.

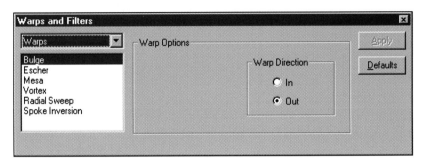

Figure 3.25 The Warps and Filters palette with Warps selected.

Using the **Warps** options, you can distort the look of the interior of a sprite while maintaining the outer dimensions:

◆ **Bulge** pushes or pulls the pattern of the interior from the middle of the sprite.

◆ **Escher** spreads the middle part, pushing the upper part up and lower part down.

◆ **Mesa** moves the pattern around a radius within the interior and pushes toward the top and bottom.

◆ **Vortex** works like a completely vertical tornado within the sprite.

◆ **Radial Sweep** eventually forms an oval within the sprite.

◆ **Spoke Inversion** moves the interior of the sprite along invisible spokes pointing toward the center of the sprite.

Using the **Warp Transforms** options, you can change the outer dimensions of a sprite:

◆ **Wave** changes the sprite to a sine wave. You can set the frequency, amplitude, and coordinates.

◆ **Interactive Warps** changes the sprite to one of eight shapes shown in the palette and can simulate movement. Select a sprite, click on a shape, click on **Apply**, and drag the dimensions of the selected sprite.

◆ **Rectangular** changes the interior of the sprite using mathematical functions: sine, cosine, and linear knee. You can set the axis of the sprite.

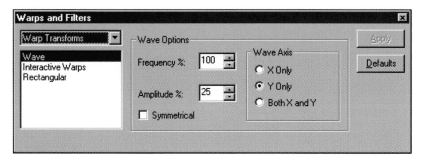

Figure 3.26 The Warps and Filters palette with Warp Transforms selected.

Using the Outlines options, you can apply shadows and outlines to a sprite:

◆ **Shadow** places a shadow box below and to the right of the sprite using the color specified in the color box, the offset values, and the opacity setting in the palette.

◆ **Edge** places a border around the outside of the sprite using the color specified in the color box, the thickness, and the opacity setting in the palette.

◆ **Edge Only** places a border around the outside of the sprite using the color specified in the color box, the thickness, and the opacity setting in the palette. This option removes the color from the sprite itself.

◆ **Recess** adds a black border to the top and left side of the sprite and a white border to the right and bottom of the sprite.

◆ **Relief** adds a white border to the top and left side of the sprite and a black border to the right and bottom of the sprite.

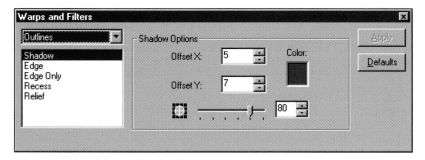

Figure 3.27 The Warps and Filters palette with Outlines selected.

Using the **Filters** options, you can change a sprite pixel by pixel, based on the colors and characteristics of nearby pixels within the sprite:

♦ **Blur** blurs all the pixels in the selected sprite, even outside the original dimensions of the sprite. If you choose low values in the Horizontal and Vertical text/option boxes, you can still see the colors. Higher values result in a greater blur.

♦ **Soften** lightly blurs all the pixels in the selected sprite.

♦ **Sharpen** reverses a blur but does not reverse the change in dimensions caused by the **Blur** or **Soften** options. Repeatedly clicking on **Apply** continues to sharpen the pixels and brighten their colors.

♦ **Sharpen Lite** gradually reverses a blur but does not reverse the change in dimensions caused by the **Blur** or **Soften** options. Repeatedly clicking on **Apply** continues to sharpen the pixels and brighten their colors.

♦ **Outline** outlines some colors and darkens other colors in a sprite. You can use this effect to draw multicolored frames around sprites. It is a good idea to experiment with this effect after applying patterns and fills to sprites.

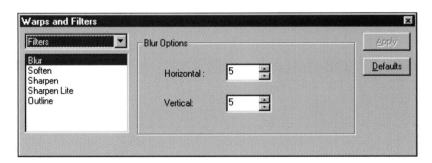

Figure 3.28 The Warps and Filters palette with Filters selected.

Using the **Color Enhancement** options, you can change the color effects within the selected sprite:

♦ **Wash** applies a translucent effect to a sprite and dims the colors. The level of translucency depends on the selected level of opacity.

♦ **Luminance** replaces the colors with similar levels of gray.

♦ **Complement Color** replaces all the colors in the sprite with their complementary colors (for example, black with white and blue with yellow).

♦ **Color Atop** washes the current foreground color over all the colors of the sprite except for the clear pixels.

◆ **Color Over** washes the current foreground color over all the colors of the sprite including the clear pixels.

◆ **Tint** washes a thin coating of the current foreground color over the sprite.

◆ **Colorize** washes the current foreground color over the sprite but does not change its level of darkness or lightness.

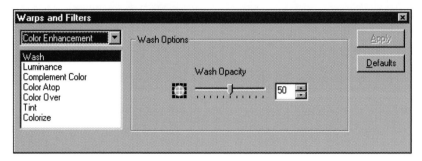

Figure 3.29 The Warps and Filters palette with Color Enhancement selected.

APPLYING ART EFFECTS

Use the Art Effects palette (Figures 3.30, 3.31, 3.32, 3.33, and 3.34) to change the appearance of a sprite—especially a fine-resolution sprite that has been scanned in. Using the many artistic effects available with this palette, you can modify the appearance of the selected sprite in many ways. To open the Art Effects palette, click on the **Art Effects** button, choose **Tools: Art Effects**, or press **Alt+7.** Click on the **Apply** button to change the selected sprite.

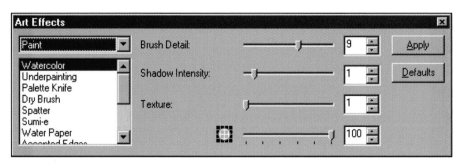

Figure 3.30 The Art Effects palette with Paint and its first option, Watercolor, selected.

Using the **Paint** options, you can change the appearance of the selected sprite by simulating painting techniques: **Watercolor**, **Underpainting**, **Palette Knife**, **Dry Brush**, **Spatter**, **Sumi-e**, **Water Paper**, **Accented Edges**, **Paint Daubs**, **Sponge**, **Sprayed Strokes**, **Dark Strokes**, or **Fresco**. To master a technique, you should experiment by selecting various colors and palette options.

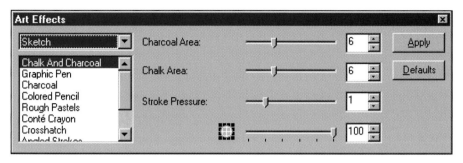

Figure 3.31 The Art Effects palette with Sketch and its first option, Chalk And Charcoal, selected.

Using the **Sketch** options, you can change the appearance of the selected sprite by simulating drawing techniques: **Chalk And Charcoal**, **Graphic Pen**, **Charcoal**, **Colored Pencil**, **Rough Pastels**, **Conté Crayon**, **Crosshatch**, **Angled Strokes**, **Smudge Stick**, and **Ink Outlines**. To master a technique, you should experiment by selecting various colors and palette options.

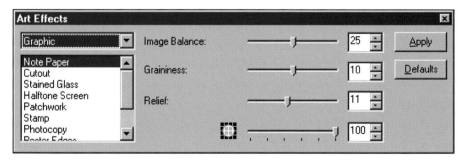

Figure 3.32 The Art Effects palette with Graphic and its first option, Note Paper, selected.

Using the **Graphic** options, you can change the appearance of the selected sprite with miscellaneous patterns: **Note Paper**, **Cutout**, **Stained Glass**, **Halftone Screen**, **Patchwork**, **Stamp**, **Photocopy**, **Poster Edges**, **Reticulation**, and **Torn Edges**. To master a technique, you should experiment by selecting various colors and palette options.

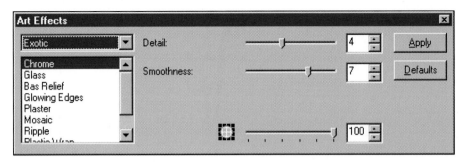

Figure 3.33 The Art Effects palette with Exotic and its first option, Chrome, selected.

Using the **Exotic** options, you can change the appearance of the selected sprite with miscellaneous patterns: **Chrome**, **Glass**, **Bas Relief**, **Glowing Edges**, **Plaster**, **Mosaic**, **Ripple**, **Plastic Wrap**, and **Craquelure**. To master a technique, you should experiment by selecting various colors and palette options.

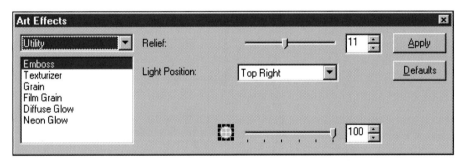

Figure 3.34 The Art Effects palette with Utility and its first option, Emboss, selected.

Using the **Utility** options, you can change the appearance of the selected sprite with miscellaneous patterns and colors: **Emboss**, **Texturizer**, **Grain**, **Film Grain**, **Diffuse Glow**, and **Neon Glow**. To master a technique, you should experiment by selecting various colors and palette options.

SCANNING AND ANIMATING A SPRITE

If you have access to a scanner, you can produce unique animations using scanned images from a variety of sources.

Before you scan an image for the first time in Image Composer, choose **File: Scan: Select Scan Source**. Select the name of the scanner with which you want to acquire the image and click on **OK**.

To acquire an image, follow these steps:

1. Choose **File: Scan: Acquire Scan**. Image Composer starts your scanner software.
2. Run your scanner software to scan and edit the image.
3. When you have completed the scan, close the scanner software window. The scanned image appears in the Image Composer window where you can edit the image.

INTRODUCING MICROSOFT GIF ANIMATOR

Using Microsoft GIF Animator, you can animate a series of GIF files. To open GIF Animator from within Image Composer, choose **Tools: Microsoft GIF Animator**. To open GIF Animator, the Image Composer Composition Guide must be onscreen with or without a composition.

 SHORTCUT If you have created a shortcut icon on your desktop for GIF Animator, double-click on it to start the program.

 NOTE When you need to edit an animation, plan on using the same program that you used to create the animation. Otherwise, small incompatibilities between animation programs may result in your spending unnecessary time in additional editing.

The GIF Animator is composed of a small window (Figure 3.35) with a toolbar and three sections.

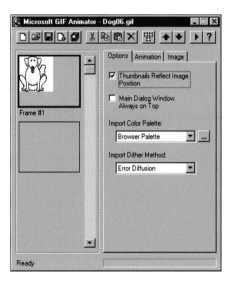

Figure 3.35 The GIF Animator window with the first frame in place and the Options section open.

The GIF Animator Window

The GIF Animator window contains a variety of elements, including a toolbar and three sections.

The GIF Animator Toolbar

In most Windows-based programs, toolbar buttons are shortcuts for menu commands. Using the GIF Animator toolbar buttons or shortcut keys described below, you can perform all the actions necessary to create an animation.

New–Click on this button or press **Ctrl+N** to create a new animation file.

Open–Click on this button or press **Ctrl+O** to open an existing file to start the animation. If you use this while a file is open, GIF Animator warns that current changes will be lost and prompts you to save your changes.

Save–Click on this button or press **Ctrl+S** to save the animation file using the name of the first file you opened.

Insert–Click on this button or press **Ctrl+I** to insert the next GIF file into the current animation in the frame preceding the current frame.

Save As–Click on this button or press **Ctrl+A** to open the Save As dialog box so that you can save the animation file under a different name.

Cut–Click on this button or press **Ctrl+X** to remove the contents of the selected frame to the Windows Clipboard.

Copy–Click on this button or press **Ctrl+C** to place a copy of the contents of the selected frame to the Windows Clipboard.

Paste–Click on this button or press **Ctrl+V** to place the contents of the Windows Clipboard into the selected frame.

Delete–Click on this button or press **Del** to permanently delete the contents of the selected frame. Although you have deleted the contents of the frame, you do not delete the actual GIF file.

Select All–Click on this button or press **Ctrl+L** to select the contents of all the frames in the current animation.

Move Up–Click on this button or press the **Up Arrow** key to move the contents of the selected frame to the previous frame in the current animation.

Move Down–Click on this button or press the Down Arrow key to move the contents of the selected frame to the next frame in the current animation.

Preview—Click on this button or press **Ctrl+R** to play the animation without having saved it first.

 Help—Click on this button or press **F1** to open the help file window.

The Options Section

The Options section contains the following options with which you can manage your GIF files.

Thumbnails Reflect Image Position—Check this check box (the default) to view an image in the specified space using the values set in the Animation section. A check mark shows the image position and its current proportions within the thumbnail window.

Main Dialog Window Always on Top—Check this check box to keep the GIF Animator window on top of every other window onscreen. When the check box is checked, you can use drag-and-drop to move an image from Image Composer to a GIF Animator frame.

Import Color Palette—From this drop-down list box, select a palette to be used for the current animation.

- If you select **Browser Palette**, GIF Animator uses one palette matching the most commonly used Web browsers throughout the animation.
- If you select **Optimal Palette**, GIF Animator selects a separate palette for each frame of the animation.
- If you click on the button to the right of this drop-down list box, you can open a custom palette to use.

Import Dither Method—From this drop-down list box, select a method with which the current animation will be drawn onscreen.

- If you select **Solid**, the result is a fast display, which is best for animations with few colors.
- If you select **Pattern**, the result is a relatively coarse display.
- If you select **Random**, the result is a relatively fine display.
- If you select **Error Diffusion**, the result is a fine, relatively slow display.

The Animation Section

The Animation section (Figure 3.36), which is available after you load the first file in an animation, controls the workings of your animation.

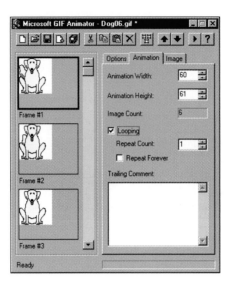

Figure 3.36 The GIF Animator window with the Animation section open and Looping checked.

The Animation section contains the following options.

....

Animation Width–Type or select the width of the area in which the animation is located and plays. The starting value is the width of the GIF file.

Animation Height–Type or select the height of the area in which the animation is located and plays. The starting value is the height of the GIF file.

Image Count–Image Composer displays the number of frames in the current animation–saved or not.

Looping–Check this check box to loop your animation (that is, have it play more than once).

Repeat Count–Type or select the number of loops in this text/option box.

Repeat Forever–Check this check box to play this animation as long as the page is onscreen. Select this option very carefully.

Trailing Comment–In this text box, type a comment attached to the animation.

....

The Image Section

The Image section (Figure 3.37), which is available after you load the first file in an animation, controls characteristics of specific frames in your animation.

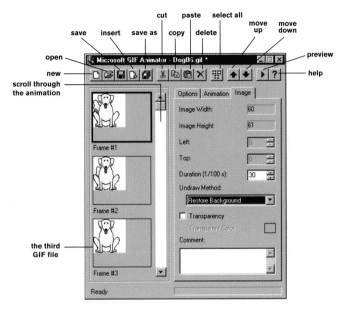

Figure 3.37 The GIF Animator window with the Image section open and Looping checked.

The Image section contains the following options.

Image Width–Image Composer displays the width of the image in the selected frame.

Image Height–Image Composer displays the height of the image in the selected frame.

Left–If this option is available, you can specify the position of the left side of the image in the selected frame.

Top–If this option is available, you can specify the position of the top of the image in the selected frame.

Duration (1/100 s)–Type or select the amount of time that the current image displays when the animation plays. This means that you can vary the display time for each of the images in an animation.

Undraw Method–From this drop-down list box, select one of the following:

- ◆ If you choose **Undefined**, the Web browser will not change the background of the current image before playing the following image.
- ◆ If you choose **Leave**, the Web browser will superimpose the following image on the current image.
- ◆ If you choose **Restore Background**, the Web browser will display the following image in its entirety.
- ◆ If you choose **Restore Previous**, the Web browser will display the current image when it displays the following image.

Transparency–Check this check box to specify a transparent color, which will not appear in the current image. Click on the color block to open a palette from which you can choose the transparent color.

Transparent Color–Click the box to display a palette from which you can choose a color that GIF Animator will treat as the transparent portion of the image. You can choose only one transparent color.

Comment–In this text box, type a comment attached to the current image.

Creating an Animation

To animate a series of images in GIF Animator, follow these steps:

1. Select a palette and dithering method from the Options section.

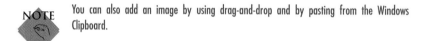

2. Click on the **Open** button or press **Ctrl+O**, and choose a file from the Open dialog box. Your selection should be the last file in the series.

3. To insert a subsequent file, click on the **Insert** button or press **Ctrl+I**, and choose a file from the Insert dialog box. Insert files from the next to last to the first in the animation series.

> **NOTE** You can also add an image by using drag-and-drop and by pasting from the Windows Clipboard.

4. Repeat step 3 to add images to the animation.

5. Whenever you want to view the animation (Figure 3.38), click on the **Preview** button or press **Ctrl+R**.

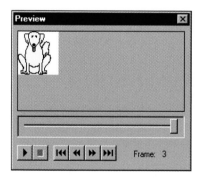

Figure 3.38 The Preview window in which you can play your animation before or after saving it.

6. To save the animation using the name of the file that you first opened, click on the **Save** button or press **Ctrl+S**.

7. To save the animation using a different name, click on the **Save As** button or press **Ctrl+A**. Then type the file name in the Save As dialog box.

Working with Paint Shop Pro

Paint Shop Pro is a shareware paint program with which you can create and edit images—down to the pixel level—using an assortment of easy-to-use tools, each of which you can adjust to obtain the best effects. Paint Shop Pro allows you to open and save graphic files in about 30 formats. This means that you can use the program to convert a variety of files—including some obscure types—to the GIF format. Program features include a screen capture utility, many special effects, and support for TWAIN scanners.

As a Windows-based program, Paint Shop Pro includes many functions with which Windows users are familiar. For example, you can copy, move, and paste selections and undo your actions using familiar toolbar buttons and Edit menu commands. Paint Shop Pro also includes a robust help system.

NOTE Shareware programs are not free. Producers of shareware allow you to try out their programs, usually for a few weeks, before you register and make a nominal payment.

STARTING PAINT SHOP PRO

To start Paint Shop Pro, follow these steps:

1. Click on the **Start** button and select **Programs**. Windows opens the Programs menu.

2. Move the mouse pointer over Paint Shop Pro. Windows opens a submenu.

3. Click on **Paint Shop Pro**. The Paint Shop Pro window (Figure 4.1) opens.

SHORTCUT If you have created a shortcut icon on your desktop for Paint Shop Pro, double-click on it to start the program.

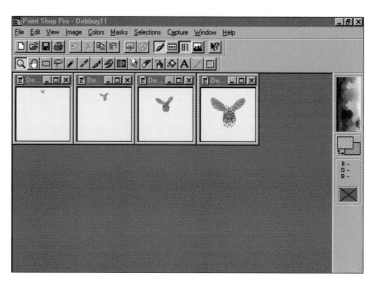

Figure 4.1 The Paint Shop Pro window with four frames of Deborah Eddy's debbug.gif animation.

 SHORTCUT Rather than installing Paint Shop Pro on your computer, you can run the program from its CD disk, thereby saving on hard drive space. After you insert the CD disk in your CD drive, a splash screen automatically appears on your desktop. To start the program, click on **Run Paint Shop Pro**.

THE PAINT SHOP PRO WINDOW

The Paint Shop Pro window contains several elements. Many of these elements are familiar to Windows users, but some are unique to Paint Shop Pro.

The Title Bar and Menu Bar

The Paint Shop Pro title bar and menu bar are standard Windows elements. The title bar includes the name of the program and the current saved file. The menu bar contains menus from which you select commands with which you can perform actions. When you open a menu and highlight a command, Paint Shop Pro displays a short description of the command in the status bar at the bottom of the window.

The Toolbar

Below the menu bar is the toolbar, with standard Windows buttons on the left and some buttons that are unique to Paint Shop Pro on the right.

 NOTE The set of buttons immediately below the toolbar is the tool palette, which is covered in the following section.

New–Click on this button to start a new image. This is equivalent to choosing **File: New** or pressing **Ctrl+N**.

Open–Click on this button to open an existing image file. This is equivalent to choosing **File: Open** or pressing **Ctrl+O**.

Save–Click on this button to save the current file. This is equivalent to choosing **File: Save** (or pressing **Ctrl+S**) or choosing **File: Save As** (or pressing **F12**) if you are saving a new file.

Print–Click on this button to print the current file. This is equivalent to choosing **File: Print** or pressing **Ctrl+P**.

Undo–Click on this button to undo the most recent action. This is equivalent to choosing **Edit: Undo** or pressing **Ctrl+Z**. If this button is dimmed, you have not performed an action, you can't undo the action, or you have already performed one undo.

Cut–Click on this button to remove the current selection and place it in the Windows Clipboard. This is equivalent to choosing **Edit: Cut** or pressing **Ctrl+X**. If this button is dimmed, you have not selected an object. For more information about selecting and cutting, see the "Manipulating an Image–Example 2" section later in the chapter.

Copy–Click on this button to copy the current selection into the Windows Clipboard. This is equivalent to choosing **Edit: Copy** or pressing **Ctrl+C**. If this button is dimmed, you have not selected an object. For more information about selecting and copying, see the "Manipulating an Image–Example 2" section later in the chapter.

Paste as New Image–Click on this button to paste the contents of the Windows Clipboard at the current location in the image. This is equivalent to choosing **Edit: Paste: As New Image** or pressing **Ctrl+V**. If this button is dimmed, the Windows Clipboard is empty. For more information about pasting a selection, see the "Manipulating an Image–Example 2" section later in the chapter.

Full Screen Preview–Click on this button to view the current image in a window without the title bar, menu bar, toolbar, Tool palette, or status bar on display. This is equivalent to choosing **View: Full Screen** Preview or pressing **Ctrl+Shift+F**. To return to a normal window, press **Esc**.

Normal Viewing–Click on this button to display the current image at its actual size. This is equivalent to choosing **View: Normal Viewing (1:1)** or pressing **Ctrl+Alt+N**. If this button is dimmed, the image is already at its actual size.

Toggle Tool Palette–Click on this button to display the tool palette if it is hidden or hide it if it is displayed. This is equivalent to choosing **View: Tool Palette**. For more information, see the "The Tool Palette and the Style Bar" section later in the chapter.

Toggle Style Bar–Click on this button to display the style bar if it is hidden or hide it if it is displayed. This is equivalent to choosing **View: Style Bar**. For more information, see the "The Tool Palette and the Style Control Bar" section later in the chapter.

Toggle Color Palette–Click on this button to display the color palette if it is hidden or hide it if it is displayed. This is equivalent to choosing **View: Color Palette**. For more information, see the "The Color Palette" section later in the chapter.

Toggle Histogram Window–Click on this button to display the histogram window if it is hidden or hide it if it is displayed. This is equivalent to choosing **View: Histogram Window**.

Help–Click on this button and then click on an object onscreen to display context-sensitive help about that object or the help window. This is equivalent to pressing **Shift+F1**. You can open two help windows simultaneously by choosing **Help: Help Topics** or by pressing **F1**. To "deselect" context-sensitive help, press **Esc**.

Learning More about Toolbars

Paint Shop Pro button bars, such as the toolbar and the tool palette (described in the following section) have certain common characteristics.

◆ When you move the mouse pointer over a toolbar button, Paint Shop Pro displays a small yellow box that states the name of the button and, in the status bar at the bottom of the window, provides a brief explanation of the button.

◆ You can change the location of a toolbar by pointing to an area above, below, or next to a button and dragging.

◆ You can move the toolbar to any part of the window. If you move the toolbar away from the top, left or right side, or bottom, it floats (Figure 4.2).

◆ You can drag a floating toolbar around by its title bar or any area away from a button.

◆ You can change the size of a floating toolbar by pointing to an edge and, when the mouse pointer changes to a double-pointed arrow, dragging the edge. Release the mouse button when the toolbar is the desired size. Double-click on the floating toolbar to anchor it to its default position below the menu bar or toolbar above it. Double-click on the fixed toolbar to float it at its last position and shape. Note that you can also move a fixed toolbar to the left or the right.

 NOTE In other Windows-based programs with the ability to float toolbars, when you move a floating toolbar to its former fixed location, it seems to snap into position. However, in Paint Shop Pro, you can move a toolbar to almost any location—above or next to a toolbar, to the left or right, or even on top of the menu bar.

Hiding and Displaying the Toolbar

Sometimes, particularly when working on a large or magnified picture, it's easier to edit or draw in a work area temporarily cleared of toolbars. To hide or display the toolbar, choose **View: Toolbar**. A check mark preceding the command indicates that the toolbar is on display.

fig 4.2

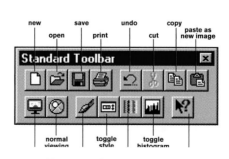

Figure 4.2 The floating toolbar.

The Tool Palette and the Style Control Bar

By default, the tool palette appears immediately below the toolbar. The tool palette contains 16 buttons with which you can create and manipulate images. When you click on a button, the style control bar displays options.

Zoom—Click on this button to zoom in (see the details of an image) or zoom out (see all or most of an image). When you click on the **Zoom** button, the style control bar contains the Zoom Factor drop-down list box from which you can select the level of zoom. Clicking on the Zoom button is equivalent to choosing **View: Zoom In** or **View: Zoom Out** and selecting a zoom factor. For more information, see the "Zooming the Image" section later in the chapter.

Mover—Click on this button with the left mouse button to move the area of the image that you can see in the workspace; right-click to move the area that you have selected. When you click on the **Mover** button, the style control bar contains the Zoom Factor drop-down list box from which you can select the level of zoom. For more information, see the "Moving the Image or Selection" section later in the chapter.

Selection—Click on this button to select an area of the image. When you click on the **Selection** button, the style control bar contains the Selection Type drop-down list box from which you can select a geometric selection area: **Rectangle**, **Square**, **Ellipse**, or **Circle**. The style control bar also includes the Feather text/option box with which you can determine the sharpness or softness of the edge of the selection. For more information, see the "Modifying an Image" section later in the chapter.

Freehand—Click on this button to select an irregular area of the image. When you click on the **Freehand** button, the style control bar contains the Feather text/option box with which you can determine the sharpness or softness of the edge of the selection. For more information, see the "Modifying an Image" section later in the chapter.

Magic Wand—Click on this button to select one of the color characteristics of the image. When you click on the **Magic Wand** button, the style control bar contains the Match Mode drop-down list box from which you can select a characteristic: **RGB Value** (color), **Hue**, or **Brightness**. It also displays the Tolerance text/option box with which you can determine how close the selection must be to the Match Mode option and the Feather text/option box with which you can determine the sharpness or softness of the edge of the selection. For more information, see the "Modifying an Image" section later in the chapter.

Dropper—Click on this button to change the foreground or background color. When you click on the **Dropper** button, the style control bar contains the Zoom Factor drop-down list box from which you can select the level of zoom. For more information, see the "Changing the Foreground and Background Colors" section later in the chapter.

Paint Brushes—Click on this button to enable a drawing tool. When you click on the **Paint Brushes** button, the style control bar contains the Brush Type drop-down list box from which you can select a drawing tool, the Size text/list box from which you can select a point size, the Shape drop-down list box from which you can select the shape of the drawing tool, and the Paper Texture drop-down list box from which you can simulate brush or pencil strokes on textured paper. For more information about using paintbrushes, see the "Creating an Image—Example 1" section later in the chapter.

Clone Brush–Click on this button to copy part of an image to another part of the image or to another image. When you click on the **Clone Brush** button, the style control bar contains the Clone Mode drop-down list box from which you can select whether the area from which you copy moves or does not move after the selection and the Size text/list box from which you can select a point size. It also provides the Shape drop-down list box from which you can select the shape of the drawing tool, the Opacity text/option box from which you can select the level of opacity or transparency, and the Paper Texture drop-down list box from which you can select the texture of the freeform drawing.

 Color Replacer–Click on this button to replace one color with another in the image. When you click on the **Color Replacer** button, the style control bar contains the Size text/list box from which you can select the width of the replacer (in pixels), the Shape drop-down list box from which you can select the shape of the replacer tool, the Tolerance text/option box from which you can determine how close the color must be to be replaced, and the Paper Texture drop-down list box from which you can select the texture of the drawing. Double-click on the button to replace the color of the entire image.

 Retouch–Click on this button to retouch 24-bit color or 8-bit grayscale images. When you click on the **Retouch** button, the style control bar contains the Retouch Mode drop-down list box from which you can select the type of retouch action, the Size text/list box from which you can select the width of the retouch tool (in pixels), and the Shape drop-down list box from which you can select the shape of the retouch tool. It also contains the Opacity text/option box from which you can select the level of opacity or transparency and the Paper Texture drop-down list box from which you can select the texture of the drawing.

 Eraser–Click on this button to erase part of the image. When you click on the **Eraser** button, the style control bar contains the Size text/list box from which you can select the fineness of the eraser and the Shape drop-down list box from which you can select the shape of the eraser. It also provides the Opacity text/option box from which you can select the level of opacity or transparency and the Paper Texture drop-down list box from which you can select the texture of the erased area.

 Airbrush–Click on this button to add an airbrush effect to part of the image. When you click on the **Airbrush** button, the style control bar contains the Size text/list box from which you can select the fineness of the airbrush effect, the Shape drop-down list box from which you can select the shape of the effect, the Opacity text/option box from which you can select the level of opacity or transparency, and the Paper Texture drop-down list box from which you can select the texture of the airbrushed area.

 Flood Fill–Click on this button to fill an enclosed area of the image with the current foreground color. When you click on the **Flood Fill** button, the style control bar contains the Match Mode drop-down list box from which you can select a color characteristic: **RGB Value** (color), **Hue**, **Brightness**, or **None**. It also provides the Tolerance text/option box from which you can determine how close the selection must be to the Match Mode option; the Fill Style drop-down list box from which you can select the type of fill (solid, pattern, or a gradient), and the Options button, which includes options determined by the selected fill style.

 Text–Click on this button to add text to the image. When you click on **Text**, the style control bar contains the Zoom Factor drop-down list box from which you can select the level of zoom. For more information, see the "Adding Text" section later in the chapter.

Line—Click on this button to draw a line in the image. When you click on the **Line** button, the style control bar contains the Width text/option box from which you can select the width (in pixels) of the line. For more information, see the "Drawing Lines" section later in the chapter.

 Shapes—Click on this button to draw a geometric shape in the image. When you click on **Shapes**, the style control bar contains the Line text/option box from which you can select the width (in pixels) of the line, the Shape drop-down list box from which you can select the shape, and the Style drop-down list box from which you can choose to outline or fill the drawn shape. For more information, see the "Creating Geometric Shapes" section later in the chapter.

Hiding and Displaying the Tool Palette and the Style Control Bar

 To hide or display the tool palette, click on the **Toggle Tool Palette** button or choose **View: Tool Palette**. A check mark preceding the command indicates that the tool palette is on display.

 To hide or display the style control bar, click on the **Toggle Style Bar** button or choose **View: Style Bar**. A check mark preceding the command indicates that the style control bar is on display.

The Workspace

The Paint Shop Pro workspace is the entire area below the style control bar, to the left of the color palette on the right side of the computer screen, and above the status bar at the bottom. If you are working on an image, the workspace includes the window in which it is located.

Paint Shop Pro allows you to open more than one window in the workspace. Simply choose **Window: New Window** or press **Shift+W** to open a new window. Then, select **Window: Cascade** to display one window behind the other with both title bars showing. Or, select **Window: Tile Horizontally** or **Window: Tile Vertically** to display both windows, either one above the other or side by side, respectively. To close a window, click on the **Close** button (the *X* in the upper-right corner of the window). To maximize or restore the remaining window, click on the **Maximize** or **Restore** button, respectively, to the left of the **Close** button. Another way to maximize the remaining window, to fill in the empty space left by a closed window, is to choose **Window: Tile Horizontally** or **Window: Tile Vertically**.

The most important reason for opening more than one window at a time is to view and work with your image in two different ways. For example, you can show it at its actual size (that is, Normal Viewing) in one window and magnify or zoom in on it in another window. When you change the image in one window, it automatically changes in the other. For more information about zooming, refer the section, "Zooming the Image" later in the chapter.

If you work with more than one window at a time, consider providing more space in which to work by hiding the parts of the window. Choose one or more of the following commands: **View: Histogram Window**, **View: Toolbar**, **View: Tool Palette**, **View: Color Palette**, **View: Style Bar**, or **View: Status Bar**. To display a hidden window element, simply issue the command again.

The Image Window

The image window is the area in the workspace that contains the current image. By default, the image window is a 500 × 500-pixel square.

The Color Palette

The Color palette (Figure 4.3), which is located on the right side of the screen, shows the current foreground and background colors and other color information. At the top of the palette, you'll find a range of colors from which you can select. Immediately below that are the current colors; the foreground color is within the box that is above and to the left, and the background color is within the box that is below and to the right. Below that are the red-green-blue values of the current location of the mouse pointer. (If the pointer is not pointing to a color in the color palette or the image, the R, G, and B labels are followed by dashes. At the bottom of the palette is a sample box containing the color on which the mouse pointer rests.

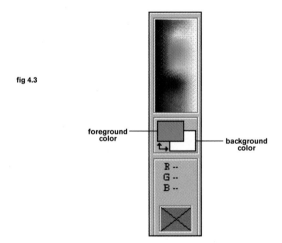

fig 4.3

foreground color

background color

Figure 4.3 The color palette shows the current foreground and background colors and other color values.

You can change the location of the color palette by pointing to an area very near a box or border and dragging. You can move the palette to any part of the window, but you cannot change its shape or size. Note that you can move the color palette elements up and down the gray bar on which the palette is located.

To display a hidden color palette or to hide a displayed color palette, either click on the **Toggle Color Palette** button or choose **View: Color Palette**.

Changing Color Preferences

By default, Paint Shop Pro uses the RGB (red-green-blue) color format, which is the best choice for Web graphics. If you are more comfortable with HSL (hue-saturation-luminance, also known as hue-saturation-value), you can change your preferences. For more information about RGB colors, see the "About RGB Colors" section in Chapter 3. For information about HSL colors, see the "About HSV Colors" section, which is also in Chapter 3. While you are changing color format, you can also choose to display numeric color values in decimal (the default) or hexadecimal. To change your color preferences, follow these steps:

1. Choose **File: Preferences: General Program Preferences**.
2. In the Paint Shop Pro Preferences dialog box, click on the **Palettes** tab. Paint Shop Pro displays the Palettes section (Figure 4.4).

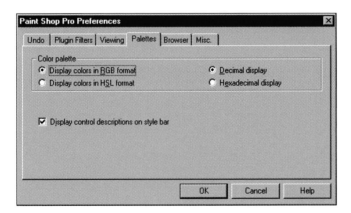

Figure 4.4 The Palettes section of the Paint Shop Pro Preferences dialog box.

3. To choose a color format, click on the **Display Colors in RGB Format** or **Display Colors in HSL Format** option button.
4. To choose a numeric display, click on the **Decimal Display** or **Hexadecimal Display** button.
5. To display the labels above the drop-down list boxes and text/option boxes in the style control bar, check the **Display Control Descriptions on Style Bar** check box (the default). To hide the labels, clear the **Display Control Descriptions on Style Bar** check box.

6. When you have completed your selections, click on **OK**.

Changing the Foreground and Background Colors

 To change the foreground and background colors, use the **Dropper** tool. You can choose a color from within the color palette or from an image (for example, to match an existing color when editing an image). To specify a color, follow these steps:

1. Click on the **Dropper** tool.
2. Move the mouse pointer around the color palette or the current image. Look at the color in the sample box as you move the pointer.
3. To choose a foreground color, left-click when the sample box color is as desired.
4. To choose a background color, right-click when the sample box color is appropriate.

 SHORTCUT You can create an image file of colors with which you like to work. For example, when moving the **Dropper** around the color palette, you may have a hard time finding a pure color, such as a Red with an R value of 255 and G and B values of 0. If you collect good colors in their own image file, you can open the file, move the **Dropper** to the desired color, and left-click or right-click to make it the new foreground or background color.

 NOTE When you start Paint Shop Pro, the last foreground and background colors selected are the current colors.

Editing, Saving, and Loading the Color Palette

You can edit the color palette for the current image. For example, you might want to work with several shades of a particular color, you might want to add more colors to the palette, or you might want to use a 216-color palette compatible with Web graphics. On the CD-ROM disk, you'll find 216color.pal. To be able to load it, move it into the directory in which you have installed Paint Shop Pro.

 NOTE Colors vary according to the graphics board and associated software installed in a computer, so it's best to view all colors and see how they work together before making a final color choice. Regardless of your color choice, there is a very good chance that some browser will interpret your colors in a very strange way.

To edit the color palette, follow these steps:

1. Choose **Colors: Edit Palette** or press **Shift+P**. Paint Shop Pro opens the Edit Palette dialog box (Figure 4.5).

2. If you wish, sort the colors by opening the Sort Order drop-down list box and selecting **Palette Order**, **By Luminance**, or **By Hue**.

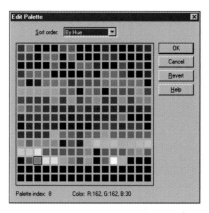

Figure 4.5 The Edit Palette dialog box.

3. To change the color of a particular color, double-click on its square. Paint Shop pro opens the Color dialog box (Figure 4.6).

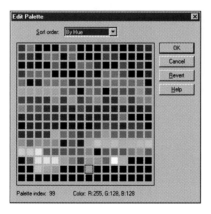

Figure 4.6 The Color dialog box after editing some yellows and oranges near the bottom of the color grid.

4. You can adjust the color in various ways:

   ◆ by sliding the mouse pointer around the large color refiner box.

   ◆ by sliding the mouse pointer up and down the vertical luminosity bar.

   ◆ by typing hue, saturation, and/or luminosity values in the Hue, Sat, and/or Lum text boxes, respectively.

   ◆ by typing red, green, and/or blue values in the Red, Green, and/or Blue text boxes, respectively.

SHORTCUT You can specify a color value by clicking on the square of a color that resembles the desired color in the Edit Palette dialog box. Write down the R, G, and B values at the bottom of the dialog box. Then, in the Color dialog box, try Red, Green, and Blue values similar to the values that you wrote down. To fine-tune your selection, slide up and down the vertical luminosity bar.

5. When you have selected the desired color value, click on **OK** to close the dialog box.

6. Change other colors by repeating steps 3 to 5, or close the dialog box by clicking on **OK**.

To save the palette so that you can use it for future images, choose **Colors: Save Palette**. Then, to load the palette, choose **Colors: Load Palette** or press **Shift+O**.

The Status Bar

A status bar (Figures 4.7 and 4.8), which displays Paint Shop Pro information, appears at the bottom of the window.

Left click to move the visible area of the image; right click to move the selection area

Figure 4.7 The Paint Shop Pro status bar with the mouse pointer pointing to the Mover button.

(336, 112)   Image: 500 x 500 x 16 - 246.9 KBytes

Figure 4.8 The Paint Shop Pro status bar with the mouse pointer within an image.

◆ If you have selected a menu command, the status bar contains a short description. The default description tells you how to get help.

◆ If you are pointing to an area within an image, the status bar displays the current X-Y coordinates on the left side. On the right side of the status bar are the image size (in pixels), the number of colors, and the computer memory (RAM) needed to create this image.

SHORTCUT You can control the memory used by an image by changing the number of colors (1 bit requires the smallest memory and 24 bits requires the largest) or changing the dimensions (a small size results in smaller memory use). GIF files are 8 bit, or 256 colors.

To hide a displayed status bar or to display a hidden status bar, choose **View: Status Bar**.

Zooming the Image

When you view an image at its actual size, you may not be able to work on its details, or, conversely, you may not be able to see it completely—especially if it extends beyond the limits of your computer screen. Paint Shop Pro allows you to zoom in (that is, see the details as small as a pixel, depending on the percentage you have zoomed in) or zoom out (that is, see a greater part of a large image). You can zoom in up to 16 times the actual size; you can zoom out to 1/16 of the actual size.

You can zoom in using several methods:

◆ Click on the **Zoom** button. Then, move the magnifying-glass mouse pointer to the image and left-click repeatedly until the image looks as large as you want (up to 16 times the actual size). In the title bar of the image window, you can see the current zoom-in factor (from 2:1 to 16:1).

◆ Press the plus sign (+) on the numeric keypad repeatedly until the image looks as large as you want (up to 16 times the actual size).

◆ Choose **View: Zoom In** and select a value from 2:1 to 16:1 from the cascading menu.

You can zoom out using several methods:

◆ Click on the **Zoom** button. Then, move the magnifying-glass mouse pointer to the image, and right-click repeatedly until the image looks as small as you want (down to 1/16 the actual size). In the title bar of the image window, you can see the current zoom-in factor (from 1:2 to 1:16).

◆ Press the minus sign (-) on the numeric keypad repeatedly until the image looks as small as you want (down to 1/16 the actual size).

◆ Choose **View: Zoom Out** and select a value from 1:2 to 1:16 from the cascading menu.

 To return to the actual size of the image, click on the **Normal Viewing** button, zoom in or zoom out until the image is 1:1, choose **View: Normal Viewing (1:1)**, or press **Ctrl+Alt+N**.

Figure 4.9 shows three windows containing images of Rodin's Thinker. Thinker:1 shows the image at its actual size, Thinker:2 shows the zoomed-in head, and Thinker:3 is zoomed-out.

Figure 4.9 Three views of the Thinker: actual, zoomed in, and zoomed out.

Turning on the Grid

After you zoom in 10 times (10:1) or more, Paint Shop Pro allows you to work with a grid that shows each pixel in your image. To enable the grid display, choose **View: Grid When Zoomed** or press **Ctrl+Alt+G**. If the grid is turned on, a checkmark precedes the command. To turn off the grid, choose **View: Grid When Zoomed** or press **Ctrl+Alt+G** again.

Working with a grid allows you to create or edit an image at the pixel level. For example, you can round sharp corners by removing a pixel or two at the very point of a corner, or you can add narrow shadows by selecting a slightly darker color and painting a line along the borders of an image. You can also touch up text to make it easier to read. Figure 4.10 shows the grid for an image zoomed to 10:1.

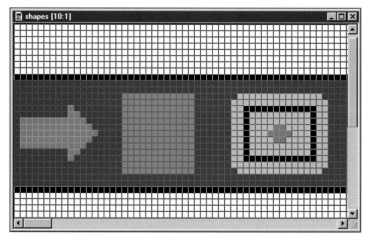

Figure 4.10 Shapes shown at 10:1 with an active grid.

Moving the Image or Selection

The image does not always have to be in the same location in the workspace. You can move the image window, the image, or a selection using the following techniques:

- You can move the window as you would any window or dialog box, simply drag it by its title bar.
- You can move the image around its window by clicking on the **Mover** button, holding down the left mouse button, and dragging.
- You can move a selection around the window by clicking on the **Mover** button, holding down the right mouse button, and dragging.

CREATING AN IMAGE—EXAMPLE 1

Paint Shop Pro enables you to create images by combining several geometric shapes and drawing with a number of brush tools.

Creating Geometric Shapes

 Use the **Shapes** tool to draw rectangles, squares, ovals, and circles using the foreground color. To draw a shape, follow these steps:

1. Click on the **Shapes** tool.
2. From the Shape drop-down list box in the style control bar, select a shape: **Rectangle**, **Square**, **Oval**, or **Circle**.
3. From the Style drop-down list box in the style control bar, select **Outlined** to create an outlined shape or **Filled** to create a filled shape.
4. Move the mouse pointer to a starting point, drag the mouse pointer to the opposite corner of the shape, and release the mouse button.

 SHORTCUT   If you have created an outlined shape and want to fill it with color, if you want to change the color of a filled shape, or if you want to apply a color to an shape completely enclosed within a border or another color, select a foreground color and click on the **Flood Fill** tool.

Drawing Lines

 Use the **Line** tool to draw lines of varying widths. To draw a line, follow these steps:

1. Click on the **Line** tool.
2. From the Width text/option box in the style control bar, select a width from 1 to 100.

3. Move the mouse pointer to a starting point, drag the mouse pointer to the opposite end of the line, and release the mouse button. If you want to draw a line at a multiple of 45 degrees, press and hold down the **Shift** key before drawing the line.

Drawing Freeform Shapes, Curves, and Lines

 Use the **Paint Brushes** tool to draw free-form shapes, curves, and lines with a variety of looks, depending on your selection of options from the style control bar. To use the **Paint Brushes** tool, follow these steps:

1. Click on the **Paint Brushes** tool.
2. From the Brush Type drop-down list box in the style control bar, select a brush type: **Normal**, **Pen**, **Pencil**, **Marker**, **Crayon**, **Chalk**, or **Charcoal**.
3. From the Size drop-down list box in the style control bar, select a size, which sets the width of the free-form shapes that you draw. Valid values range from 1 to 200.
4. From the Shape drop-down list box in the style control bar, select a shape: **Square**, **Round**, **Left Slash**, **Right Slash**, or **Horizontal**. The shape that you select determines the look of the top and bottom of the free-form shape that you draw.
5. From the Paper Texture drop-down list box in the style control bar, select a texture from a long list. The texture option simulates the look of a free-form shape drawn on a particular paper texture.
6. Move the mouse pointer to a starting point and drag it to create a free-form shape.
7. When the free-form shape is complete, release the mouse button. Figure 4.11 shows a series of sequential frames from the duck.gif animation. Each frame uses lines and freeform shapes and curves.

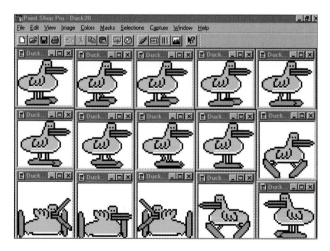

Figure 4.11 A series of sequential frames using lines and freeform shapes and curves.

Adding Text

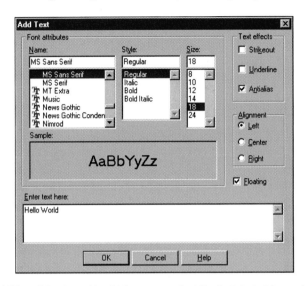

Use the **Text** button to add text to the image window. After you click on the **Text** button and click at the location at which you want to insert the text, Paint Shop Pro opens the Add Text dialog box (Figure 4.12) in which you can insert text; change the font (using fonts installed on your computer), point size, or style; and specify text effects and alignment.

Figure 4.12 The Add Text dialog box with which you can adjust the font, font style, or size of text in a image.

The options in the Add Text dialog box described below.

Name–A text/list box from which you can select a font that is installed on your computer.

Style–A text/list box from which you can select the text style: **Regular** (not enhanced), **Italic**, **Bold**, or **Bold Italic**.

Size–A text/list box in which you can type a point size or from which you can choose from the point sizes available for the selected font.

Strikeout–A check box that, when checked, draws a line through the text that you type. The default is a cleared check box.

Underline–A check box that, when checked, underlines the text that you type. The default is a cleared check box.

Antialias–A check box that, when checked (the default), smoothes jagged pieces of the text by shading it. This option is available only for 256-color (or greater) images.

Alignment–A group of option buttons from which you can select the alignment of the text within its bounding box.

Floating—A check box that, when checked (the default), draws the typed-in text in the foreground color and in a bounding box that floats in a separate layer above the image. When the check box is cleared, the text is drawn in the color at the current location and in the same layer as the image.

Enter Text Here—A text box in which you type the text to be inserted in the image window.

 NOTE

After you have added text to a image, you cannot edit it as text. The only way to change the text is to delete it and add a new version, or edit it as you would a graphic.

MODIFYING AN IMAGE

After creating an image, you can modify it in several ways.

◆ Use the Selections menu commands to select part or all of an image.

◆ Use the Edit menu commands to copy, cut, paste, or delete part or all of an image.

◆ Use the Image menu commands to flip, mirror, rotate, crop, or resize an image; add a border; or change an image using special effects, deformations, and filters.

Selecting an Image

Sometimes you can work with an image without selecting it. For example, if you add shapes, lines, or text to an image window, you don't need to make a selection. However, at other times, you must make a selection before working on an image. For example, if you want to copy, move, or remove part of an image, you must select it. Paint Shop Pro provides several tools for making selections.

Selecting a Geometric Area

 Click on the **Selection** button to select a geometric area of an image. You can specify a selection type of **Rectangle**, **Square**, **Ellipse**, or **Circle**. Figure 4.13 shows an image with a rectangular area selected and moved. Notice that the selection is surrounded with a moving marquee of dashes. While the marquee is active, you can continue to work with the selection.

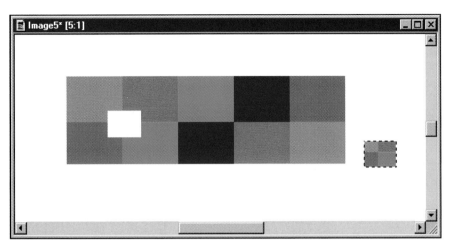

Figure 4.13 A rectangular selection.

Selecting an Irregular Area

 Click on the **Freehand** button to select an irregular area of an image. Because you define a selection area by drawing it on the image, there is no need to specify a selection type. To draw a selection area, use the cross hairs as a guide. Figure 4.14 shows an irregular selection above the image and the Freehand mouse pointer.

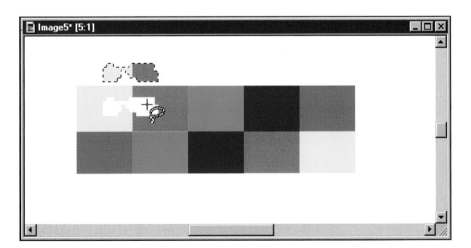

Figure 4.14 An irregular selection and the Freehand mouse pointer.

Selecting by Color Characteristics

 Click on the **Magic Wand** button to select one of the color characteristics (**RGB Value**, **Hue**, or **Brightness**) of an image. This allows you to choose one section of an image with one click. You can also specify the closeness of the match by typing or selecting a value from the Tolerance text/option box. Figure 4.15 shows a Magic Wand selection.

 Feather, which is available for all three selection tools, allows you to select a specific area. A smaller Feather value results in a very "tight" selection; a larger value includes more pixels in the selection.

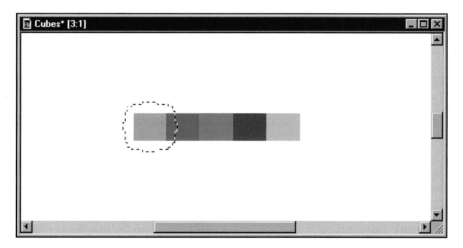

Figure 4.15 A Magic Wand selection, which is based on an RGB value and a large Feather value.

Selecting an Entire Image

To select the entire image, choose **Selections: Select All** or press **Shift+A**. Paint Shop Pro draws a bounding box around the edges of the image window.

Inactivating a Selection

To inactivate a selection (that is, make it permanent in its current location and remove the selection bounding box), choose **Selections: Select None** or press **Shift+N**.

Inverting a Selection

To invert the selection (that is, select the unselected area and "unselect" the selected area), choose **Selections: Invert** or press **Shift+V**. Paint Shop Pro draws a bounding box around the edges of the image window. Figures 4.16 and 4.17 show a selection and an inverted selection of the same image.

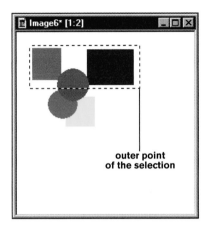

Figure 4.16
A small portion of an image is selected.

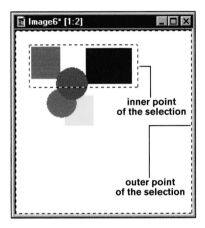

Figure 4.17
The entire image except for the original selection is now selected.

Modifying a Selection

After you have made a selection, you can adjust it in three ways: you can feather it, change its *opacity* (its level of transparency), and make selected pixels transparent.

Feathering a Selection

To feather the current selection, choose **Selections: Modify: Feather** or press **Ctrl+H**. In the Feather Selection dialog box (Figure 4.18), change the value in the Feather text/list box. Paint Shop Pro feathers the selection.

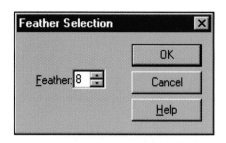

Figure 4.18
The Feather Selection dialog box.

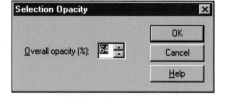

Figure 4.19
The Selection Opacity dialog box.

 Many animation programs do not recognize transparency information from art programs.

Changing the Opacity of a Selection

To change the opacity of the current selection, choose **Selections: Modify: Overall Opacity** or press **Ctrl+Y**. In the Selection Opacity dialog box (Figure 4.19), change the percent value in the Overall Opacity text/list box. Paint Shop Pro makes the image more opaque or more transparent.

Making a Color Transparent

Animated GIFs should be transparent to allow the background color of the page to show through. To choose a transparent color for an image, choose **File: Preferences: File Format Preferences**. When the File Preferences dialog box (Figure 4.20) opens, click on the **GIF** tab, if needed, and click on an option button:

Maintain Original File's Transparency Information–Select this option to keep the current transparency settings.

Do Not Save Any Transparency Information–Select this option to remove the current transparency settings.

Set the Transparency Value to the Background Color–Select this option to set the color that will be made transparent to the current background color (or the closest match on the current palette).

Set the Transparency Value to Palette Entry *n*–Select this option to set the color that will be made transparent to a selected color from the current palette.

Preview–Click on this button to see the effects of your choice on the current image.

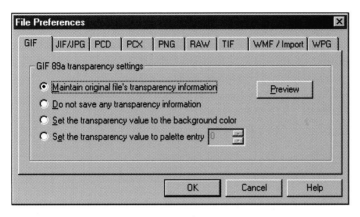

Figure 4.20 The File Preferences dialog box.

Another way to make a specific color transparent is to choose **Selections: Modify: Transparent Color** or press **Ctrl+T**. Paint Shop Pro opens the Transparent Color Select dialog box (Figure 4.21). From the Transparent Color drop-down list box, select a color: **Foreground Color**, **Background Color**, **White**, **Black**, **Red**, **Green**, or **Blue**. You can adjust the level of tolerance, so that Paint Shop Pro can make transparent a color that is close to one of those in the Transparent Color drop-down list box but is not an exact match.

SHORTCUT   Making the background of an image transparent helps you to create GIF files (thus, animations) that take as little storage space as possible.

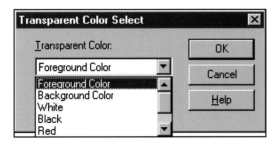

Figure 4.21 The Transparent Color Select dialog box with an open Transparent Color drop-down list box.

Moving a Selection

To move a selection, move the mouse pointer to it. When the mouse pointer changes to a four-headed arrow, hold down the left mouse button and drag the selection to its new location. Then, release the mouse button.

Copying, Cutting, and Pasting Selections

Most Windows-based programs include an Edit menu that includes commands with which you can copy, cut, paste, and delete objects. In Paint Shop Pro, you can use Edit menu commands to work with images.

Copying a Selection

 To copy the current selection to the Windows Clipboard, click on the **Copy** button, choose **Edit: Copy**, or press **Ctrl+C**. When you copy a selection, Paint Shop Pro leaves the selection in place and places a copy in the Clipboard. If the **Copy** button or **Copy** command is dimmed, you have not made a selection.

Cutting a Selection

 To remove the current selection and place it in the Windows Clipboard, click on the **Cut** button, choose **Edit: Cut**, or press **Ctrl+X**. When you cut a selection, Paint Shop Pro fills the space left by the selection with the background color. If the **Cut** button or **Cut** command is dimmed, you have not selected an object.

Pasting a Selection

Paint Shop Pro has four Paste commands: **As New Image**, **As New Selection**, **As Transparent Selection**, and **Into Selection**. If the Paste as New Image button or the commands on the Paste cascading menu are dimmed, the Windows Clipboard is empty.

- ◆ To paste the contents of the Windows Clipboard into a new window, click on the **Paste as New Image** button, choose **Edit: Paste: As New Image**, or press **Ctrl+V**.
- ◆ To paste the contents of the Windows Clipboard in the current image window, choose **Edit: Paste: As New Selection** or press **Ctrl+E.** Paint Shop Pro inserts the selection in the lower right corner of the window with a four-headed mouse pointer over it. Move the selection to the desired location in the image window and click to place it.

- To paste the contents of the Windows Clipboard in the current image window and make all the pixels with the background color transparent, choose **Edit: Paste: As Transparent Selection** or press **Ctrl+Shift+E**.

- To replace the current selection in the current image window with the contents of the Windows Clipboard, choose **Edit: Paste: Into Selection** or press **Ctrl+L**.

Deleting a Selection

To delete a selection permanently, either choose **Edit: Clear** or press the **Del** key. After you have deleted a selection, the only way to restore it is to choose **Edit: Undo** or press **Ctrl+Z**. However, remember that after you have performed another action, you cannot undo the deletion; Paint Shop Pro allows you to undo only the last action.

CREATING IMAGES FOR ANIMATION

Slight changes from one image to another simulate motion. So, to animate a movie-marquee sign, you can make two variations: with a "light bulb" border with alternately changing colors and with text that flashes in two different colors and two different sizes.

ABOUT THIS ANIMATION— MOVIE-MARQUEE NEW SIGN

*marqnew.gif **2K 71 × 35** Level: Easy*

The movie-marquee NEW sign has a running marquee border and a flashing NEW sign within.

- This animation is composed of two GIFs.
- The sign was created in Windows Paint and edited in Paint Shop Pro.
- The lights in the marquee are yellow with white highlights and gray with no highlights or shadows. The highlights and shadows were painted pixel by pixel.
- Many browsers do not recognize animations. Both GIFs in this animation are acceptable as static GIFs.
- This animation is set to loop infinitely.
- Consider setting this animation to a medium speed.

MANIPULATING AN IMAGE—EXAMPLE 2

Use the Image menu commands to flip, mirror, rotate, crop, or resize an image; add a border; or change an image using special effects, deformations, and filters.

Flipping an Image

You can create a simple animation by repeatedly flipping an image from top to bottom. For example, you can simulate changing colors from black to white and from white to black by flipping a black-and-white checkerboard pattern. To flip an image from top to bottom, choose **Image: Flip** or press **Ctrl+I**. To flip the image back to its original appearance, choose **Image: Mirror** or press **Ctrl+M** again.

Mirroring an Image

Mirroring an image actually flips it from left to right. To mirror an image, choose **Image: Mirror** or press **Ctrl+M**. To flip the image back to its original appearance, choose **Image: Mirror** or press **Ctrl+M** again.

Rotating an Image

Paint Shop Pro allows simple rotation of 90, 180, and 270 degrees for images less than 256 color grayscale or 16 million color. For 256 color grayscale or 16 million color, you can rotate by degrees. To rotate an image, choose **Image: Rotate** to open the Rotate dialog box (Figure 4.22).

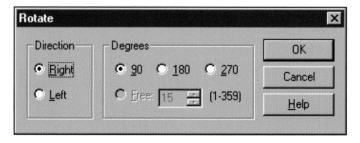

Figure 4.22 The Rotate dialog box.

The options in this dialog box are described below.

Direction—To rotate the image toward the right (the default), click on the **Right** option button. To rotate toward the left, click on the **Left** option button.

90—Click on this option button to rotate the image 90 degrees.

180—Click on this option button to rotate the image 180 degrees.

270—Click on this option button to rotate the image 270 degrees.

Free—Select or type the number of degrees to rotate the image in this text/option box.

WARNING When you rotate an image, its center does not always remain in the same place. Sometimes, a wobble is a good effect in an animation. If you want little or no wobble, you may have to select rotated images and move the center of each toward standard coordinates (look on the left side of the status bar). In addition, when Paint Shop Pro rotates an image, it may change its width and height. Fortunately, many animation programs (such as Microsoft GIF Animator) adjust the dimensions of each image as you construct an animation.

SHORTCUT If the **Free** option is not available, the current image does not have sufficient depth of color to be rotated by degrees. To rotate this type of image using the **Free** option, choose **Colors: Increase Color Depth: 16 Million Colors** (24 Bit). After rotating the image, choose **Colors: Decrease Color Depth** and choose a command from the cascading menu.

Adding a Border to an Image

You can add a border, using the current background color, to an image, which means that you will increase its size. To add a border, follow these steps:

1. If needed, change the background color.
2. Choose **Image: Add Borders**. Paint Shop Pro opens the Add Borders dialog box, which contains the values of the last border that you entered.
3. To make the border the same size on all four sides, check the **Symmetric** check box.
4. Type or select values from the Top, Bottom, Left, and/or Right text/option boxes. (If you have checked **Symmetric**, Paint Shop Pro inserts identical values in all four text/option boxes.)
5. Click on **OK**. Paint Shop Pro adds the border to the image, thereby increasing the size of the image window; the image remains the same size (Figure 4.23).

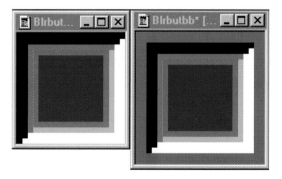

Figure 4.23 Two images—one with an added border.

Cropping an Image

When you crop an image, you remove unnecessary portions of the image. In Paint Shop Pro, you change the dimensions of an image when you crop, resulting in both a smaller size and a smaller file. To crop an image, follow these steps:

1. Select the image using one of the Selection tools: the **Selection**, **Freehand**, or **Magic Wand** button.

2. Choose **Image: Crop** or press **Shift+R**. (If the command is dimmed, you have forgotten to select the image.) Paint Shop Pro crops the area around the image or the image itself, depending on the area of the selection.

Enlarging the Canvas

Enlarging the canvas also changes the image size, filling in the new area with the background color. To enlarge the canvas, follow these steps:

1. If needed, change the background color.

2. Choose **Image: Enlarge Canvas**. Paint Shop Pro opens the Enlarge Canvas dialog box, which contains the last values that you entered.

3. To center the image in the enlarged image window, check the **Center Image** check box.

4. Type or select values from the Width and Height text/option boxes.

5. Click on **OK**. Paint Shop Pro increases the size of the image window; the image remains the same size (Figure 4.24).

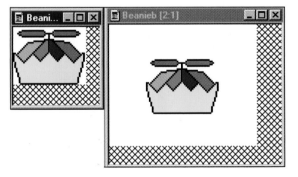

Figure 4.24 Two images—one with an enlarged canvas.

Resampling an Image

When you resample an image, you change the image size while Paint Shop Pro maintains tight control of image resolution. Use resampling to change the dimensions for photographs and similar fine images. To resample an image, follow these steps:

1. Choose **Image: Resample** or press **Shift+S**. Paint Shop Pro opens the Resample dialog box (Figure 4.25).

2. To select a predefined size, click on one of the five option buttons on the left side of the dialog box.

3. If you plan to use custom dimensions and want to keep the current *aspect ratio* (the proportions of width and height), check the **Maintain Aspect Ratio** check box.

4. To select a custom size, type the width and height in the text boxes on the right side of the dialog box.

5. Click on **OK**. Paint Shop Pro changes the size of the image.

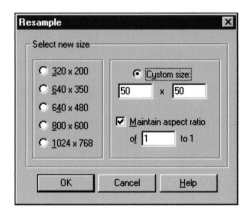

Figure 4.25 The Resample dialog box.

Resizing an Image

When you resize an image, you change the image size. Use resizing to change the dimensions for simple or reduced-color images using the Resize dialog box, which is identical to the Resample dialog box. To resize an image, choose **Image: Resize** and follow the steps in the preceding section.

Adding a Drop Shadow Behind a Selection

You can add a shadow behind the current selection by following these steps:

1. If you want to select a specific shadow color, change the foreground or background color.

2. Choose **Image: Special Effects: Add Drop Shadow**. Paint Shop Pro opens the Drop Shadow dialog box.

3. To change the shadow color from the default black, open the Color drop-down list box and select a color: **Foreground Color**, **Background Color**, **White**, **Black**, **Red**, **Green**, or **Blue**.

4. To change the level of opacity, type or select a number from the Opacity text/option box. A high value is more opaque, and a low value is more transparent.

5. To blue the edges of the shadow, type or select a value from the Blur text/option box.

6. To change the position of the shadow behind the selection, move the Offset sliders vertically or horizontally. To review the results, look at the sample. You can also type values in the Vertical or Horizontal text boxes.

7. Click on **OK**. Paint Shop Pro adds a drop shadow (Figure 4.26).

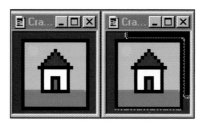

Figure 4.26
Two images—one with a drop shadow.

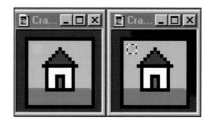

Figure 4.27
Two images—one with a selected and changed sun.

Cutting Out a Selection

You can cut a selection out of an image and apply other effects by using the Cutout dialog box. Simply follow these steps:

1. If you want to fill the cutout area or a shadow behind the selection with a particular foreground or background color, change the foreground or background color.

2. Choose **Image: Special Effects: Cutout**. Paint Shop Pro opens the Cutout dialog box (Figure 4.27).

3. To change the interior color, check the **Fill Interior with Color** check box, open the Interior Color drop-down list box and select a color: **Foreground Color**, **Background Color**, **White**, **Black**, **Red**, **Green**, or **Blue**.

4. Follow steps 3 to 7 in the preceding section.

Adding a Chisel Border to a Selection

You can make a selection look as though it is sitting on top of a three-dimensional four-sided border by following these steps:

1. If you want to select a specific background color to comprise part of a background-color chisel, change the background color.

2. Choose **Image: Special Effects: Chisel**. Paint Shop Pro opens the Chisel dialog box.

3. To change the border width, type or select a number from the Size text/option box.

4. To create a semi-transparent border that allows the current background of the image to shine through, click on the **Transparent** option button.

5. To create a semi-transparent border that allows the current background color to shine through, click on the **Background Color** option button.

6. Click on **OK**. Paint Shop Pro adds a chisel border (Figure 4.28).

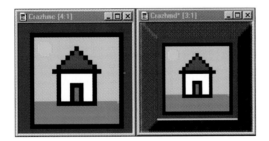

Figure 4.28 Two images—one with a dark chisel border.

Buttonizing an Image or Selection

You can make an image or selection look as though it is a toolbar button with the buttonize special effects. To buttonize an image, follow these steps:

1. If you want to select a specific background color to comprise the edge of the button, change the background color.

2. Choose **Image: Special Effects: Buttonize**. Paint Shop Pro opens the Buttonize dialog box (Figure 4.29).

3. To change the border width, type or select a percentage from the Edge Size text/option box. The preview picture shows the chosen options.

4. To create a semi-transparent narrow edge, click on the **Transparent Edge** option button. The preview picture shows the chosen options.

5. To create a semi-transparent thick border, click on the **Solid Edge** option button. The preview picture shows the chosen options.

6. Click on **OK**.

Figure 4.29 The Buttonize dialog box.

Adding a Hot-Wax Finish to an Image or Selection

You can apply a coating on top of an image or selection by choosing **Image: Special Effects: Hot Wax Coating**. Remember that you can undo the last action performed by choosing **Edit: Undo** or pressing **Ctrl+Z**.

Deforming an Image

Paint Shop Pro provides a variety of commands with which you can change the form of an image—if it has over 256 colors. The best way to view these effects on the current image is to choose **Image: Deformation Browser**. When Paint Shop Pro opens the Deformation Browser dialog box (Figure 4.30), you can browse the Deformation Name list box, clicking on names and viewing the Sample Preview window.

SHORTCUT   The best way to use deformation effects in an animation is to save several versions of an image. Then, open an image file, apply the deformation, and save the file. After you have changed a series of images, test the results using an animation program. For example, animating an unchanged image and the same image changed with the **Circle** effect might simulate the image breathing. Or, alternating an image deformed with **Perspective – Horizontal** and **Skew** shows back-and-forth movement.

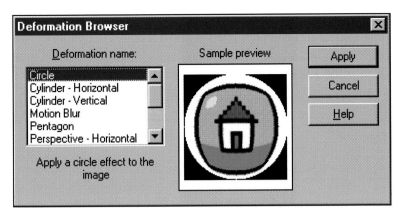

Figure 4.30 The Deformation Browser dialog box with the effects of the Circle deformation shown in the Sample Preview window.

You can both select and fine-tune the deformations in the Deformation Browser dialog box by choosing **Image: Deformations** and choosing a command from the cascading menu. The commands followed by an ellipsis (…) open a dialog box from which you can select options to adjust the selected effect.

Filtering an Image

Paint Shop Pro filters allow you to apply other special effects to an image—if it has over 256 colors. The best way to view these effects on the current image is to choose **Image: Filter Browser**. When Paint Shop Pro opens the Filter Browser dialog box (Figure 4.31), you can browse the Filter Name list box, clicking on names and viewing the Sample Preview window.

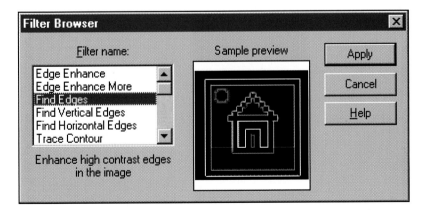

Figure 4.31 The Filter Browser dialog box with Find Edges selected.

You can both select and fine-tune the filter effects in the Filter Browser dialog box by choosing **Image: Edge Filters**, **Image: Normal Filters**, or **Image: Special Filters**, and choosing a command from the cascading menu. The commands followed by an ellipsis (…) open a dialog box from which you can select options to adjust the selected effect. You can also define your own filter by choosing **Image: User Defined Filters** and selecting options from the User Defined Filters dialog box.

ABOUT THIS ANIMATION—CRAZY HOME SIGN

crazhome.gif 3K 51 × 48 Level: Easy

The crazy HOME sign uses Paint Shop deformations to change the dimensions of a simply drawn house.

- ◆ This animation is composed of three GIFs—all repeated more than once.
- ◆ The sign was created in Paint Shop Pro.
- ◆ To be able to apply deformations, the GIF color depth was increased to 16 million colors.
- ◆ The first GIF (**crazhom1**) is undistorted and was saved and named twice (**crazhom2** and **crazhom3**) as the basis for the other two GIFs.
- ◆ The second GIF was elongated using the **Cylinder–Horizontal** deformation. Then, its colors were touched up using the **Dropper** and **Paintbrushes** tools. It was elongated further by selecting the roof and moving it toward the top of the window. The sun from the original GIF was copied and pasted as a new selection into the upper-left corner. The lawn area was increased in height.
- ◆ The third GIF was widened using the **Cylinder–Vertical** deformation. Then, its colors were touched up using the **Dropper** and **Paintbrushes** tools. It was widened further by selecting either side of the door and moving the selections toward the left and right sides of the window. The sun from the original GIF was copied and pasted as a new selection into the upper-left corner. The lawn area was decreased in height. A new line of sky was painted under the house to simulate the house jumping above the ground.
- ◆ Distorting the images resulted in some narrow borders, so the borders of each image were checked and modified where needed to ensure that they were all 2 pixels wide.
- ◆ Many browsers do not recognize animations. The beginning and end GIFs in this animation are standard HOME signs.
- ◆ This animation is set to loop 10 times.
- ◆ Consider setting this animation to a relatively slow speed.

SCANNING AND ANIMATING AN IMAGE — EXAMPLE 3

If you have access to a scanner, you open the door to many possibilities. You can use images from books, magazines, catalogs, and newspapers as a starting point for unique animations.

Before you scan an image for the first time in Paint Shop Pro, choose **File: Select Source**. Select the name of the scanner with which you want to acquire the image and click on **OK**.

To acquire an image, follow these steps:

1. Choose **File: Acquire**. Paint Shop Pro starts your scanner software.

2. Run your scanner software to scan and edit the image.

3. When you have completed the scan, close the scanner software window. The scanned image appears in the Paint Shop Pro workspace (Figure 4.32).

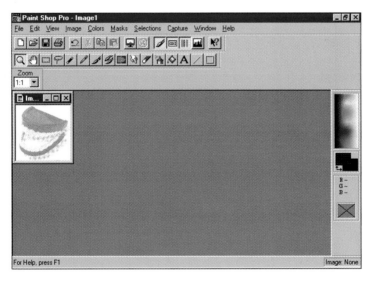

Figure 4.32 A scanned image in the Paint Shop Pro workspace.

ABOUT THIS ANIMATION—ANIMATED TEETH

teeth.gif 2K 80 × 72 Level: Medium

The teeth animation simulates the behavior of a false teeth windup toy.

- ◆ This animation is composed of two GIFs.
- ◆ The first file (**teetha**) was scanned in from a catalog and then made larger, repainted, and further edited in Paint Shop Pro. The file was a 16-million-colors (24-bit) bit-mapped (BMP) file.
- ◆ Before making new images, the file was cropped and scaled down.
- ◆ The second image in the animation was saved as **teethb**. After zooming to 2:1, the **Freehand** tool selected the top part of the teeth. After choosing **Image: Rotate**, the selected area was rotated 20 degrees, to open the teeth.
- ◆ Both image files were opened in the workspace.
- ◆ The rotated file needed to be edited and repainted. Comparisons were made in order to match colors, shadows, and highlights; many times, the **Dropper** tool was moved to the adjacent image to match colors for the current image.
- ◆ Both images were aligned with the left and bottom margins of the image window.
- ◆ A blue background was added. Blue is the transparent color.
- ◆ The edited images were saved as GIF files.
- ◆ Many browsers do not recognize animations. The beginning and end GIFs in this animation are the original image.
- ◆ This animation was set to loop infinitely. This animation should run at a fast delay time.

Working with GIF Construction Set

5

GIF Construction Set is a shareware program with which you can animate a series of GIF files automatically or build an animation block by block (that is, line by line). GIF Construction Set also enables you to make GIF files transparent, manage color palettes, view individual GIFs and animations, add comments, and adjust animation settings. In addition, the program provides tools with which you can create a banner of moving text and create transitions from one image to another.

NOTE Shareware programs are not free. Producers of shareware allow you to try out their programs, usually for a few weeks, before you register and make a nominal payment.

With GIF Construction Set, you can work on these types of blocks:

- **Header blocks** define screen dimensions and optionally specify a *global color palette* (that is, it affects all the images and text) for the animation file. For more information, see the "Editing a Header Block" section.

- **Loop blocks** specify the number of times that an animation runs, or loops. For more information, see the "Editing a Loop Block" section.

- **Control blocks** define one transparent color, user input, and the behavior of the image as it is replaced by the following image. For more information, see the "Editing a Control Block" section.

- **Image blocks** define the location and attributes of the image, including an optional *local color palette* (that is, a palette for the current image). For more information, see the "Editing an Image Block" section.

- **Plain text blocks** define the current image's text and its attributes.

- **Comment blocks** describe the image: its creator, the date it was created and any other pertinent information. Comments are not displayed with the image.

109

STARTING GIF CONSTRUCTION SET

To start GIF Construction Set, follow these steps:

1. Click on the **Start** button and select **Programs**. Windows opens the Programs menu.
2. Move the mouse pointer over GIF Construction Set. Windows opens a submenu.
3. Click on **GIF Construction Set**. The program window (Figure 5.1) opens.

 Shortcut: If you have created a shortcut icon on your desktop for the GIF Construction Set, double-click on it to start the program.

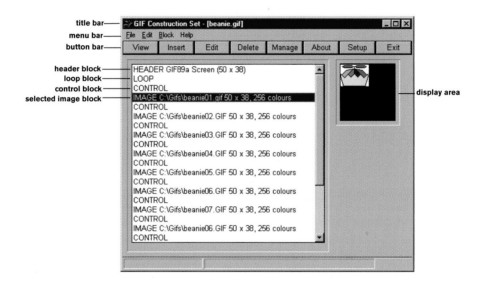

Figure 5.1 The GIF Construction Set window with a sample animation loaded and the first frame selected.

THE GIF CONSTRUCTION SET WINDOW

The GIF Construction Set is composed of a small window with a menu bar, button bar, display area, and preview box.

The Title Bar and Menu Bar

The GIF Construction Set title bar and menu bar are standard Windows elements. The title bar includes the name of the program and the current saved file. The menu bar contains menus from which you select commands with which you can perform actions.

The Button Bar

The GIF Construction Set button bar contains buttons with which you can perform the most common actions supported by the program.

View–Click on this button, press **Block: View,** or press **Ctrl+W** to preview the animation. To return to the GIF Construction Set window, press Esc or right-click.

Insert–Click on this button, choose**Block: View,** or press **Ctrl+I** to open the Insert Object bar, which contains buttons with which you can insert an object: an image, control, comment, plain text, or loop. Click on the Cancel button or press Esc to close the Insert Object bar. For more information, see "Inserting Objects in an Animation."

Edit–Click on this button, choose **Block: Edit**, or press **Ctrl+E** to edit the selected block. For more information, see the following section, "Modifying an Animation."

Delete–Click on this button or choose **Block: Delete** to delete the selected block.

WARNING

GIF Construction Set has no undo function and does not prompt you to confirm a deletion. So, when you inadvertently delete a line and want to undo the action, exit the program without saving the file. This means that when you are working on an animation, it is important to save from time to time. Then, if you must exit the program without saving, you'll have less work to redo.

Manage–Click on this button or choose **Block: Manage** to open the Block Management dialog box with which you can adjust the location of control and image blocks. For more information, see the "Managing Control and Image Blocks" section.

About–Click on this button to display the About dialog box, which is equivalent choosing **Help: About** in other Windows applications. The About dialog box displays the version number, copyright information, name of the person to whom the program is registered, amount of memory free for processing, and number of colors that your current Windows screen driver can display.

Setup–Click on this button or choose **File: Setup** to open the Setup dialog box with which you can customize the GIF Construction Set.

Exit–Click on this button, choose **File: Exit,** or press **Alt+F4** to exit GIF Construction Set. If you have changed the current file, you will be prompted to save it before the program ends.

The Display Area

When you start GIF Construction Set, the display area contains a list of the GIF files in the last folder you accessed from within the program. If you are starting GIF Construction Set for the first time, the display area contains the list of GIFs in the GIF ConstructionSet folder. After you have opened a file, the display area changes: Now it displays the blocks making up the open GIF file.

The Preview Box

The preview box, which appears when you select an image block (which is preceded by the word *IMAGE*), contains a picture of the selected image.

USING THE ANIMATION WIZARD

The easiest way to create an animation is to use the Animation Wizard, which will lead you through all the required steps and allow you to animate files that are not GIFs.

NOTE When you add a file to the animation, the Animation Wizard does not include its transparency information. Therefore, if you want to specify a transparent color, you must edit the animation file. For this and other reasons, after running the Wizard, you may want to edit the file "manually" to get the best effects.

To run the Animation Wizard, locate the GIFs with which you want to make the animation, start GIF Construction Set, and follow these steps:

1. Choose **File: Animation Wizard** or press **Ctrl+A**. GIF Construction Set opens a Welcome dialog box (Figure 5.2).

2. Click on **Next**. GIF Construction Set opens a dialog box (Figure 5.3).

Figure 5.2
A dialog box that welcomes you to the Animation Wizard.

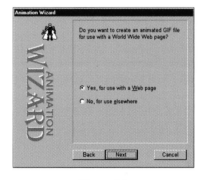

Figure 5.3
Select the location of your animation.

3. To use the animation on a page on the World Wide Web, select **Yes**, the default. This automatically specifies a color palette that presents the optimal display of your animation under Netscape Navigator. Then, click on **Next**. GIF Construction Set opens a dialog box (Figure 5.4).

4. To repeat the animation the entire time the page is on a visitor's screen, select **Loop Indefinitely** (the default). To play the animation once, select **Animate Once and Stop**. Then, click on **Next**. GIF Construction Set opens a dialog box (Figure 5.5).

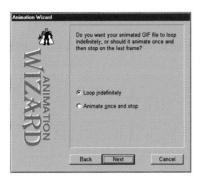

Figure 5.4
Select the number of times that the
animation loops.

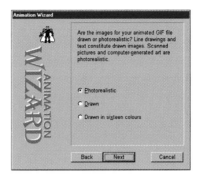

Figure 5.5
Select whether the image is photorealistic or drawn.

5. Select an option button that best describes the type of image with which you are creating the animation. If you have scanned, captured, or created an image that is photographic quality, select **Photorealistic**. If you have drawn the image, select either **Drawn** (a line drawing) or **Drawn in Sixteen Colors** (a line drawing using the Windows 16-color palette). Then, click on **Next**. GIF Construction Set opens a dialog box (Figure 5.6).

6. From the list box, select the delay between the display of the current image and the following image throughout the animation. You can change the delay for the entire animation or selected frames later, if you edit the animation. Then, click on **Next**. GIF Construction Set opens a dialog box (Figure 5.7).

7. Click on **Select** to open an Open dialog box.

8. Click on the name of the image to be included in the animation file, and click on **OK**.

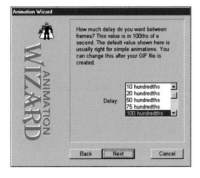

Figure 5.6
Select the delay between image displays.

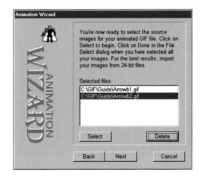

Figure 5.7
Select the image file to be inserted
in the animation.

SHORTCUT It is best to place all the files for the animation in a single folder that has an eight-character (or less) folder name. Otherwise, GIF Construction Set may import folder information in addition to the image file.

9. Repeat step 8 until you have selected all the images in the animation.

10. Click on **Done** to signal that you have completed the animation.

11. Click on **Next**. GIF Construction Set opens a dialog box (Figure 5.8) that displays a message indicating that the wizard has completed the animation.

Figure 5.8
GIF Construction Set displays a
completion message.

12. Click on **Done**. GIF Construction Set builds the animation, showing the progress in the status bar, and loads the animation in the display area.

13. Click on the **View** button to run and test the animation.

14. Unless you need to edit individual images in the animation, choose **File: Save** to save the file. (You can edit the animation whether or not you save it first.) Figure 5.9 shows a completed animation file.

Figure 5.9
A completed animation file in the
GIF Construction Set window.

MODIFYING AN ANIMATION

In order to change an animation's characteristics, you can edit it block by block using a set of Edit dialog boxes.

Editing a Header Block

To edit the header block, in which you can define screen dimensions and specify a global color palette, either double-click on the block in the display area, or select the block and click on the **Edit** button. GIF Construction Set opens the Edit Header dialog box (Figure 5.10).

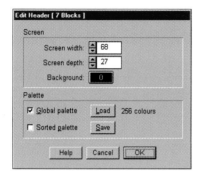

Figure 5.10
The Edit Header dialog box.

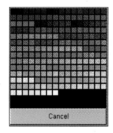

Figure 5.11
The background color palette.

The options in this dialog box are described below.

....

Screen Width–In this text/list box, type or select the width of the animation, in pixels.

Screen Depth–In this text/list box, type or select the height of the animation, in pixels.

Background–Click on this button to open a palette (Figure 5.11) from which you can select the color behind the animation.

 NOTE The background should be transparent for most animations, so setting the Background color is not important.

Global Palette–Check this check box to use the global palette for the current animation. This is the default and the best setting for any animation.

Load–Click on this button to load a saved global or local palette.

Sorted Palette–Check this check box to specify a sorted palette, which may have an affect on the way other programs see the current image. Most times, you will leave this check box unchecked.

Save–Click on this button if you want to save the current palette.

....

Editing a Loop Block

To edit the loop block, in which you can specify the number of times that an animation plays, either double-click on it in the display area or select the loop block and click on the **Edit** button. GIF Construction Set opens the Edit Loop Block dialog box (Figure 5.12).

Figure 5.12
The Edit Loop Block dialog box.

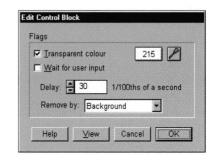

Figure 5.13
The Edit Control Block dialog box.

The only option in this dialog box is:

Iterations–In this text/list box, type or select the number of times that you want to run the animation.

NOTE   Older versions of Netscape Navigator ignore the number of loops set in the Iterations text/list block. When viewed in a Navigator version before 2.0, an animation will either run forever or not run at all.

Editing a Control Block

For every image in an animation, there is an accompanying control block, in which you can specify certain characteristics of the image. To edit a control block, either double-click on it in the display area or select the control block and click on the **Edit** button. GIF Construction Set opens the Edit Control Block dialog box (Figure 5.13).

The options in this dialog box described below.

Transparent Colour–Check this check box to be able to identify one of the global palette colors as being transparent. Typically, you will select the background color as the transparent color. (The reason behind the spelling of the word *colour* is that Alchemy Mindworks, Inc., the developers of GIF Construction Set, is a Canadian company.)

There are two ways to specify a transparent color for the current image. After opening the Edit Control Block dialog box, check the Transparent Colour check box and either:

◆   Click on the first button to the right of the check box. Then, click on a color in the palette.

◆ Click on the dropper button. When the view window opens, click on the desired transparent color in the image. The second option isn't always available, so your best choice is to select a color from the palette.

Wait for User Input—Check this check box to have a user viewing the current image respond by pressing a key or clicking before continuing the animation. In most cases, this check box will remain unchecked.

NOTE Remember that all the options in this dialog box affect only the current image. If you want to edit settings for all the images in an animation, you must edit each control block, or choose the most appropriate option when running the Animation Wizard. You can also edit all control blocks at once by clicking on the **Manage** button and selecting options from the Block Management dialog box. For more information see "Managing Control and Image Blocks" section.

Delay—In this text/list box, type or select the number representing the number of 1/100ths of a second before the next image in the animation is displayed.

Remove by—From this drop-down list box, select the way that the current image will be replaced by the next image.

◆ **Nothing**—The following image completely replaces the current image. For animations with images that are all the same dimensions and no transparent colors, this is probably the best choice.

◆ **Leave as is**—The current image remains and the following image overlays it (that is, any of the current image's pixels that are not overlaid remain in view).

◆ **Background**—The background color replaces the current image, and then the next image appears. This is a good choice for most animations.

◆ **Previous Image**—The previous image completely replaces the current image.

View—Click on this button to see the current animation.

SHORTCUT If clicking on **View** doesn't work, click on **OK** to close the dialog box. Then, click on the **View** button in the GIF Construction Set window.

NOTE After changing settings in this dialog box, it's a good idea to view the results both in the GIF Construction Set View window and also in the Netscape Navigator and Microsoft Internet Explorer browser windows. An animation that does not run smoothly in GIF Construction Set might look fine in a browser window.

Editing an Image Block

To edit an image block, in which you can define the location and some attributes of the image, either double-click on an image block, or select an image block and click on the **Edit** button. GIF Construction Set opens the Edit Image dialog box (Figure 5.14).

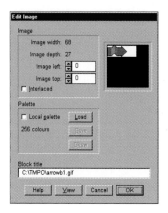

Figure 5.14 The Edit Image dialog box with the current image displayed.

The options in this dialog box are described below.

Image Width–This displays the width, in pixels, of the current image.

Image Depth–This displays the height, in pixels, of the current image.

Image Left–In this text/list box, type or select a number representing the distance, in pixels, of the current image from the left corner of the computer screen. To see the change, view it in the view window or open the animation in a Web browser.

Image Top–In this text/list box, type or select a number representing the distance, in pixels, of the current image from the top of the computer screen. To see the change, view it in the view window or open the animation in a Web browser.

Interlaced–Check this check box to interlace the current image. Most animations should not be interlaced, so you should leave this check box unchecked.

Local Palette–Check this check box to use the local palette for the current image. In most cases, you should leave this check box unchecked and use the global palette instead.

Load–Click on this button to load a saved global or local palette.

Save–Click on this button if you want to save the current palette.

Show–Click on this button to display the local palette. If you have not selected the local palette, this button is dimmed.

Block Title–In this text box, you can edit the location and name of the current image file.

View–Click on this button to see the current image.

SHORTCUT

If clicking on **View** doesn't work, click on **OK** to close the dialog box. Then, click on the **View** button in the GIF Construction Set window.

ABOUT THIS ANIMATION—ARROW BEND

arrobend.gif 2K 68x27 Level: Easy

The arrow bend animation emphasizes an object by pointing to it in alternate bent and straight positions.

- ◆ This animation is composed of two GIFs.
- ◆ The images are drawn in Windows Paint; the animation is created using GIF Construction Set.
- ◆ The width of both arrows is identical.
- ◆ Draw the bent arrow (arrowb1) first. Add white dots to indicate the highlighted part of the arrow; add black dots to indicate the shadowed part. After saving the file, save it again as arrowb2.
- ◆ In arrowb2, select the front part of the arrow and drag it to the right border. Fill in the missing middle section with red, and join the borders.
- ◆ Set the animation to loop infinitely.
- ◆ This animation works best at a medium to high speed.

Inserting Objects in an Animation

You can insert objects and blocks to an existing animation. For example, you might have skipped a particular file, or you might want to smooth an animation by creating images that include intermediate movements (such as moving an arrow 20 pixels to the right instead of the original 40). To add an object, click on the block after which you want to insert the new object, click on the **Insert** button, choose **Block: Insert**, or press **Ctrl+I**. Then, click on a button in the Insert Object bar (Figure 5.15).

Figure 5.15
The Insert Object bar.

The buttons in this window are described below.

Image–Click on this button to insert an image using the same Open dialog box from which you select image files using the Animation Wizard.

Control–Click on this button to insert a control block.

Comment–Click on this button to insert a comment block.

Plain Text–Click on this button to insert a plain text block.

Loop–Click on this button to insert a loop block. If the animation already includes a loop block, you must delete it first; only one loop block is allowed in an animation.

Cancel–Click on this button or press **Esc** to close the Insert Object bar without taking an action.

More about Inserting Images

When you insert an image file in an animation, you may have to specify a palette—particularly if you have specified the global palette—using the Palette dialog box (Figure 5.16).

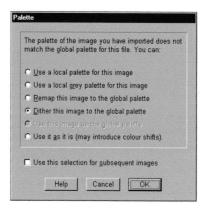

Figure 5.16
The Palette dialog box.

The options in this dialog box are described below.

Use a Local Palette for This Image–Click on this option button to specify a local palette for the new image file. If you have already specified a global palette, the two palettes may clash.

Use a Local Gray Palette for This Image–Click on this option button to specify a local grayscale palette for the new image file. If you have already specified a global palette, the two palettes may clash.

Remap This Image to the Global Palette–Click on this option button to specify the global palette for the new image file. Use this option for drawings.

Dither This Image to the Global Palette–Click on this option button to specify the global palette for the new image file. Use this option for photographs and other scanned images.

Use This Image As the Global Palette–Click on this option button to specify the global palette for the first image file in an animation. This option button is dimmed if you have previously inserted other image blocks in the animation.

Use It As It Is–Click on this option button to not associate the image with a palette. Choose this option if the new image includes opaque or transparent colors that are in the global palette and that you want to preserve.

Merging a File into an Animation

You can merge a file consisting of a single image or several images (that is, an animation) into the current animation. Simply choose **Block: Merge** or press **Ctrl+M**, select a file, and click on **OK**. GIF Construction Set merges the entire file except for its header block into the animation. Then, delete and/or edit the new blocks as needed.

Exporting an Image from an Animation

You can export a single image in an animation to a separate file. For example, you might want to base a new animation on the image, or you might want to edit it and insert it back into the animation. To export an image, follow these steps:

1. Click on its image block in the GIF Construction Set window.
2. Choose **Block: Export** or press **Ctrl+P**. GIF Construction Set opens the Save As dialog box.
3. Name the image and click on **OK**.

Extracting a Block from an Animation

You can export one or more blocks in the current animation to a separate file. This is a good method of "grabbing" frames from other animations or of studying an animation frame by frame. For example, you can extract images from the CD-ROM disk and edit them: change their speed or position or modify them in your art program.

1. Choose **Block: Extract**. GIF Construction Set opens the Extract dialog box (Figure 5.17).
2. To select all the blocks, click on the **Select All** button.
3. To select one block, click on it.
4. To select several contiguous blocks, click on the block at one end of the range, press and hold down the **Shift** key, and click on the block at the other end of the range.
5. To select several noncontiguous blocks, click on a block to be selected, press and hold down the **Ctrl** key, and continue clicking on blocks to add them to the selection.
6. To deselect all selected blocks, click on the **Clear All** button.

7. Click on **Save**. GIF Construction Set opens the Save As dialog box.

8. Type a unique file name in the File Name text box, and click on **OK**.

9. Click on **Done**.

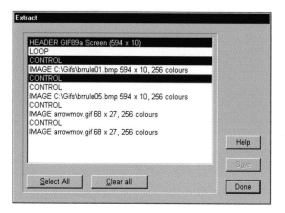

Figure 5.17
The Extract dialog box with three blocks selected.

ABOUT THIS ANIMATION— SNAPPING SCISSORS RULE

snapscis.gif 3K 561x20 Level: Medium

The snapping scissors animation is comprised of opening and closing gold scissors on a red background.

♦   This animation is composed of two GIFs.

♦   The images are drawn in Windows Paint; the animation is created using GIF Construction Set.

♦   The open scissors started as a symbol inserted into Microsoft Word. After zooming in to the pixel level, the first scissors' foreground was painted with yellow (255-255-0) and the background was painted with a mustard (128-128-0) that is not part of the 216-color palette. Save the scissors as a temporary file.

♦   The closed scissors was created by selecting and dragging both the handles and blades together in two separate operations. After repairing some paint damage, the closed scissors were saved.

♦   Create a red rule. Paste a series of open and closed scissors along the length of the rule, separating each by eight pixels.

♦   Save the rule as snapscs1.gif. Save the rule again as snapscs2.gif. Erase the first scissors in the second rule.Section by section, select the visible part of the rule and drag it toward the left. Insert open scissors at the end.

♦   Set the animation to loop infinitely.

♦   This animation works best at a medium to high speed.

Managing Control and Image Blocks

You can perform wholesale additions and changes to an animation by either clicking on **Manage** or choosing **Block: Manage** and then selecting options in the Block Management dialog box (Figure 5.18).

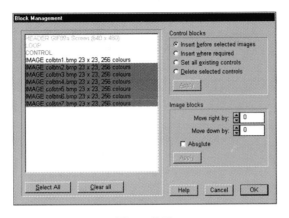

Figure 5.18
The Block Management dialog box with six images selected.

The options in this dialog box are described below.

Select All–Click on this button to select all the blocks in the animation. This is the only way to undim the dimmed buttons.

Clear All–Click on this button to deselect all the selected blocks in the animation.

Insert Before Selected Images–Click on this option button to insert control blocks before each image block.

Insert Where Required–Click on this option button to insert control blocks before each image block that doesn't already have them.

Set All Existing Controls–Click on this option button to change values for all the control blocks using the Edit Control Block dialog box.

Delete Selected Controls–Click on this option button to delete all the control blocks after responding to a confirmation message.

Apply–Click on this button to apply the selected options and keep the dialog box open to change options or select other options.

Move Right by–Type or select a value, in pixels, to move the images in the animation toward the right side of the screen.

Move Down by–Type or select a value, in pixels, to move the images in the animation toward the bottom of the screen.

Absolute–Check this check box to set a delay in the speed of the animation.

When you add control blocks to an animation, GIF Construction Set opens the Edit Control Block dialog box (see Figure 5.13). For information in selecting options in this dialog box, refer to the "Editing a Control Block" section.

CREATING AN ANIMATION FROM SCRATCH

An alternate to the Animation Wizard is creating an animation from scratch. This method takes longer, but you can edit the animation as you build it. In addition, you can add one or several images in one step, and you can also add and edit multiple control blocks at the same time.

NOTE Before creating a new animation, click on the **Setup** button and make sure that the default palette is either **216 Colours/Netscape** or **16 Colours** (the Windows palette). These two choices are the best for Web-based animations.

To create an animation file from scratch, follow these steps:

1. Choose **File: New** or press **Ctrl+N**. GIF Construction Set adds a header block with a default screen size of 640 × 480.

2. If you know the screen dimensions, double-click on the header block and change the Screen Width and Screen Depth settings. If you don't know the dimensions, you can edit at a later time.

3. To insert a control block, which must accompany each image file, click on **Insert**, choose Block: **Insert**, or press **Ctrl+I**. Then, click on **Control**. GIF Construction Set adds a control block with default settings.

4. To insert an image, click on **Insert**, choose **Block: Insert**, or press **Ctrl+I**. Then, click on **Image**. Select a file name from the Open dialog box and click on **OK**.

SHORTCUT You can insert multiple images in the animation at one time. To select several contiguous files, click on the file at one end of the range, press and hold down the **Shift** key, and click on the file at the other end of the range. To select several noncontiguous files, click on the first file to be selected, press and hold down the **Ctrl** key, and continue clicking on files to add them to the selection. Be sure to insert control blocks before each image.

5. If the Palette dialog box appears, click on an option button and click on **OK**. (If you have selected several images, the Palette dialog box will appear once for each image.) For more information about the options, refer to the "More about Inserting Images" section.

6. To insert additional images, repeat steps 3, 4, and 5.

7. To loop the animation, click on **Insert**, and click on **Loop**.

8. Save the animation.

CREATING SPECIAL-EFFECTS ANIMATIONS

GIF Construction Set enables you to create animations using two special effects: scrolling banners and transitions. Each effect is easy to do: You can complete an animation in just a few minutes.

Making a Scrolling Banner

Scrolling banners show moving text on a background. To create a banner, choose **Edit: Banner** and fill in the Edit Banner dialog box (Figure 5.19).

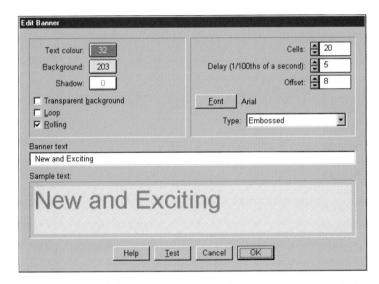

Figure 5.19 The Edit Banner dialog box with a large sample banner on display.

The options in this dialog box are described below.

Text Colour—Click on this button to open a palette from which you can choose the color of the scrolling text.

Background—Click on this button to open a palette from which you can choose the color of the banner background.

Shadow—Click on this button to open a palette from which you can choose the color of a shadow behind the scrolling text. This button is available only if you choose a drop shadow type.

Transparent Background—Check this check box to make the background color transparent. An unchecked check box uses the background color that you specified in the Background option. The only way to test transparency in a banner is to view it in a Web browser.

Loop—Check this check box to loop the banner forever. An unchecked check box displays the banner one time.

Rolling—Check this check box to scroll the banner from right to left. An unchecked check box indicates that the banner text appears as a static image.

Banner Text–Type the banner text in this text box.

Sample Text–In this sample box, view the banner text and colors.

Cells–Type or select the number of frames in the banner in this text/option box.

Delay (1/100ths of a Second)–Type or select the delay between the display of the current frame and the next.

Offset–Type or select the number of pixels that a drop shadow is offset from the text or the perceived depth of embossed text. The higher the value, the more distance there appears to be between the shadow and the text.

Font–Click on this button to open a Font dialog box from which you can select a font, font style (regular, italic, bold, or bold italic), or font size. A smaller font size results in a smaller GIF file.

Type–From this drop-down list box, select the type of text:

- ◆ **Simple** is two-dimensional text. If you have selected a two-color palette, Simple is the only available text type.
- ◆ **Shadow** displays a shadow offset below and to the right of the scrolling text.
- ◆ **Embossed** displays slightly three-dimensional text.

Test–Click on this button to view the banner before you save it. Press **Esc** or right-click to return to the Edit Banner dialog box.

After you have completed your selections, click on **OK**. GIF Construction Set creates an animation (Figure 5.20).

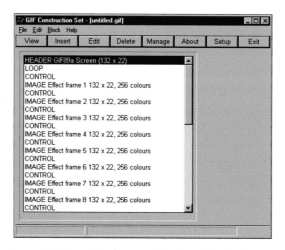

Figure 5.20 A scrolling banner animation in the display area.

Making an Animation with a Transition Effect

A transition animation is actually a static image that appears or disappears using one of 10 effects. For example, an interesting way to present a picture of a building, a chart, or even an "Old Master" is to apply a transition effect.

NOTE Transition animations can be very large. For example, the Mona Lisa animation shown on the following page is over 360,000 kilobytes—so large that the loading time would be excessive.

To create a transition, choose **Edit: Transition**. In the Edit Transition dialog box (Figure 5.21), click on **Select** to select an image, and then select options.

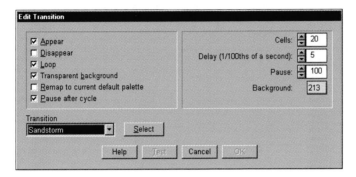

Figure 5.21 The Edit Transition dialog box.

The options in this dialog box are described below.

....

Appear–Check this check box to introduce the display of the image with a transition effect.

Disappear–Check this check box to conclude the display of the image with a transition effect.

Loop–Check this check box to loop the transition forever. An unchecked check box displays the transition one time.

Transparent Background–Check this check box to make the background color transparent. The only way to test transparency in a transition is to view it in a Web browser.

Remap to Current Default Palette–Check this check box to apply the default palette to the selected image. This may improve the appearance of drawn images but not photographs or scanned images.

Pause After Cycle–Check this check box to display the image for a set time period before or after a transition effect occurs. Specify the time delay using the Pause text/option box.

Cells–Type or select the number of frames in the transition in this text/option box.

Delay (1/100ths of a Second)–Type or select the delay between the display of the current frame and the next.

Pause–Type or select the time period during which the image is displayed without a transition effect occurring.

Background–Click on this button to open a palette from which you can select the background color. This button does not appear until you have selected an image.

Transition–From this drop-down list box, select a transition effect:

- ◆ **Adam Seven Interlace** interlaces the image a few pixels at a time.
- ◆ **Horizontal Split** displays the image in two sections—the top half from the left side of the screen and the bottom half from the right side.

- **Raster** displays the image in several narrow horizontal sections—half from the left side of the screen and half from the right side.
- **Sandstorm** displays the image one pixel at a time; the background pixels are gradually replaced with pixels from the image.
- **Tile** displays the image in blocks of pixels, several at a time.
- **Vertical Split** displays the image in two sections—the left half from the top of the screen and the right half from the bottom.
- **Wipe in from Bottom** scrolls the image up from the bottom of the frame.
- **Wipe in from Left** scrolls the image to the right from the left side of the frame.
- **Wipe in from Right** scrolls the image to the left from the right side of the frame.
- **Wipe in from Top** scrolls the image down from the top of the frame.

Select—Click on this button to open an Open dialog box from which you can select an image file. You must select a file before choosing other options from the Edit Transition dialog box.

Test—Click on this button to view the banner before you save it. Press **Esc** or right-click to return to the Edit Transition dialog box.

Figure 5.22 shows an image of the Mona Lisa with the Sandstorm transition.

Figure 5.22 The Mona Lisa in a sand storm.

Working with Adobe Photoshop

Adobe Photoshop is a true paint program. You can paint and draw just as if you were working with oils and water colors. You can make images from scratch or use and edit scanned, captured, or imported images. Photoshop is a superior art-editing program that includes many types of effects that you can apply to images—regardless of their source.

Photoshop allows you to copy, move, and paste images and selections and to undo an action using Edit menu commands. Photoshop's extensive help system also includes CD-based tutorials and demonstrations. Its *User Guide* provides detailed information about most of Photoshop's features.

Table 6.1 lists the file formats that Photoshop reads from, saves to, imports from, and exports to.

NOTE

In Windows, you can open files using the **File: Open** and **File: Open As** commands. The Macintosh version of Photoshop provides the **File: Open** command. Both versions save with the **File: Save**, **File: Save As**, and **File: Save a Copy**. With Windows and Macintosh computers, you can import files using **File: Import** and **File: Export**, respectively.

Table 6.1 Photoshop-Supported File Formats

Format	Reads from	Saves to	Imports from	Exports to
Anti-Aliased PICT	No	No	Yes (Mac only)	No
BMP (*.BMP, *.RLE)	Yes	Yes	No	No
CompuServe GIF (*.GIF)	Yes	Yes (Mac only)	No	See GIF89a
EPS PICT Preview	Yes	No	No	No
Filmstrip (*.FLM)	Yes	Yes (Mac only)	No	No
Generic EPS (*.AI, *.AI)	Yes	No	No	No
GIF89a	See CompuServe GIF	See CompuServe GIF	See CompuServe GIF	Yes
Illustrator Paths	Yes (Mac only)	No	No	Yes
JPEG (*.JPG, *.JPE)	Yes	Yes	No	No
Kodak CMS Photo CD	Yes (Mac only)	No	No	No

Table 6.1 Photoshop-Supported File Formats (continued)

Format	Reads from	Saves to	Imports from	Exports to
Kodak Photo CD (*.PCD)	Yes (Windows only)	No	No	No
PCX (*.PCX)	Yes	Yes	No	No
PDF (*.PDF)	Yes	Yes	No	No
Photoshop (*.PSD, *.PDD)	Yes	Yes	No	No
Photoshop EPS (*.EPS)	Yes	Yes	No	No
PICT File (*.PCT, *.PIC)	Yes	Yes	No	No
PICT Resource	Yes (Mac only)	Yes (Mac only)	Yes (Mac only)	No
Pixar (*.PXR)	Yes	Yes	No	No
PNG (*.PNG)	Yes	Yes	No	No
Raw (*.RAW)	Yes	Yes	No	No
Scitex CT (*.SCT)	Yes	Yes	No	No
Targa (*.TGA, *.VDA, *.ICB, *.VST)	Yes	Yes	No	No
TIFF (*.TIF)	Yes	Yes	No	No

Photoshop also supports *plug-ins* (programs, utilities, or libraries that can add features to the current program).

SHORTCUT When you want to save an image to a GIF89a-compliant file, choose **File: Export: GIF89a Export**. In the GIF89a Export Options dialog box, clear the Interlaced check box, accept all the options, and click on **OK**. In the Export GIF89 dialog box, type a file name, and click on **Save**.

STARTING ADOBE PHOTOSHOP

To start Adobe Photoshop on a Windows computer, follow these steps:

1. Click on the **Start** button and select **Programs**. Windows opens the Programs menu.
2. Move the mouse pointer over Adobe. Windows opens a submenu.
3. Click on **Adobe Photoshop**. The Photoshop window (Figure 6.1) opens with a tool box on the left side and three tool palettes on the right.

SHORTCUT If you have created a **shortcut** icon on your desktop for Photoshop, double-click on it to start the program.

title bar
menu bar
toolbox
palettes
work area
status bar

Figure 6.1 The Photoshop window with the default palettes and three open from the tutorial.

To start Adobe Photoshop on the Macintosh platform, open the Adobe Photoshop folder and double-click on the **Photoshop** icon.

THE PHOTOSHOP WINDOW

The Photoshop window contains a variety of elements, many that are familiar to Windows and Macintosh users and some that require more explanation.

The Title Bar and Menu Bar

The Photoshop title bar and menu bar are standard elements. The title bar includes the name of the program, and the menu bar contains menus from which you select commands with which you can perform actions. Photoshop also contains *context menus*, which contain commands associated with objects on the desktop.

To use a context menu, right-click on an object in the current window or a small arrow in palettes to open the menu; then, move the mouse pointer to the desired command, and left-click to select the command.

To use a context menu, move the mouse pointer to an object, press and hold down the **Control** key, click the mouse button, move the mouse pointer to the command, and click to select it.

The Work Area

The Photoshop work area is the space below the menu bar and above the status bar at the bottom of the window. The work area includes the toolbox and three palette boxes on the right. The work area can also contain image windows, if you have opened any image files.

You can work on more than one image file at a time. This means that you can copy a color from one image and use it in another. When working on animations, you can open each frame in the work area, place them in order, and see the potential motion. You can also open the same image in more than one window. For example, you can show it at its actual size in one window and magnify or zoom in on it in another window. (For more information about zooming, refer to the section "Zooming the Image" later in the chapter.) When you change the image in one window, it automatically changes in the other.

To open the current image in a second window, you can:

- ◆ Choose **View: New View**.
- ◆ Open the File menu and select its filename from the bottom of the menu, if the image is one of the last you opened.
- ◆ Choose **File: Open** and select the image file. Photoshop displays a message box. Click on **OK**.

The Toolbox

The Photoshop toolbox is, by default, on the left side of the window. The toolbox contains several sections, which separate groups of tools by purpose.

 Click on this topmost button to display the opening splash screen from which you can click on a button (in the upper-left corner) to access the Adobe Internet site using your default Web browser, view your serial number, and see the names of those who worked on Photoshop. To close the splash screen, click on it.

The largest part of the toolbox is composed of many drawing and editing tools. All but one tool have associated context menus. Six toolbox buttons, which contain small arrows in their lower-right corners, open small palettes from which you can select currently hidden buttons to replace the default buttons permanently—until you replace them again.

To view the choices related to a particular button and select one, click and hold down the mouse button to view all the buttons. Then, slide the mouse pointer to the button to be selected and release the mouse button.

To cycle through all the choices related to a particular button and select one:

 Press and hold down **Alt** and repeatedly click on the button until the desired choice appears.

Press and hold down **Option** and repeatedly click on the button until the desired choice appears.

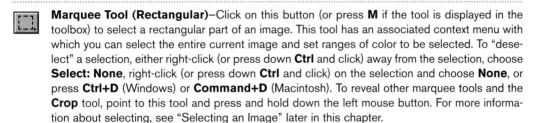 **Marquee Tool (Rectangular)**–Click on this button (or press **M** if the tool is displayed in the toolbox) to select a rectangular part of an image. This tool has an associated context menu with which you can select the entire current image and set ranges of color to be selected. To "dese-lect" a selection, either right-click (or press down **Ctrl** and click) away from the selection, choose **Select: None**, right-click (or press down **Ctrl** and click) on the selection and choose **None**, or press **Ctrl+D** (Windows) or **Command+D** (Macintosh). To reveal other marquee tools and the **Crop** tool, point to this tool and press and hold down the left mouse button. For more informa-tion about selecting, see "Selecting an Image" later in this chapter.

Marquee Tool (Elliptical)–Click on this button (or press **M** if the tool is displayed in the tool-box) to select an oval part of an image. To reveal other marquee tools and the **Crop** tool, point to this tool and press and hold down the left mouse button. For more information about select-ing, see "Selecting an Image" later in this chapter.

Single Row Marquee Tool–Click on this button (or press **M** if the tool is displayed in the tool-box) to select a rectangular 1-pixel-high part of an image. To reveal other marquee tools and the **Crop** tool, point to this tool and press and hold down the left mouse button.

Single Column Marquee Tool–Click on this button (or press **M** if the tool is displayed in the toolbox) to select a rectangular 1-pixel-wide part of an image. To reveal other marquee tools and the **Crop** tool, press and hold down the left mouse button.

Crop Tool–Click on this button (or press **C**) to crop, or cut away, part of an image but not change its scale. To reveal the marquee tools, point to this tool and press and hold down the left mouse button. For more information about using the marquee tools, see the "Selecting an Image" section later in this chapter. For more information about the **Crop** tool, see the "Cropping an Image with the Crop Tool" section later in this chapter.

Move Tool–Click on this button (or press **V**) to move an image, *layer* (similar to an application of paint over a canvas or a sheet of acetate placed over an animation background), or guide with-in the current window. For more information about using the **Move** tool, see the "Moving an Image or Selection" section later in this chapter. For more information about layers, see the "Working with Layers" section later in this chapter.

Lasso Tool–Click on this button (or press **L** if the tool is displayed in the toolbox) to select an irregular area of an image. This tool has an associated context menu with which you can select all elements of the current image and set ranges of color to be selected. To "deselect" a selec-tion, either right-click (or press down **Ctrl** (Windows) or **Command** (Macintosh) and click) away from the selection, choose **Select: None**, right-click (or press down **Ctrl** and click) on the selec-tion and choose **None**, or press **Ctrl+D** (Windows) or **Command+D** (Macintosh). To reveal the **Polygon Lasso** tool, point to this tool and press and hold down the left mouse button.

Polygon Lasso Tool–Click on this button (or press **L** if the tool is displayed in the toolbox) to select a polygonal area of an image. This tool has an associated context menu with which you can select all elements of the current image and set ranges of color to be selected. To "dese-lect" a selection, either right-click (or press down **Ctrl** and click) away from the selection, choose **Select: None**, right-click (or press down **Ctrl** and click) on the selection and choose **None**, or press **Ctrl+D** (Windows) or **Command+D** (Macintosh). To reveal the **Lasso** tool, point to this tool and press and hold down the left mouse button. For more information about using the **Lasso** tools, see the "Selecting an Image" section later in this chapter.

Magic Wand Tool–Click on this button (or press **W**) to select one or more color characteristics of the image. This tool has an associated context menu with which you can select all elements of the current image and set ranges of color to be selected. To "deselect" a selection, either right-click (or press down **Ctrl** and click) away from the selection, choose **Select: None**, right-click (or press down **Ctrl** and click) on the selection and choose **None**, or press **Ctrl+D** (Windows) or **Command+D** (Macintosh). For more information, see the "Modifying an Image" section later in this chapter.

Airbrush Tool–Click on this button (or press **A**) to add an airbrush effect to part of the image using the foreground color. With associated context menu, you can apply special effects using the **Airbrush** tool.

Paintbrush Tool–Click on this button (or press **B**) to paint the image using the foreground color. With the associated context menu, you can apply special effects using the **Paintbrush** tool. For more information about using the Paintbrush Tool, see the "Creating an Image–Example 1" section later in this chapter.

Eraser Tool–Click on this button (or press **E**) to erase part of the image, replacing the erased part with the background color. With the associated context menu, you can select the shape and size of the **Eraser** tool as well as other tools.

Pencil Tool–Click on this button (or press **Y**) to draw on the image with the foreground color. This tool has an associated context menu with which you can apply special effects.

Rubber Stamp Tool–Click on this button (or press **S**) to copy an area of an image to another area of the image or to a different image. This tool has an associated context menu with which you can apply special effects.

Smudge Tool–Click on this button (or press **U**) to smear the colors on the image. With the associated context menu, you can select the shape and size of the **Smudge** tool as well as select color effects.

Blur Tool–Click on this button (or press **R** if the tool is displayed in the toolbox) to lessen the contrast between colors in the image. With the associated context menu, you can select the shape and size of the **Blur** tool as well as select color effects. To reveal the **Sharpen** tool, point to this tool and press and hold down the left mouse button.

Sharpen Tool–Click on this button (or press **R** if the tool is displayed in the toolbox) to increase the contrast between colors in the image. With the associated context menu, you can select the shape and size of the **Sharpen** tool and can select color effects. To reveal the **Blur** tool, point to this tool and press and hold down the left mouse button.

 NOTE The Filter menu contains the **Sharpen** command and several subcommands.

Dodge Tool–Click on this button (or press **O** if the tool is displayed in the toolbox) to lighten an area of the image. With the associated context menu, you can select the shape and size of the **Dodge** tool as well as select the part of the image to be affected. To reveal the **Burn** tool or the **Sponge** tool, point to the **Dodge** tool and press and hold down the left mouse button.

Burn Tool–Click on this button (or press **O** if the tool is displayed in the toolbox) to darken an area of the image. With the associated context menu, you can select the shape and size of the **Burn** tool as well as the part of the image to be affected. To reveal the **Dodge** tool or **Sponge** tool, point to the **Burn** tool and press and hold down the left mouse button.

 Sponge Tool–Click on this button (or press **O** if the tool is displayed in the toolbox) to add color to or remove color from an area of the image. With the associated context menu, you can select the shape and size of the **Sponge** tool and can select the part of the image to be affected. To reveal the **Dodge** tool or **Burn** tool, point to the **Sponge** tool and press and hold down the left mouse button.

 Pen Tool–Click on this button (or press **P** if the tool is displayed in the toolbox) to draw painting or selection *paths* (very fine lines or curves) to an image. With the associated context menu, you can select the image, act on the current layer of the image, or select color effects. To reveal the **Direct Selection** tool, **Add Anchor Point** tool, **Delete Anchor Point** tool, or **Convert Anchor Point** tool, point to the **Pen** tool and press and hold down the left mouse button.

 Direct Selection Tool–Click on this button (or press **P** if the tool is displayed in the toolbox) to select or drag *anchor points* (the beginning or ending of a path). With the associated context menu, you can select the image, act on the current layer of the image, or select color effects. To reveal the **Pen** tool, **Add Anchor Point** tool, **Delete Anchor Point** tool, or **Convert Anchor Point** tool, point to the **Direct Selection** tool and press and hold down the left mouse button.

 Add Anchor Point Tool–Click on this button (or press **P** if the tool is displayed in the toolbox) and then move the tool to the path to add an anchor point to it. With the associated context menu, you can select the image, act on the current layer of the image, or select color effects. To reveal the **Pen** tool, **Direct Selection** tool, **Delete Anchor Point** tool, or **Convert Anchor Point** tool, point to the **Add Anchor Point** tool and press and hold down the left mouse button.

 Delete Anchor Point Tool–Click on this button (or press **P** if the tool is displayed in the toolbox) and then move the tool to an anchor point to remove it from a path. With the associated context menu, you can select the image, act on the current layer of the image, or select color effects. To reveal the **Pen** tool, **Direct Selection** tool, **Add Anchor Point** tool, or **Convert Anchor Point** tool, point to the **Delete Anchor Point** tool and press and hold down the left mouse button.

 Convert Anchor Point Tool–Click on this button (or press **P** if the tool is displayed in the toolbox) and then move the tool to an anchor point on a curve to convert it to an angled anchor point. Click and drag to revert the angled anchor point. With the associated context menu, you can select the image, act on the current layer of the image, or select color effects. To reveal the **Pen** tool, **Direct Selection** tool, **Add Anchor Point** tool, or **Delete Anchor Point** tool, point to the **Convert Anchor Point** tool and press and hold down the left mouse button.

 Type Tool–Click on this button (or press **T** if the tool is displayed in the toolbox) to open the Type Tool dialog box in order to add foreground-color formatted text to the image at the insertion point. This tool has an associated context menu with which you can select the image, act on the current layer of the image, or select color effects. To reveal the **Type Mask** tool, point to the **Type** tool and press and hold down the left mouse button.

Type Mask Tool–Click on this button (or press **T** if the tool is displayed in the toolbox) to open the Type Tool dialog box in order to make a foreground-color formatted selection in the form of typed text at the insertion point. This tool has an associated context menu with which you can change the selection, act on the current layer of the image, or select effects. To "deselect" a selection, either right-click (or press down on **Ctrl** and click) away from the selection, choose **Select: None**, right-click (or press down on **Ctrl** and click) on the selection and choose **None**, or press **Ctrl+D** (Windows) or **Command+D** (Macintosh). To reveal the **Type** tool, point to the **Type Mask** tool and press and hold down the left mouse button. For more information, see the "Modifying an Image" section later in the chapter.

Line Tool–Click on this button or press **N** to draw a line on the image. Press and hold down **Shift** and click on this button to draw a line at 45 degrees or a multiple. This tool has an associated context menu with which you can affect a selection, layer, or color.

Gradient Tool–Click on this button or press **G** to fill a particular area with a selected range of colors. This tool has an associated context menu with which you can select many effects for the gradient.

Paint Bucket Tool–Click on this button or press **K** to fill an enclosed area with the foreground color.

Eyedropper Tool–Click on this button or press **I** to change the foreground color to a selected color within the image or fill a particular area with a selected range of colors. This tool has an associated context menu with which you can select the size of the area from which you get the color. To turn on the Eyedropper tool temporarily:

Press down the **Alt** key.

Press down the **Option** key.

Hand Tool–Click on this button or press **H** to move an image within its window, if it is smaller than its window. This tool has an associated context menu with which you can select an image size.

Zoom Tool–Click on this button or press **Z** to zoom in on the image. This tool has an associated context menu with which you can select an image size, zoom in, or zoom out.

The foreground/background color section (Figure 6.2) of the toolbox not only shows the current foreground and background colors but also contains tools with which you can manipulate the colors.

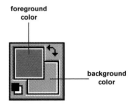

Figure 6.2 The foreground/background section of the toolbox.

Switch Foreground and Background Colors–Click on this button or press **X** to change the foreground color to the background color and the background color to the foreground color.

Default Foreground and Background Colors–Click on this button or press **D** to change the foreground color to the default black and the background color to the default white.

Edit in Standard Mode–Click on this button (or press **Q** to cycle between this and the following edit mode) to view the image without working on a *mask* (a type of selection in which the contents are protected from the changes around it). Standard Mode is the default editing mode.

Edit in Quick Mask Mode–Click on this button (or press **Q** to cycle between this and the prior edit mode) to view the image and temporary masks. This is the alternate to **Edit in Standard Mode**.

Standard Screen Mode–Click on this button (or press **F** to cycle through screen modes) to display the Photoshop window with the title bar, menu bar, toolbox, status bar, image window(s), and palettes. This is the default application view.

Full Screen Mode with Menu Bar–Click on this button (or press **F** to cycle through screen modes) to display the Photoshop window with the menu bar, toolbox, status bar, image window(s), and palettes.

Full Screen Mode–Click on this button (or press **F** to cycle through screen modes) to display the Photoshop window with the toolbox, status bar, image window(s), and palettes.

When you move the mouse pointer over a toolbox button, Photoshop displays a Tool Tip, a small yellow box that states the name of the button and its shortcut key. When you click on the tool, the status bar at the bottom of the window contains a brief explanation.

You can change the location, but not the dimensions, of the toolbox by pointing to the title bar and dragging. You can move the toolbox anywhere in the window.

You can hide or display the toolbox and all the palettes on the right side of the window by pressing the **Tab** key.

You can hide the toolbox by choosing **Window: Hide Tools**. You can reveal a hidden toolbox by choosing **Window: Show Tools**.

The Photoshop Palettes

On the right side of the work area are three small windows that contain three or more palettes each. There are nine Photoshop palettes.

The Navigator palette (Figure 6.3) enables you to zoom in or out on an image. For more information about zooming, see the "Changing the View of an Image" section later in the chapter.

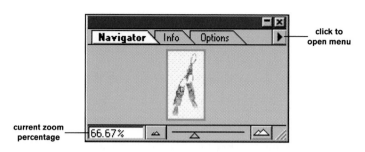

click to
open menu

current zoom
percentage

Figure 6.3 The Navigator palette.

The Info palette (Figure 6.4) provides color values, the current coordinates of the mouse pointer, and other information, depending on the currently selected tool.

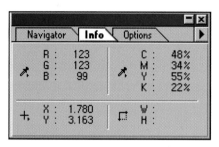

Figure 6.4
The Info palette.

Figure 6.5
The Hand Tool Options palette.

The Options palette contains options related to the currently selected tool. For example, Figure 6.5 shows the palette for the **Hand** tool. As you continue reading this chapter, you'll find out about specific palettes in sections devoted to particular tools.

The Color palette (Figure 6.6) enables you to set the foreground and background colors. For more information, see the "Changing the Foreground and Background Colors" section later in the chapter.

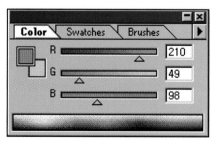

Figure 6.6
The Color palette.

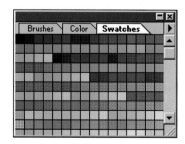

Figure 6.7
A 216-color special Swatches palette.

You can also use the Swatches palette (Figure 6.7), which contains the colors for the current image, to set foreground and background colors. You can also create a custom palette by adding and deleting colors and saving it for use in other images.

NOTE 216-color.aco, a 216-color palette for Photoshop, is included on the CD-ROM disk bundled with this book.

The Brushes palette contains brushes for drawing and some editing tools. For example, Figure 6.8 shows the default brush palette when the **Paintbrush** tool is selected.

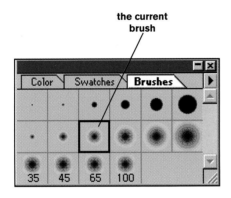

Figure 6.8 The Brushes palette.

The Layers palette (Figure 6.9) enables you to edit particular elements of an image, including the background, shadows behind the image, and the bits and pieces that make up the image itself. For more information, see the "Working with Layers" section later in the chapter.

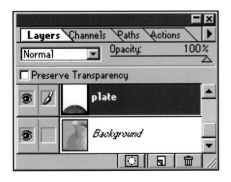

Figure 6.9
The Layers palette with two layers.

Figure 6.10
The Channels palette.

The Channels palette (Figure 6.10) shows how the image's colors break down into *channels*, or their basic color elements (such as an RGB image's red, green, and blue channels or a CMYK image's cyan, magenta, yellow, and black channels).

The Paths palette (Figure 6.11) shows the paths that you have created in the image.

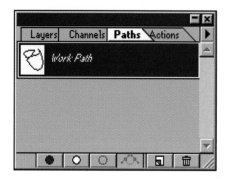

Figure 6.11
The Paths palette.

Figure 6.12
The Actions palette.

The Actions palette (Figure 6.12) lists standard and user-recorded *actions* (which are like macros in other programs). From within this palette, you can record, play, save, or delete actions.

- All palettes offer context menus. Simply click on the right-pointing arrow to open a menu of commands that are related to the palette.

- Some palettes have buttons arranged along the bottom margin. Click on a button to take a particular action, which is related to the palette. Active buttons have associated Tool Tips; inactive buttons are dimmed.

- To display a particular palette, either click on its tab immediately below the title bar, double-click on its tool in the toolbox, or choose a show command from the Window menu.

- You can hide or display the toolbox and all the palettes on the right side of the window by pressing the **Tab** key.

- You can hide or display the palettes without affecting the display of the toolbox by pressing **Shift+Tab**.

The Status Bar

A status bar (Figure 6.13), which displays Photoshop information, appears at the bottom of the window.

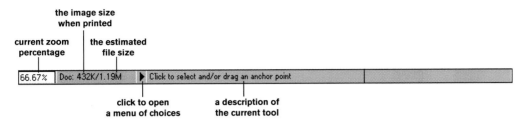

Figure 6.13 The Photoshop status bar.

The status bar is composed of three sections.

At the left side is a text box that displays the current percentage of zoom. You can zoom in or out a certain percentage by typing a value in the text box and pressing **Enter**.

The next section displays one of four pieces of information: Document Sizes, Scratch Sizes, Efficiency, or Timing. Click on the right-pointing arrow to select the type of information to be displayed.

◆ Document Sizes (Doc)—On the left, the size of the image when printed and, on the right, the current size if the image is saved as a .PSD file. The two values give you a range so that you can predict the file's ultimate size.

◆ Scratch Sizes (Scr)—On the left, the amount of random access memory (RAM) currently used by Photoshop and, on the right, the RAM available to Photoshop.

◆ Efficiency (Eff)—The percentage of RAM used versus the percentage used by a *scratch disk*, which is Photoshop's name for virtual memory.

◆ Timing—The time that it took to perform the most recent action.

The rightmost section contains a short description of the currently-selected tool and informs you when you can use the **Shift**, **Alt**, and **Ctrl** keys. The status bar on the Macintosh does not provide this information.

To hide the status bar, choose **Window: Hide Status Bar**. To display the hidden status bar, choose **Window: Show Status Bar**.

PREPARING TO CREATE AN IMAGE

Before you create an image, you may have to go through some steps, such as changing the foreground and background colors, turning on a grid, and displaying the rulers. In addition, before you start working, you should learn how to change the view of an image, so that you can work on your image at a pixel-by-pixel level or in its entirety.

Changing the Foreground and Background Colors

Photoshop enables you to choose foreground and background colors in several ways—by clicking on a small section of the toolbox to selecting from a dialog box or palette.

Switching Colors

You can return to the default foreground and background colors or switch colors with a single click.

◆   To change the foreground and background colors to their default black and white, respectively, click on **Default Foreground and Background Colors** tool in the toolbox or press **D**.

◆   To change the foreground color to the background color and the background color to the foreground color, click on **Switch Foreground and Background Colors** tool in the toolbox or press **X**.

Using a Color from an Image

You can select a new foreground or background color from an open image file using the **Eyedropper** tool. To select a color, follow these steps:

1.   Click on the **Eyedropper** tool or press **I**.
2.   To select a foreground color, click on a color in the current image.
3.   To select a background color:

 Press and hold down the **Alt** key and click on a color in the image.

 Press and hold down the **Option** button and click on a color in the image.

Using the Color Picker Dialog Box

You can select a new foreground or background color by clicking on the foreground color or background color in the toolbox or the currently selected foreground or background color box (that is, the box with a double-line border) in the Color palette and choosing from the Color Picker dialog box (Figure 6.14). The Color Picker dialog box provides support for four color standards: HSB, RGB, Lab, and CMYK.

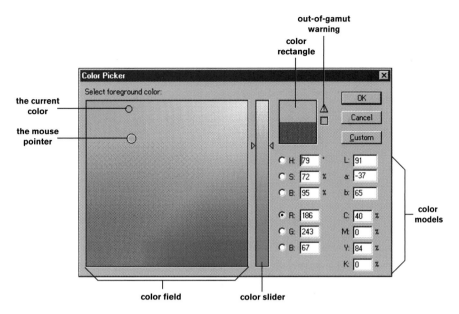

Figure 6.14 The Color Picker dialog box.

The Color Picker dialog box contains the following elements.

Color Field–A large box containing a range of colors from which you can select. Either click on the desired color or slide the mouse pointer around until it points to the desired color.

Color Slider–A vertical box containing a range of colors related to the currently-selected or pointed-to color. You can slide the pointers up and down the color slider to find the desired color.

Color Rectangle–A small box containing the current foreground or background color in the bottom half and the currently selected color, which may replace the foreground or background color, in the top half.

HSB Color Model–The hue-saturation-brightness model contains three values: the hue (the actual color), saturation (lesser or greater amounts of gray in the color), and brightness (the lightness or darkness of the color). Valid values for the hue range from 0 to 360; valid values for saturation and brightness range from 0 to 100. For more information about HSB colors, which are also known as HSL and HSV colors, see the "About HSV Colors" section in Chapter 3.

RGB Color Model–The red-green-blue model contains three values that show the amounts of red, green, and blue in a particular color. Valid values ranges from 0 to 255 for each color. For more information about RGB colors, see the "About RGB Colors" section in Chapter 3.

Lab Model–The CIE L*a*b* model contains three values: luminance, a green-to-red saturation, and a blue-to-yellow saturation. Valid values for L range from 0 to 100; valid values for a and b range from -128 to 127.

CMYK Color Model–The cyan-magenta-yellow-black model contains four values. The model is based on process-color inks used for color separations. Valid values for all four colors range from 0 to 100.

NOTE CMYK provides fewer color choices than RGB or HSB, so if you choose a color that is beyond the range of CMYK colors, the out-of-gamut warning appears accompanied by the CMYK color that is the closest to your choice. If you plan to use the CMYK Color Model, click on the warning to change to the valid color. However, remember that GIF files use a maximum of 256 colors, the RGB color palette.

Custom–Click on this button to open a dialog box from which you can select custom colors from standard color systems: ANPA, DIC, FOCOLTONE, PANTONE, TOYO, and TRUMATCH.

Using the Color Palette

As you learned in the previous section, you can click on the currently selected foreground or background color in the Color palette (Figure 6.15) to select a new color from the Color Picker dialog box. You can also use the Color palette itself to quickly change the foreground or background color.

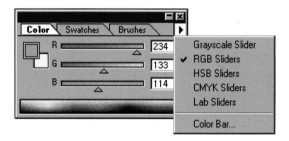

Figure 6.15 The Color palette with an open menu.

To select a new foreground or background color, follow these steps:

1. Click on the color box that is currently selected (that is, the one that has a double-line border).
2. Select a color by:
   ◆ sliding the sliders to "mix" the desired color.
   ◆ typing a value in the text boxes to "mix" the desired color.
   ◆ clicking in the color bar to select a color.

As the color changes in the Color palette, it also changes in the toolbox.

NOTE If you select a color that is out of the CMYK range of values, Photoshop displays the out-of-gamut warning in the Color palette. Click on it to choose the closest CMYK color, if you wish.

THE GIF ANIMATOR'S GUIDE

You can select a new color model by following these steps:

1. Click on the right-pointing arrow. Photoshop opens the Color palette menu.
2. Select a slider from the menu.

Using the Swatches Palette

You can use the color boxes in the Swatches palette (Figure 6.16) to select a foreground or background color. To select a new foreground color, follow these steps:

1. Open the Swatches palette. When you move the mouse pointer over the color boxes in the palette, it changes to the **Eyedropper** tool.
2. To select a foreground color, click on a color box.
3. To select a background color:

   Press and hold down the **Alt** key and click on a color box.

   Press and hold down the **Option** button and click on a color box.

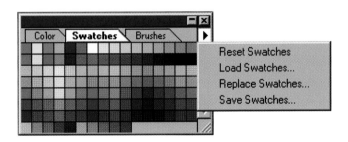

Figure 6.16 The Swatches palette with an open menu.

Showing the Grid

By default, Photoshop provides a hidden grid that controls the placement of image elements. When you add an element to an image, Photoshop "snaps" it to the grid. You can view the grid by choosing **View: Show Grid** or press **Ctrl+"**. To hide the grid, choose **View: Hide Grid** or press **Ctrl+"** (Windows) or **Command+"** (Macintosh).

Working with a grid also allows you to create or edit an image more easily at the pixel level. For example, you can round sharp corners by removing a pixel or two at the very point of a corner. Or, in a paint program such as Photoshop, you can shade or highlight an image pixel by pixel. Figure 6.17 shows one of Photoshop's tutorial images with a visible grid.

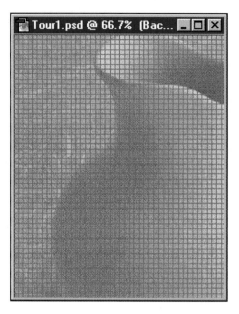

Figure 6.17 A Photoshop image with a visible grid.

You can specify grid options by following these steps:

1. Choose **File: Preferences: Guides & Grid**. Photoshop opens the Guides & Grid section of the Preferences dialog box (Figure 6.18).

2. To choose a gridline color, either select from the Color drop-down list box or click on the color box and select options from the Color Picker dialog box (see Figure 6.14).

3. To choose a gridline style, open the Style drop-down list box and select **Lines**, **Dashed Lines**, or **Dots**.

4. To set space between gridlines, type a number in the Gridline Every text box and select a unit of measure (**pixels**, **inches**, **centimeters**, **points**, or **picas**) from the drop-down list box.

5. To display heavier gridlines at regular intervals, type a number in the Subdivisions text box.

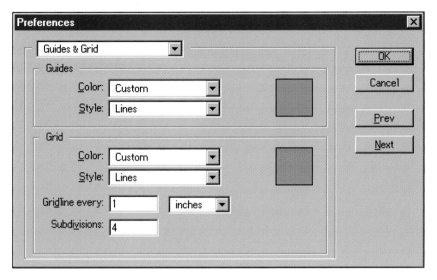

Figure 6.18 The Guides & Grid section of the Preferences dialog box.

NOTE

Guides, which are not covered in this book, are lines that mark limits within a particular image window. So, if you want to line up several images, you can set guidelines to which the images will snap.

Turning on the Rulers

To measure all or part of an image, you can display vertical and horizontal rulers (Figure 6.19) within all the open image windows. When you turn on the rulers, they remain on display until you explicitly hide them—in this or a later Photoshop session. To display the rulers, choose **View: Show Rulers** or press **Ctrl+R**. To hide the rulers, choose **View: Hide Rulers** or press **Ctrl+R** (Windows) or **Command+R** (Macintosh).

The rulers use the current unit of measure: inches, pixels, centimeters, points, or picas. To change the unit of measure, choose **File: Preferences: Units & Rulers**, and select an entry in the Units drop-down list box.

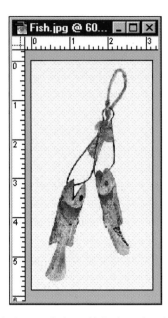

Figure 6.19 An image window with horizontal and vertical rulers.

Changing the View of an Image

When you view an image at its actual size, you may not be able to work on its details, or, conversely, you may not be able to see it completely—especially if it extends beyond the limits of your computer screen. Photoshop allows you to zoom in (that is, see the details as small as a pixel, depending on the percentage you have zoomed in) or zoom out (that is, see a greater part of a large composition). You can zoom in up to 1,600% of the actual size; you can zoom out to 0.19% of the actual size.

Zooming In on an Image

You can zoom in using several methods:

- Choose **View: Zoom In**.
- Press **Ctrl++** (Windows) or **Command++** (Macintosh) repeatedly until the image looks as large as you want.
- Press **Ctrl+=** (Windows) or **Command+=** (Macintosh) repeatedly until the image looks as large as you want.
- Click on the **Zoom** tool or press **Z**. Drag the magnifying-glass mouse pointer to form a bounding box around the area on which you want to zoom in.

SHORTCUT   To activate the **Zoom In** tool, press **Ctrl+spacebar** in the Windows version, or press **Command+spacebar** in the Macintosh version.

◆ Click on the **Zoom** tool or press **Z**. Then, move the magnifying-glass mouse pointer to the image, and left-click repeatedly until the image looks as large as you want.

◆ Open the Navigator palette (Figure 6.20) and slide the Zoom Slider to the right. The red box in the preview window in the Navigator palette surrounds the part of the image that appears in the image window.

SHORTCUT   As you scroll around the image, you can use the box as a guide for locating the part of the image on which you want to work.

◆ To zoom in to a certain percentage, type the value in the text box in the lower-left corner of the Navigator palette and press **Enter**.

◆ To zoom in to the maximum zoom level, press **Ctrl+Alt+=** (Windows) or **Command+Option+=** (Macintosh).

Figure 6.20 The Navigator palette.

Zooming Out on an Image

You can zoom out using several methods:

◆ Choose **View: Zoom Out**.

◆ Press **Ctrl+-** (Windows) or **Command+-** (Macintosh) repeatedly until the image looks as large as you want.

◆ Click on the **Zoom** tool or press **Z**. Then, move the magnifying-glass mouse pointer to the image. Press and hold down the **Alt** key (Windows) or press and hold down the **Option** Key (Macintosh). Then, left-click repeatedly until the image looks as small as you want.

To activate the **Zoom Out** tool: press **Ctrl+Alt+spacebar** (Windows) or press **Command+Option+spacebar** (Macintosh).

◆ Open the Navigator palette (Figure 6.20) and slide the Zoom Slider to the left. The red box in the preview window in the Navigator palette surrounds the part of the image that appears in the image window.

◆ To zoom out to a certain percentage, type the value in the text box in the lower-left corner of the Navigator palette and press **Enter.**

◆ To zoom out to the minimum zoom level, press **Ctrl+Alt+-** (Windows) or **Command+Option+-** (Macintosh).

Figure 6.21 shows three windows containing images of the Photoshop sample **Frame.jpg**. One window shows the image at its actual size, another shows the image zoomed in to 300%, and the remaining image is zoomed out to 40%.

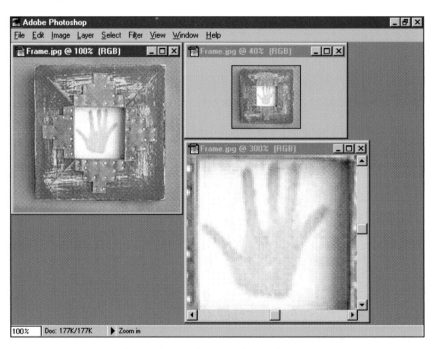

Figure 6.21 Three views of Photoshop's sample Frame.jpg image: 100%, zoomed in to 300%, and zoomed out to 40%.

Displaying an Image at 100%

You can display an image at its true size (that is, 100%) by taking one of the following actions:

- ◆ Double-click on the **Zoom** tool.
- ◆ Choose **View: Actual Pixels**.
- ◆ Press **Alt+Ctrl+0** (Windows).
- ◆ Press **Command+Option+0** (Macintosh).
- ◆ Press **Actual Pixels** on the Zoom Tool Options palette (Figure 6.22).

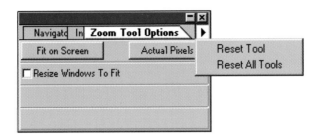

Figure 6.22 The Zoom Tool Options palette and its menu.

Fitting an Image to the Application Window

You can adjust the view of an image to fit the application window. Photoshop is intelligent enough that, when it carries out the command, it senses whether palettes or hidden or displayed. To fit an image to the window:

- ◆ Double-click on the **Hand** tool.
- ◆ Choose **View: Fit on Screen**.
- ◆ Press **Ctrl+0** (Windows).
- ◆ Press **Command+0** (Macintosh).
- ◆ Click on **Fit on Screen** in the Zoom Tool Options palette.

Viewing an Image as It Will Print

You can view an image at the size at which it will print. This means that GIF animators can get a preview of some images as they will appear in a browser window. To view an image as it will print, choose **View: Print Size**.

SHORTCUT There is no substitute for viewing an image in one or more Web browser windows—many times during its development. Then, you'll be able to see its progress and make quick changes along the way.

CREATING AN IMAGE—EXAMPLE 1

To create an image from scratch, click on a toolbox tool and start working. Keep in mind that Photoshop is a painting program, so you will work in the same way that an artist paints on a canvas. Therefore, the toolbox does not contain tools for drawing rectangles, ellipses, and polygons.

Learning About the Painting Tools

The best way to learn about the tools with which you'll paint images is to use them. However, before you get started, it's a good idea to find out how these tools work and how to change their characteristics.

Each of the tools described in this section is associated with a Brushes palette, an Options palette, and a shortcut menu.

SHORTCUT As you work with a tool, it's a good idea to have its Brushes palette and Options palette on display.

Using the Brushes Palette

The Brushes palette (Figure 6.23) for any tool provides several predefined brushes, which vary depending on the tool. To choose a predefined brush, click on it.

NOTE Although you can use the same predefined brush for several tools (the **Airbrush**, **Paintbrush**, **Pencil**, and **Line** tools), the results vary. For example, if you select the finest brush, a Pencil line will be very thin with a sharp edge and the Airbrush line will be faint but somewhat thicker.

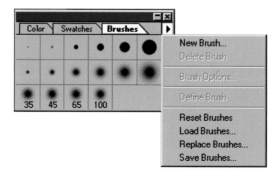

Figure 6.23 The Paintbrush tool's Brushes palette with its menu.

You can create a new brush by selecting options in the New Brush dialog box (Figure 6.24).

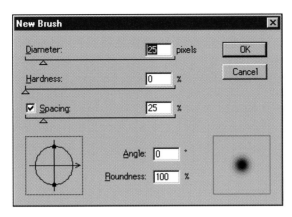

Figure 6.24 The New Brush dialog box.

The options in this dialog box are described below.

. . . .

Diameter–Slide the slider to select the size (that is, diameter) of the brush. Valid values range from 1 (the smallest) to 999 pixels (the largest). The preview box in the lower-right corner shows the effects.

SHORTCUT   You can check the settings for the current brush by selecting it, choosing the **Brush Options** command from the menu, and looking at the values in the Brush Options dialog box, which is identical to the New Brush dialog box.

Hardness–Slide the slider to select the sharpness or blurriness of the edges of the brush. Valid values range from 0 (the blurriest) to 100% (the sharpest). The preview box in the lower-right corner shows the effects.

Spacing–Check the check box and slide the slider to specify the spacing between the pixels drawn or painted by the selected tool. The higher the value, the more chance that there will be gaps in a brush-stroke. Valid values range from 1 (tight spacing) to 999% (loose spacing).

Angle–To set the angle at which a brush stroke is drawn, either type a value in this text box or drag the wheel in the preview box in the lower-left corner.

Roundness–To set the percent of roundness of the brush stroke, type a value in this text box. Valid values range from 0 (the most flat) to 100% (the most round).

. . . .

To create a new brush, follow these steps:

1. Click on the right-pointing arrow in the Brushes palette.
2. Select **New Brush**.
3. Select options from the New Brush dialog box.
4. Click on **OK**. Photoshop adds the new brush to the Brushes palette and selects it.

To delete a brush, open the Brushes menu and select **Delete Brush**. Photoshop deletes the brush without prompting you for confirmation.

 SHORTCUT You can insert a circle within an image window using the current foreground color. First, select a tool. In the New Brush dialog box, specify the diameter of the potential circle, select **100%** hardness, and click on **OK**. Then, move the mouse pointer to the point at which the center of the circle will be located. Finally, click to create the circle. You can also create an ellipse, rectangle, or irregularly shaped object by clicking on a selection tool, drawing a selection circle in the work area, and using the **Paint Bucket** tool to fill it with the foreground color.

The Paintbrush Tool

 Use the **Paintbrush** tool to paint blurry-edged strokes (using the default brush) with the foreground color. Every time you click on the **Paintbrush** tool, it acts as though you have added more paint to a paintbrush; you can add more paint to an image. You can modify the Paintbrush using the Paintbrush Options palette (Figure 6.25).

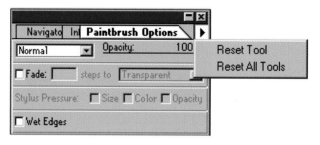

Figure 6.25 The Paintbrush Options palette with its menu.

The options in this palette are described below.

Blending Mode–Opening this drop-down list box reveals a menu with many painting effects, which affect the application of color or paint.

Opacity–Slide this slider or press numbers on the keyboard or numeric keypad (if the **Num Lock** key has been activated) to vary the brush stroke from transparent to opaque. Valid values range from 1 (the most transparent) to 100% (the most opaque).

Fade–Check this check box to fade the brush stroke rather than end it abruptly. Specify the rate of fade by typing a value from 1 (an abrupt end) to 9999 (a fade that ends in 9999 increments). After you specify a rate of fade, you can open the drop-down list box and select the type of fade: **Transparent** (to fade to transparent) or **Background** (to fade to the background color).

Stylus Pressure–The options–**Size**, **Color**, and **Opacity**–are available only if you are working with a pressure-sensitive digitizing tablet.

Wet Edges–Check this check box to simulate painting with watercolors.

To use the Paintbrush, follow these steps:

1. Click on the **Paintbrush** tool.
2. Change the brush size in the Brushes palette and select options in the Paintbrush Options palette, if needed.
3. Move the paintbrush mouse pointer to the image window and drag to apply paint. (To paint a straight line, press and hold down **Shift,** and drag.)

The Pencil Tool

Use the **Pencil** tool to draw sharp-edged strokes (using the default brush) with the foreground color.

You can modify the Pencil using the Pencil Options palette (Figure 6.26).

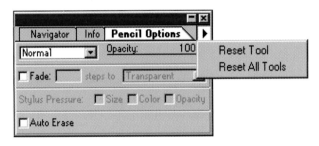

Figure 6.26 The Pencil Options palette with its menu.

With one exception, this palette contains the same options as the Paintbrush Options palette. The one different option is:

Auto Erase–Check this check box to draw with the foreground color in some areas and the background color in others. If you draw over an area that has been drawn or painted with the current foreground color, the Pencil replaces the foreground color with the background color. If you draw over an area in any other color, the Pencil draws in the foreground color.

To use the Pencil, follow these steps:

1. Click on the **Pencil** tool.
2. Change the brush size in the Brushes palette and select options in the Pencil Options palette, if needed.
3. Move the pencil mouse pointer to the image window and drag to insert pencil strokes.

To use the **Auto Erase** option, follow these steps:

1. Open the Pencil Options palette.
2. Check the **Auto Erase** check box and change other options, if needed.
3. Change the brush size in the Brushes palette, if needed.
4. Select a foreground color that will be replaced with the background color.
5. Select a background color that will replace the foreground color.
6. Move the pencil mouse pointer to the image window and drag to insert pencil strokes only over the areas having the current foreground color.

The Line Tool

 Use the **Line** tool to draw a line with the foreground color. You can modify the **Line** tool using the Line Tool Options palette (Figure 6.27).

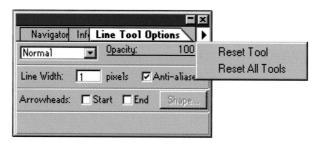

Figure 6.27 The Line Tool Options palette with its menu.

The options in this palette are described below.

Blending Mode–Opening this drop-down list box reveals a menu with many painting effects that affect the application of color or paint.

Opacity–Slide this slider or press numbers on the keyboard or numeric keypad (if the **Num Lock** key has been activated) to vary the line from transparent to opaque. Valid values range from 1 (the most transparent) to 100% (the most opaque).

Line Width–In this text box, specify the width, in pixels, of the line. If you type *0*, you can use the **Line** tool to measure distances within the image.

Anti-Aliased–Check this check box to smooth the line.

Arrowheads–Check the **Start** check box, **End** check box, or both to insert arrowheads at the beginning, the end, or both ends of the line.

Shape–Click on this button, which is available only if you have selected an arrowhead option, to open the Arrowhead Shape dialog box (Figure 6.28). This button is available only if you check the **Start** check box, **End** check box, or both.

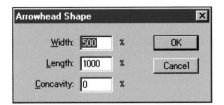

Figure 6.28 The Arrowhead Shape dialog box.

The options in this dialog box are described below.

Width–To set the width of the arrowhead, type its percentage of the width of the line.

Length–To set the length of the arrowhead, type its percentage of the length of the line.

Concavity–To set the curve of the bottom of the arrowhead, type a value from -50 (curved toward the center of the line) to 50 (curved toward the arrowhead point).

To use the **Line** tool, follow these steps:

1. Click on the **Line** tool.
2. Change the brush size in the Brushes palette and select options in the Line Tool Options palette, if needed.
3. Move the line-tool mouse pointer to the image window and drag to insert straight lines.
4. To insert lines that are at 45-degree multiples (that is, 45 degrees, 90 degrees, 135 degrees, 180 degrees, and so on), press and hold down the **Shift** key and drag the line-tool mouse pointer.

The Smudge Tool

 Use the **Smudge** tool to smear the colors on the image. You can modify the **Smudge** tool using the Smudge Tool Options palette (Figure 6.29).

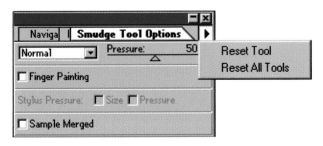

Figure 6.29 The Smudge Tool Options palette with its menu.

The options in this palette are described below.

Blending Mode–Opening this drop-down list box reveals a menu with many painting effects, which affect the application of color or paint.

Pressure–Slide this slider or press numbers on the keyboard or numeric keypad (if the **Num Lock** key has been activated) to vary the effect of smudging the image. Valid values range from 1 (the lightest smear effect) to 100% (the heaviest effect).

Finger Painting–Check this check box to start a smudge with the foreground color. Otherwise, the smudge uses the color at the current location of the mouse pointer.

Stylus Pressure–The options–**Size**, **Color**, and **Opacity**–are available only if you are working with a pressure-sensitive digitizing tablet.

Sample Merged–Check this check box to smudge all the layers of the image. Clear this check box to smudge only the current layer. For more information about layers, see the "Working with Layers" section later in the chapter.

To use the **Smudge** tool on painted or drawn parts of an image, follow these steps:

1. Click on the **Smudge** tool.
2. Change the brush size in the Brushes palette and select options in the Smudge Tool Options palette, if needed.
3. Move the smudge-tool mouse pointer to the image window and drag using short strokes.

NOTE

When you use the Smudge tool, you will introduce a color that is probably not part of the 216-color palette.

The Airbrush Tool

 Use the **Airbrush** tool to spray an airbrush effect with the foreground color. You can modify the **Airbrush** tool using the Airbrush Options palette (Figure 6.30).

Figure 6.30 The Airbrush Options palette with its menu.

The options in this palette are described below.

Blending Mode–Opening this drop-down list box reveals a menu with many painting effects that affect the application of color or paint.

Pressure–Slide this slider or press numbers on the keyboard or numeric keypad (if the **Num Lock** key has been activated) to vary the effect of smudging the image. Valid values range from 1 (the lightest smear effect) to 100% (the heaviest effect).

Fade–Check this check box to fade the airbrush stroke rather than end it abruptly. Specify the rate of fade by typing a value from 1 (an abrupt end) to 9999 (a fade that ends in 9999 increments). After you specify a rate of fade, you can open the drop-down list box and select the type of fade: **Transparent** (to fade to transparent) or **Background** (to fade to the background color).

Stylus Pressure–The options–**Color** and **Pressure**–are available only if you are working with a pressure-sensitive digitizing tablet.

To use the Airbrush, follow these steps:

1. Click on the **Airbrush** tool.

2. Change the brush size in the Brushes palette and select options in the Airbrush Options palette, if needed.

3. Move the Airbrush mouse pointer to the image window and drag to spray the image.

The Eraser Tool

Use the **Eraser** tool to erase part of the image. If you are working in a single-layer image, the **Eraser** tool replaces the erased area with the background color. If you are working in a multiple-layer image, the **Eraser** tool makes the erased area transparent. (For more information about layers, see the "Working with Layers" section later in the chapter.) You can modify the **Eraser** tool using the Eraser Options palette (Figure 6.31).

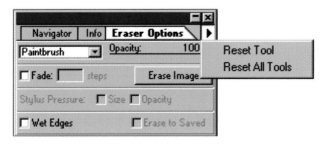

Figure 6.31 The Eraser Options palette with its menu.

The options in this palette are described below.

Tool Type–From this drop-down list box, select the tool that the Eraser will use to erase. The choices are **Paintbrush**, **Airbrush**, **Pencil**, and **Block**, which is a small square.

Opacity–Slide this slider or press numbers on the keyboard or numeric keypad (if the **Num Lock** key has been activated) to vary the line from transparent to opaque. Valid values range from 1 (the most transparent) to 100% (the most opaque).

Fade–Check this check box to fade the airbrush stroke rather than end it abruptly. Specify the rate of fade by typing a value from 1 (an abrupt end) to 9999 (a fade that ends in 9999 increments). After you specify a rate of fade, you can open the drop-down list box and select the type of fade: **Transparent** (to fade to transparent) or **Background** (to fade to the background color).

Erase Image–Click on this button to erase the entire current image after Photoshop prompts you to confirm the deletion.

Stylus Pressure–The options–**Size** and **Opacity**–are available only if you are working with a pressure-sensitive digitizing tablet.

Wet Edges–Check this check box to simulate erasing with watercolors (that is, the erasure is uneven). This option is available only if you have selected the paintbrush tool type.

Erase to Saved–Check this check box to save the erased section to a version of this image that has already been saved.

NOTE   If you have selected **Erase to Saved**, you must press and hold down a key to erase to a saved version of the image: In the Windows version, press and hold down the **Alt** key as you erase; in the Macintosh version, press and hold down the **Option** key as you erase.

To use the Eraser to erase painted or drawn areas of an image, follow these steps:

1. Click on the **Eraser** tool.
2. Change the brush size in the Brushes palette and select options in the Eraser Options palette, if needed.
3. Move the eraser mouse pointer to the image window and drag to erase parts of the image.

Painting an Image

Before you create an image in Photoshop, select options from the New dialog box (Figure 6.32). In this dialog box, you specify the image name, its size, color mode, and its background.

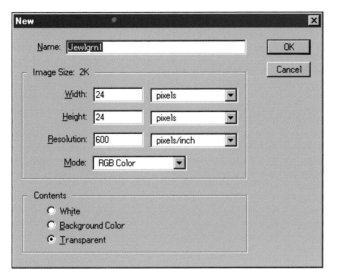

Figure 6.32 The New dialog box for a small image.

The options in the New dialog box are described below.

Name–Type the image file name in this text box.

Image Size–A display of the current approximate file size based on the dimensions and resolution.

Width–In this text box, type the width of the image. Open the drop-down list box and select the unit of measure: **pixels**, **inches**, **centimeters**, **points**, **picas**, or **columns**. As you change the dimensions, view the Image Size display.

Height–In this text box, type the height of the image. Open the drop-down list box and select the unit of measure.

Resolution–In this text box, type the desired graphic resolution of the image. The resolution depends on the type of image that you want to create. High resolutions produce fine images with small pixels but greater file sizes. Lower resolutions result in coarse images with large pixels but lower file sizes.

Mode–From this drop-down list box, select a color mode: **Bitmap**, **Grayscale**, **RGB Color**, **CMYK Color**, or **Lab Color**. For Web graphics, the most common choice is RGB Color.

Contents–To select a background for the image, click on an option button:

 ◆ **White** fills the background with white.
 ◆ **Background Color** fills the background with the current background color.
 ◆ **Transparent** makes the background transparent. Photoshop represents a transparent background with a checkerboard background. Note that most animation programs ignore transparency settings specified in art programs.

To create an image, follow these steps:

1. Start Photoshop.

2. Choose **File: New** or press **Ctrl+N** (Windows) or **Command+N** (Macintosh). Photoshop opens the New dialog box (Figure 6.32).

3. Fill in the dialog box and click on **OK** when you have finished. Photoshop opens an image window and changes settings in the palettes.

4. To work on a magnified version of the composition, zoom in. Choose **View: Zoom In** or press **Ctrl++** (Windows) or **Command++** (Macintosh). For more information about zooming in, refer to the "Zooming In on an Image" section earlier in the chapter.

5. To view a large part of the image, zoom out. Choose **View: Zoom Out** or press **Ctrl+-** (Windows) or **Command+-** (Macintosh). For more information about zooming out, refer to the "Zooming Out on an Image" section earlier in the chapter.

6. To resize the image window, drag its sides or corners.

7. If needed, select a foreground color, background color, or both. For more information, refer to the "Changing the Foreground and Background Colors" section earlier in the chapter.

8. Click on the **Paintbrush**, **Pencil**, **Airbrush**, or **Line** tool and paint or draw the image.

9. Continue working on the image by repeating steps 4 through 8, as needed. In addition, you can use the **Smudge** tool and the **Eraser** tool to change your work.

10. Save the image as a GIF file by choosing **File: Export: GIF89a Export**.

ABOUT THIS ANIMATION—LIGHTED RULE

dotrule.gif 4K 601 × 13 Level: Easy

The lighted rule animation shows flashing lights in random colors.

◆ This animation is composed of four images created in Photoshop.

◆ The original rule is a rectangle filled in black using the Paint Bucket tool.

◆ The grid is turned on and set to 1 pixel per gridline.

◆ All work is done at 100% (**View: Actual Pixels**).

◆ Lights are drawn every fourth pixel using the Pencil set at the lowest brush size. To draw a light, move the mouse pointer to the center of a pixel and quickly click. If the mouse button is held down too long, the dot is drawn slightly larger than the pixel size. To undo a light, choose **Edit: Undo**.

◆ After an image is completed, save it (for example, **dotrule1**) and save it again as the basis for the next image (**dotrule2**) in the series.

◆ Change colors in each image at random. Colors were selected for brightness and lightness. To make sure that colors don't repeat in succeeding images, it's a good idea to display several succeeding images in the work area.

THE GIF ANIMATOR'S GUIDE

- ◆ Remove pixels from both ends of each rule to make a point.
- ◆ Many browsers do not recognize animations. Each image in this animation can stand alone.
- ◆ This animation loops infinitely.
- ◆ This animation looks better at a slower speed.

MODIFYING AN IMAGE

After creating an image, you can modify it in several ways:

- ◆ Use selection tools or Select menu commands to select part or all of an image.
- ◆ Use the Edit menu commands to copy, cut, paste, and delete part or all of an image.
- ◆ Use the transform commands or the Layer menu commands to scale, rotate, skew, distort, or flip a selection.
- ◆ Use Filter menu commands to apply innumerable special effects.

 NOTE Whenever you edit an image, it's a good idea to save it from time to time. This avoids your having to redo your work unnecessarily.

Selecting an Image

Sometimes you can work with an image without selecting it. For example, if you paint or draw on an image window, you don't need to make a selection. However, at other times, you must make a selection before working on an image. For example, if you want to copy, move, or remove part of an image, you must select it. Photoshop provides several selection tools.

The selection tools have several attributes in common:

- ◆ After you select a selection tool, you can open a context menu from which you can select the entire image or select using color attributes.

- Photoshop surrounds a selection with a moving marquee of dashes.
- After you have made a selection, you can use Select menu commands to select the entire image, "deselect" the image, invert the image, and apply effects.
- You can drag a selection marquee—not the image within the selection—around the image window. (Use the Move tool to move the selection or entire image.)
- Two of the three selection tool buttons have small right-pointing arrows in their lower-right corners. This indicates the presence of other selection tools. To reveal one of these tools, point to the selection tool and press and hold down the left mouse button. A small button bar showing all the associated tools appears. To select a tool, drag the mouse pointer to it and release the mouse button.

Selecting by Color Characteristics

Click on the **Magic Wand** tool to select one or more color characteristics of an image. By default, if you drag the magic wand mouse pointer, all components of the image as well as the entire image are surrounded by selection boxes. If you specify color characteristics before dragging, you can choose one section of an image for editing. To "deselect" a selection, either right-click (or press down **Ctrl** and click) away from the selection, choose **Select: None**, right-click (or press down **Ctrl** and click) on the selection and choose **None,** or press **Ctrl+D** (Windows) or **Command+D** (Macintosh). Figure 6.33 shows Magic Wand selections.

Figure 6.33 Several Magic Wand selections.

Selecting a Rectangular Area

To select rectangular areas of an image, Photoshop provides three marquee tools: **Marquee**, **Single Row Marquee**, and **Single Column Marquee**—all in the same location on the toolbox.

NOTE   The **Crop** tool is also associated with these tools. To learn about cropping, see the "Cropping an Image with the Crop Tool" section later in the chapter.

Click on the **Marquee** tool or press **M** to select any rectangular part of an image (Figure 6.34). If you press and hold down the **Shift** key as you drag, Photoshop forces the selection to be a square.

Click on the **Single Row Marquee** tool or press **M** to select a rectangular 1-pixel-high part of an image.

Click on the **Single Column Marquee** tool or press **M** to select a rectangular 1-pixel-wide part of an image.

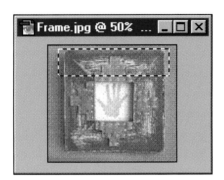

Figure 6.34 A rectangular selection.

Selecting an Elliptical Area

The Marquee tool bar also includes a tool with which you can make elliptical or circular selections. Click on this **Marquee** tool or press **M** to select an oval part of an image. If you press and hold down the **Shift** key as you drag, Photoshop forces the selection to be a circle.

Selecting an Irregular Area

Photoshop provides two lasso tools with which you can make irregular selections by drawing the borders of the selection on the image.

 Click on the **Lasso** tool or press **L** to select an irregular area of an image. Use this tool to make a selection with any shape. To use the **Lasso** tool, drag around the image to make a selection. The pointed part of the tool determines the border of the selection.

 Click on the **Polygon Lasso** tool or press **L** to select a polygonal area of an image (that is, a selection with sharp corners). To use the **Polygon Lasso** tool, follow these steps:

1. Zoom in so that you can get a better view of the image.
2. Select the **Polygon Lasso** tool.
3. Move the polygon-lasso mouse pointer to the image, and click at a starting corner.
4. Continue clicking at corners to add to the selection.
5. Complete the selection by clicking at the starting corner. Figure 6.35 shows an irregular polygonal selection.

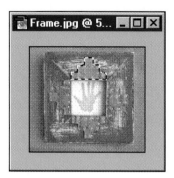

Figure 6.35 An irregular selection created with the Polygon Lasso tool.

Working with Paths

Photoshop provides a set of unique selection tools with which you can draw very fine lines or curves in an image and adjust their shapes. At any time, you can save a path for future actions. You can draw two types of paths:

- An open path (for example, a curving, bending, or straight line) starts and ends with *end points*.
- A closed path (for example, an ellipse, rectangle, or polygon) has no beginning or end.

In addition to the end points, paths are made up of line or curve segments marked by *anchor points*, which indicate a place in a line or curve at which there is a change in direction.

Photoshop provides five path tools (described below), all on the same toolbar within the toolbox.

 Click on the **Pen** tool (or press **P** if this is the current path tool) to draw a path.

 Click on the **Direct Selection** tool (or press **P** if this is the current path tool) to select or drag path segments, anchor points, end points, or *direction lines*, which show the current direction of the curve.

Click on the **Add Anchor Point** tool (or press **P** if this is the current path tool) to add an anchor point to it.

Click on the **Delete Anchor Point** tool (or press **P** if this is the current path tool) to remove the selected anchor point.

Click on the **Convert Anchor Point** tool (or press **P** if this is the current path tool) to convert an anchor point on a curve to an anchor point on an angle.

You can draw and edit paths using the **Pen** tool, the Paths palette (Figure 6.36), or both.

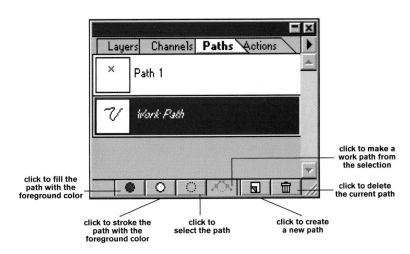

Figure 6.36 The Paths palette with two paths, including the current path on an image.

There are several ways to start a path:

◆ Click on the **Pen** tool, if you are creating the first path for an image.

◆ Make sure that no paths are selected. Then, open the Paths palette menu, and choose **New Path**.

◆ Click on the **New Path** button in the Paths palette.

◆ In the Windows version, press and hold down the **Alt** button and click on the **New Path** button in the Paths palette. Photoshop opens the New Path dialog box (Figure 6.37). Type the name in the text box, and click on **OK**. Photoshop adds the new named path in the Paths palette.

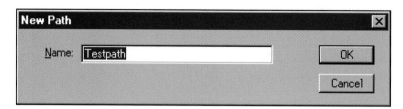

Figure 6.37 The New Path dialog box.

◆ In the Macintosh version, press and hold down the **Option** button and click on the **New Path** button in the Paths palette. Photoshop opens the New Path dialog box. Type the name in the text box, and click on **OK**. Photoshop adds the new named path in the Paths palette.

To draw a path, follow these steps:

1. Move the pen mouse pointer to the image and start drawing the path.

2. To draw a curved path segment, drag the mouse pointer. As you drag, Photoshop adds one or more direction lines.

3. To draw a straight path segment, click each time you want to change the direction of the path. Figure 6.38 shows a path that combines curved and straight lines.

4. To preview a segment, open the Pen Tool Options palette (Figure 6.39) and check the **Rubber Band** check box.

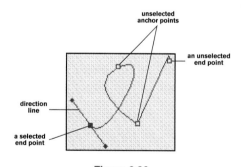

Figure 6.38
A path with both curved and straight lines.

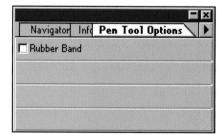

Figure 6.39
The Pen Tool Options palette provides
a single check box.

 To edit a path (that is, change the directions and angles of the lines), use the **Direct Selection** tool to select the path. Then, you can drag by the end points or anchor points. As you drag, Photoshop adds one or more direction lines, which you can also drag to modify the orientation of the curve. Or, you can drag a curve or line to a new location.

Selecting an Entire Image

To select the entire image, choose **Select: All,** or press **Ctrl+A** (Windows) or **Command+A** (Macintosh). Photoshop draws a bounding box around the edges of the image window. If a selection tool is active, right-click (or press down **Ctrl** and click) and choose **Select All** from the menu.

Inactivating a Selection

To inactivate a selection (that is, make it permanent in its current location and remove the selection bounding box), either right-click (or press down **Ctrl** and click) away from the selection, choose **Select: None**, right-click (or press down **Ctrl** and click) on the selection and choose **None**, or press **Ctrl+D** (Windows) or **Command+D** (Macintosh).

Inverting a Selection

To invert the selection (that is, select the unselected area and "unselect" the selected area), choose **Select: Inverse** or press **Shift+Ctrl+I** (Windows) or **Command+I** (Macintosh). Photoshop draws a bounding box around the edges of the image window.

Moving an Image or Selection

To move an image, click on the **Move** tool or press **V**. Then, move the mouse pointer to the image and drag. The image moves around its window. If you have made a selection and clicked on the **Move** tool, drag the selection to its new location.

Copying, Cutting, and Pasting Selections

Most Windows- and Macintosh-based programs include an Edit menu that includes commands with which you can copy, cut, paste, and delete objects. In Photoshop, you can use Edit menu commands to work with images.

Copying a Selection

To copy the current selection to the Clipboard, choose **Edit: Copy,** or press **Ctrl+C** (Windows) or **Command+C** (Macintosh). When you copy a selection, Photoshop leaves the selection in place and places a copy in the Clipboard. If the **Copy** command is dimmed, you have not made a selection.

Cutting a Selection

To remove the current selection and place it in the Clipboard, choose **Edit: Cut,** or press **Ctrl+X** (Windows) or **Command+X** (Macintosh). If the **Cut** command is dimmed, you have not made a selection.

Pasting a Selection

You can paste selections (and, at the same time, create new layers) using Photoshop's two paste commands: **Paste** and **Paste Into**. If either paste command is dimmed, the Clipboard is empty. (For more information about layers, see the "Working with Layers" section later in the chapter.)

- ◆ To paste a selection from the Clipboard as a new layer in the current image or another image, choose **Edit: Paste,** or press **Ctrl+V** (Windows) or **Command+V** (Macintosh). Photoshop turns off the selection.

- ◆ To paste a selection from the Clipboard into the current selection, choose **Edit: Paste Into,** or press **Shift+Ctrl+V** (Windows) or **Shift+Command+V** (Macintosh).

SHORTCUT — If you paste a selection from one image into another, Photoshop does not adjust for possible differences between resolution. If matching resolution is important for a particular picture, make sure that both images start with the same resolution. If resolution is less important, use the **Smudge** tool to smear the pixels in the image.

Deleting a Selection

To permanently delete a selection, either choose **Edit: Clear,** or press the **Del** key (Windows and Macintosh) or **Backspace** (Windows). After you have deleted a selection, the only way to restore it is to choose **Edit: Undo,** or press **Ctrl+Z** (Windows) or **Command+Z** (Macintosh). However, remember that after you have performed another action, you cannot undo the deletion; Photoshop allows you to undo only the last action. To learn how to delete a layer, refer to the "Working with Layers" section later in the chapter.

Changing the Size of an Image or Canvas

Occasionally, you'll find that you'll need to change the size of an image to be able to complete it. Photoshop provides two ways to change the dimensions with which you work on an image:

- ◆ The Image Size dialog box changes the actual image size. This means that you have more room to add details to an image. For example, if you want to add text to the inside of a sign, you might want to make the sign larger so that you can add medium-sized readable text.

- ◆ The Canvas Size dialog box keeps the image in its original size and proportions but increases or decreases (that is, crops) the background area around it. For example, if you want to add a section to an image but keep its current dimensions, change the canvas size to accommodate your new work.

Changing the Size of an Image

Use the Image Size dialog box (Figure 6.40) to change the size of an image:

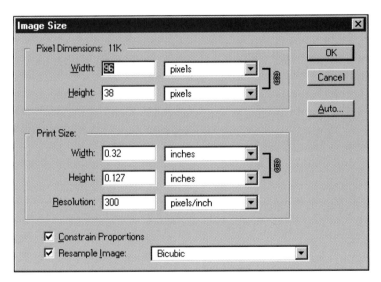

Figure 6.40 The Image Size dialog box.

The options in this dialog box are described below.

Pixel Dimensions–A display of the current size of the image file.

Print Size–A section in which you can control the width, height, and resolution of an image using resampling, which changes the dimensions of Pixels and which has little application to most GIF animations. For information about resampling, see the Adobe Photoshop User Guide.

Width–These two text boxes show width of the image in its current unit of measure and as it will print. Type a value in one of the text boxes, and select a unit of measure from the drop-down list box. If you change the value in one Width text box, Photoshop changes the value in the other Width text box.

Height–These two text boxes show height of the image in its current unit of measure and as it will print. Type a value in one of the text boxes, and select a unit of measure from the drop-down list box. If you change the value in one Height text box, Photoshop changes the value in the other Height text box.

Resolution–This text box shows the number of pixels in an image. Typing a higher resolution results in a higher file size.

Constrain Proportions–Check this check box to keep the image dimensions at its current width-height proportion. If you clear this check box, you can change the proportions.

Resample Image–Check this check box to allow Photoshop to change the number of pixels in an image as you change its dimensions. If you clear this check box, the number of pixels remains the same, regardless of a change in dimensions. From the drop-down list box, you can choose three methods for matching new pixel colors with adjacent pixel colors: **Nearest Neighbor** (takes the least time and calculations to match colors), **Bilinear** (intermediate time and calculations), or **Bicubic** (the most time and calculations to match colors).

Auto–Click on this button to open the Auto Resolution dialog box in which you can specify values if you will use a halftone screen. Halftones are not applicable to GIF animations.

To change the size of an image, follow these steps:

1. Choose **Image: Image Size**. Photoshop opens the Image Size dialog box, which shows the current dimensions of the image.

2. Check or clear the **Constrain Proportions** check box.

3. Check or clear the **Resample Image** check box and optionally select a resampling method.

4. Type values in a Width and Height text box if you have cleared the **Constrain Proportions** check box, or a Width or Height value if the **Constrain Proportions** check box is checked. If you have cleared the **Resample Image** check box, you can only change the print size width and/or height.

5. Click on **OK**. Photoshop changes the size of the image.

6. If you like the results, save the image.

NOTE

When you resize an image, it is very likely that you will need to touch it up using toolbox tools such as the **Paintbrush** and **Pencil** or commands that sharpen the edges of images. Remember that you can apply an effect and undo it (**Edit: Undo** or **Ctrl+Z**) if you don't like it.

Changing the Size of a Canvas

Use the Canvas Size dialog box (Figure 6.41) to change the size of the canvas that forms the background of an image.

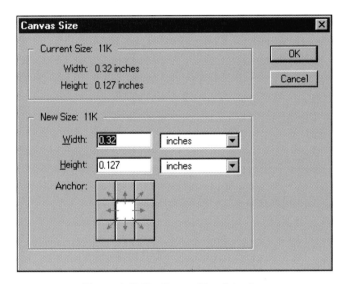

Figure 6.41 The Canvas Size dialog box.

The options in this dialog box are described below.

Current Size–This display section shows the current file size and the width and height of the image.

Width–Type a value in this text box, and select a unit of measure from the drop-down list box.

Height–Type a value in this text box, and select a unit of measure from the drop-down list box.

Anchor–The white box shows the current location of the image against its background. Click on the box representing the desired location against the new background dimensions. For example, if you want to crop from the top, bottom, and right side of an image, click on the box in the middle of the left side of **Anchor.** This protects the left side of the image from being cropped.

To change the size of the canvas, follow these steps:

1. Choose **Image: Canvas Size**. Photoshop opens the Canvas Size dialog box.
2. Type values in a Width and/or Height text boxes.

If you type a value that is smaller than the image, Photoshop displays a confirmation box. Click on the **Proceed** button to crop the image.

3. Click on an Anchor box to indicate the desired location of the image in the canvas.

4. Click on **OK**. Photoshop adds a transparent section to the canvas.

5. If you like the results, save the image.

Cropping an Image with the Crop Tool

As you have just learned, you can use the Canvas Size dialog box to crop the canvas on which an image is located. If you decrease the size of the image enough, you can even crop the image itself. You can use the **Crop** tool, which is located on the Marquee toolbar in the toolbox, to crop a canvas, image, or both, and change the cropped area using a variety of mouse pointers.

To use the **Crop** tool on the current image or its canvas, follow these steps:

1. Click on the **Crop** tool or press **C**.

2. Move the crop mouse pointer to the image window and drag a bounding box (Figure 6.42) around the part of the image and canvas that you want to keep.

3. To move the borders or corners of the bounding box, drag them by their handles.

4. To move the bounding box around the canvas, drag it.

Figure 6.42 An image showing a cropping bounding box.

5. To rotate the bounding box, drag up or down, left or right along the borders of the bounding box.

6. If you don't like the results, press **Esc** or click on another tool. If Photoshop opens a confirmation box, click on the **Don't Crop** button.

7. When the bounding box is exactly the right size and at the right location, press **Enter**. Photoshop removes the bounding box and crops the image.

8. If you like the results, save the image.

If you want to crop an image to particular dimensions (for example, to match the size of other images on a page), you can use the Cropping Tool Options palette (Figure 6.43) to do so. Simply check the **Fixed Target Size** check box and type values in the Width, Height, and Resolution text boxes. You can also select a unit of measure from the drop-down list box next to each text box.

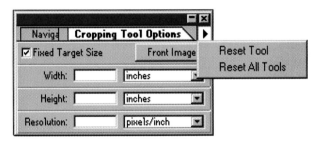

Figure 6.43 The Cropping Tool Options palette with a checked Fixed Target Size check box and an open menu.

Cropping an Image with the Crop Command

If, for some reason, you have selected part of an image, you can use the **Crop** command, which simply crops the image but does not allow you to rotate it. To crop an image using the **Crop** command, follow these steps:

1. Use a selection tool or Select menu command to select an area that you want to remain after cropping is completed.

2. Choose **Image: Crop**. Photoshop crops the image.

3. If you like the results, save the image.

Adding Text to an Image

Use the **Type** tool and the Type Tool dialog box (Figure 6.44) to add text in the foreground color to an image.

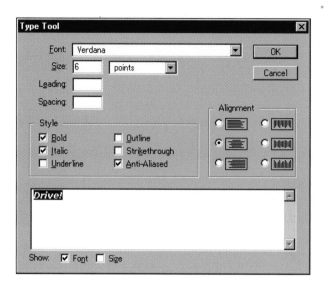

Figure 6.44 The Type Tool dialog box.

The options in the Type Tool dialog box are described below.

Font–From this drop-down list box, select one of the fonts installed on your computer system.

Size–In the text box, enter the type size; from the drop-down list box, select a unit of measure: **points** or **pixels**.

Leading–In this text box, type the value (in points or pixels) of space between multiple lines of text.

Spacing–In this text box, type the value (in points or pixels) of the space between the characters in the typed text.

Style–In this section, check the check boxes for character enhancements. You should check **Anti-Aliased** to smooth out jagged lines within characters.

Alignment–Click on an option button to align the text on a horizontal plane (from the left margin, centered between the margins, or from the right margin) or on a vertical plane (from the top of the vertical bar within the Type Tool mouse pointer, centered at the vertical bar, or from the bottom of the vertical bar).

Show Font–Check this check box to display the text in the preview box using the selected font.

Show Size–Check this check box to display the text in the preview box using the selected point size. If you clear this check box, the text will be large enough for you to see but not necessarily the same size that it will be within the image.

To use the **Type** tool, follow these steps:

1. If desired, change the foreground color.

2. Click on the **Type** tool or press **T** if the tool is displayed in the toolbox.

3. Move the type mouse pointer using the vertical bar to indicate the exact place in the image at which you want to insert the text. Photoshop opens the Type Tool dialog box.

4. Fill in the dialog box and click on **OK**. Photoshop inserts the text as a new layer within the image. (For more information about layers, see the "Working with Layers" section, which follows.)

5. If you don't like the location of the text, undo it (**Edit: Undo,** or **Ctrl+Z** (Windows) or **Command+V** (Macintosh)), click on a better location, fill in the Type Tool dialog box, and click on **OK**.

WORKING WITH LAYERS

Each Photoshop image is made up of one or more layers. When you first create an image, it is composed of one layer—the background, or canvas, on which you draw and edit. When you add certain elements to an image, Photoshop automatically creates a layer, which is like placing a sheet of acetate on top of an animation frame. As you continue to work, you can add more layers. Working with layers allows you to edit one particular part of an image without worrying about inadvertently affecting another part of the image. In addition, you can make copies of layers in order to add duplicate elements to an image or to insert exact-copy shadow boxes.

Use the Layer menu and the Layers palette (Figure 6.45) to add, edit, move, and delete layers.

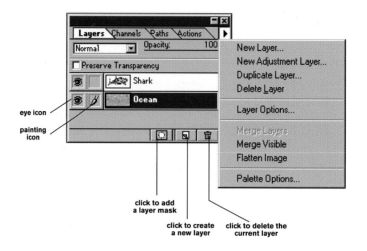

eye icon

painting icon

click to add a layer mask

click to create a new layer

click to delete the current layer

To create a new layer, click on the **New Layer** button at the bottom of the Layers palette, choose **Layer: New: Layer** or select **New Layer** from the Layers palette menu. Photoshop opens the New Layer dialog box in which you can name the layer, specify its opacity, select special effects, and/or group it with the previous layer. You can create a new layer automatically by dragging a selection to the current layer.

To hide a layer, click on the **eye** icon to its left. Click on the **eye** icon to display a hidden layer.

To name a layer, choose **Layer: Layer Options** or select **New Layer** from the Layers palette menu. In the Name text box, type a name.

To change the order of a layer among other layers, drag the layer in the Layers palette up or down to its new position. You cannot drag the background layer to a new location. To move a layer, you must click on the layer, choose **Layer: Arrange**, and then select a subcommand: **Bring to Front** (**Shift+Ctrl+]** (Windows) or **Shift+Command+]** (Macintosh)) moves the layer to the top of the order, **Send to Back** (**Shift+Ctrl+[** (Windows) or **Shift+Command+[** (Macintosh)) moves it to the bottom of the order, **Bring Forward** (**Ctrl+]** (Windows) or **Command+]** (Macintosh)) moves it one layer toward the top, and **Send Backward** (**Ctrl+[** (Windows) or **Command+[** (Macintosh)) moves it one layer toward the bottom.

To make a copy of a layer, choose **Layer: Duplicate Layer** or select **Duplicate Layer** from the Layers palette menu. In the Duplicate Layer dialog box, name the duplicate and select its destination. Then, click on **OK**.

To delete a layer, click on the **Delete Current Layer** button, choose **Layer: Delete Layer**, or select **Delete Layer** from the Layers palette menu. When you delete a layer, Photoshop does not prompt you to confirm the deletion. So, if you inadvertently delete a layer, choose **Edit: Undo** or press **Ctrl+Z** (Windows) or **Command+Z** (Macintosh).

TRANSFORMING A SELECTION OR LAYER

In addition to commands that add, edit, and delete layers, the Layer menu features the **Transform** command, which contains a comprehensive set of subcommands that you can use to manipulate selections or layers. You can use them to resize, rotate, distort, and flip.

To use a Transform subcommand, follow these steps:

1. Choose **Layer: Transform** and then select a subcommand. Photoshop places a bounding box (Figure 6.46) with handles around the selection or layer.

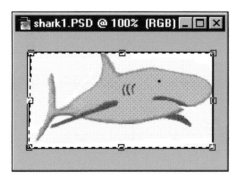

Figure 6.46 A selection ready to be transformed.

2. To transform the selection or layer, drag a handle.
3. To move the selection or layer, drag it from within its borders.
4. Press **Enter** to complete the operation. Photoshop removes the bounding box.

 SHORTCUT
Consider experimenting with some of these commands to create a series of images for animations. For example, you can repeatedly scale an object to make it seem to move away or toward the viewer, or you can distort an object to make it appear to move. After performing a transform operation, save a new file. Then, transform again and save again, and so on.

Table 6.2 describes the actions of each of the transform commands.

Table 6.2 Transform Commands and Their Actions

Command	Drag a Corner Handle to:	Drag a Mid-Line Handle to:
Layer: Transform: Scale	Change width and height	Change width or height
Layer: Transform: Rotate	Rotate left or right	Rotate left or right
Layer: Transform: Skew	Make a parallelogram	Make a polygon
Layer: Transform: Distort	Make a polygon	Increase or decrease width or height
Layer: Transform: Perspective	Proportionally increase width or height	Make a parallelogram

Rotating a Selection or Layer

Photoshop provides three commands with which you can rotate a selection or layer without dragging handles.

To rotate the selection or layer 180 degrees, choose **Layer: Transform: Rotate 180°**.

To rotate the selection or layer 90 degrees clockwise, choose **Layer: Transform: Rotate 90° CW**.

To rotate the selection or layer 90 degrees counterclockwise, choose **Layer: Transform: Rotate 90° CCW**.

Flipping a Selection or Layer

Photoshop provides two commands for flipping selections or layers horizontally or vertically. To flip a selection or layer horizontally (that is, from left to right or from right to left), choose **Layer: Transform: Flip Horizontal**. To flip a selection or layer vertically (that is, from top to bottom or from bottom to top), choose **Layer: Transform: Flip Vertical**.

Using the Numeric Transform Dialog Box

When you want to move, rotate, or skew a selection or layer by a particular measurement or percentage, use the Numeric Transform dialog box (Figure 6.47). Choose **Layer: Transform: Numeric** or press **Shift+Ctrl+T** (Windows) or **Shift+Command+T** (Macintosh) to open this dialog box.

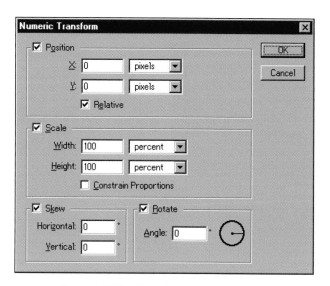

Figure 6.47 The Numeric Transform dialog box.

The options in this dialog box are described below.

Position—Check this check box to move the selection or layer. To guard against any other transformation being done inadvertently, clear the **Scale**, **Skew**, and **Rotate** check boxes or keep their values at the defaults.

X—In this text box, type a value by which you want to move the selection or layer horizontally. Optionally, select a unit of measure from the drop-down list box. The default value is 0 pixels.

Y—In this text box, type a value by which you want to move the selection or layer vertically. Optionally, select a unit of measure from the drop-down list box. The default value is 0 pixels.

Relative—Check this check box to move the selection from its current location rather than the upper-left corner of the image window (a cleared check box).

Scale—Check this check box to scale the selection or layer. To guard against any other transformation being done inadvertently, clear the **Position**, **Skew**, and **Rotate** check boxes or keep their values at the defaults.

Width—In this text box, type a value by which you want to scale the width of the selection or layer. Optionally, select a unit of measure from the drop-down list box. The default value is 100%.

Height—In this text box, type a value by which you want to scale the height of the selection or layer. Optionally, select a unit of measure from the drop-down list box. The default value is 100%.

Constrain Proportions—Check this check box to keep the width and height of the selection or layer in its original proportions.

Skew—Check this check box to skew the selection or layer. To guard against any other transformation being done inadvertently, clear the **Position**, **Scale**, and **Rotate** check boxes or keep their values at the defaults.

Horizontal—In this text box, type a value by which you want to skew selection or layer horizontally. Optionally, select a unit of measure from the drop-down list box. The default value is 0.

Vertical—In this text box, type a value by which you want to skew selection or layer vertically. Optionally, select a unit of measure from the drop-down list box. The default value is 0.

Rotate—Check this check box to rotate selection or layer. To guard against any other transformation being done inadvertently, clear the **Position**, **Scale**, and **Skew** check boxes or keep their values at the defaults.

Angle—In this text box, type the number of degrees that you want to rotate the selection or layer. The default value is 0. Another way of rotating is to drag the line within the circle.

Using the Free Transform Command

The **Free Transform** command allows you to change the dimensions of a layer or selection, or scale, rotate, or move it. To use this command, choose **Layer: Transform: Free Transform** or press **Ctrl+T** (Windows) or **Shift+Command+T** (Macintosh). When Photoshop places a bounding box around the layer or selection:

◆ Drag a corner handle diagonally to increase or decrease the width and height of the layer or selection.

◆ Drag a corner handle horizontally or vertically to increase or decrease the width or height of the layer or selection.

◆ Drag a midline handle away or toward the center of the layer or selection to increase or decrease the width or height of the layer or selection.

◆ Drag on "nonhandle" parts of the bounding box to rotate the layer or selection.

◆ Drag within the bounding box to move the layer or selection.

After you have completed the transformation, press **Enter**.

APPLYING SPECIAL EFFECTS—EXAMPLE 2

The Filters menu contains many commands with which you can apply artistic effects. To apply an effect, select a command and a subcommand. Then, you may have to choose options from a dialog box. (One example is shown in Figure 6.48.) As you select options, look at the effects in a preview box. As you might expect, the image determines both your choice of commands and the results of the effects.

SHORTCUT   If you don't like the look of an effect generated by a command, choose Edit: Undo or press **Ctrl+Z** (Windows) or **Command+Z** (Macintosh). If you are choosing effects from within a dialog box, either click on Cancel or press the Esc to close the dialog box without applying the effects. Some dialog boxes do not show a preview of the effect on your image. If this is the case, make a copy of the image file and look at the results on the copy, thereby preserving the look of the original image.

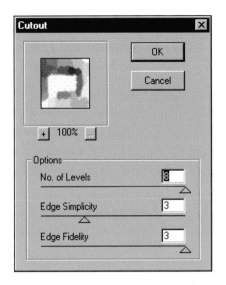

Figure 6.48 The Cutout dialog box showing the effects of the current options on rainbow-colored ovals of paint.

Photoshop provides the following special-effects commands.

Artistic—Use these subcommands and dialog boxes to apply artistic effects to images.

Blur—Use these subcommands and/or dialog boxes to blur images.

Brush Strokes—Use these subcommands and dialog boxes to apply brush-stroke effects to the interior and exterior of images.

Distort—Use these subcommands and dialog boxes to change the dimensions or the look of the surface of images. Note that the Wave and ZigZag dialog boxes include more options than most Filters dialog boxes.

Noise—Use these subcommands and/or dialog boxes to add or change the color of images.

Pixelate—Use these subcommands and/or dialog boxes to affect all or some pixels in images.

Render—Use these subcommands and/or dialog boxes to affect the lighting of surfaces or dimensions of images. Note that the Lighting Effects dialog box includes more options than most Filters dialog boxes.

Sharpen—Use these subcommands and/or dialog boxes to sharpen the surfaces and edges of images.

Sketch—Use these subcommands and dialog boxes to apply pen-and-ink or pencil-and-ink effects to images.

Stylize—Use these subcommands and/or dialog boxes to apply large-scale effects to images.

Texture—Use these subcommands and dialog boxes to apply texture effects to images. Note that the Texturizer dialog box includes more options than most Filters dialog boxes.

Video—Use these subcommands and/or dialog box to apply effects supported by television and video standards.

Other—Use these subcommands and dialog boxes to create custom filters, to change effects on masks, and to define shadows behind images.

ABOUT THIS ANIMATION—BOUNCING BALL

bounball.gif 9K 35 × 149 Level: Medium

The bouncing ball animation contains a beach ball that bounces endlessly. At the bottom of the bounce, the ball flattens in two stages. (Another bouncing ball animation on the CD-ROM disk is redball.gif: this ball bounces in two arcs.)

- ◆ This animation is composed of one ball image borrowed from a Chapter 3 animation and touched up in Photoshop.

- ◆ In Photoshop, a vertical cylinder, which represents the path of the bounce, is created.

- ◆ In the first file in the animation (**bounbl01**), the ball is selected (the **Marquee** tool) and moved (the **Move** tool) to the top of the cylinder. The image file is saved and then saved again as **bounbl02**.

- ◆ Then, select the ball, move it toward the bottom of the cylinder, save it, and save it again as the next file in the series. Continue this until saving **bounbl09**.

- ◆ Choose **Layer: Transform: Scale** to flatten the **bounbl09** very slightly on the top and bottom. Save the file, and save it again as **bounbl10**.

- ◆· Choose **Layer: Transform: Scale** again to flatten **bounbl10** a little more. This is the last file in the series.

- ◆ Many browsers do not recognize animations. For these browsers, the first file (**bounbl01**) begins and ends the animation.

- ◆ Save each file by choosing **File: Export: GIF89a Export**, clearing the **Interlace** check box, and clicking on **OK**. In the Export GIF89 dialog box, click on **Save**.

- ◆ The images making up the animation are **bounbl01**, **bounbl02**, **bounbl03**, **bounbl04**, **bounbl05**, **bounbl06**, **bounbl07**, **bounbl08**, **bounbl09**, **bounbl10**, **bounbl09**, **bounbl08**, **bounbl07**, **bounbl06**, **bounbl05**, **bounbl04**, **bounbl03**, **bounbl02**, and **bounbl01**.

- ◆ This animation is looped infinitely.

- ◆ This animation should be set as fast as possible.

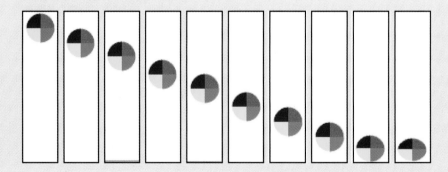

SCANNING AND ANIMATING AN IMAGE— EXAMPLE 3

If you have access to a scanner, you open the door to many possibilities: You can use images from books, magazines, catalogs, and newspapers as a starting point for unique animations.

Before you scan an image for the first time in Photoshop, choose **File: Import: Select TWAIN Source** or **Select TWAIN_32 Source**, depending on the type of scanner attached to your computer. Select the name of the scanner with which you want to acquire the image and click on **OK**.

To acquire an image, follow these steps:

1. Choose **File: Import: TWAIN or TWAIN_32**. Photoshop starts your scanner software.

2. Run your scanner software to scan and edit the image.

3. When you have completed the scan, close the scanner software window. The scanned image appears in the Photoshop workspace.

ABOUT THIS ANIMATION—COOL FAUCET

fauccool.gif 19K 90 × 86 Level: Medium

The cool faucet rotates in an infinite loop.

- This animation is composed of 20 GIFs; the first is repeated at the end.

- The faucet was scanned in from a catalog, adjusted for size, and extensively touched up.

- The text *COOL* was added using the **Type** tool and a dark gray foreground color. Characters in the word were selected and moved in order to paint thicker and darker lines to allow for clearer viewing.

- After changing the zoom level to 100% and saving the image as **faucol01**, the second image in the animation was saved as **faucol02**.

- Before beginning rotations, the background color was set to black.

- Rotations were done by choosing **Select: All** and then choosing **Layer: Transform: Numeric**. In the Angle text box, type *18* to turn the faucet 18 degrees clockwise. Finally, the image was "deselected" by choosing **Select: None**.

- Every rotation was based on the first faucet file to avoid as much text distortion as possible. Rotations of the remaining files were 36, 54, 72, 90, 108, 126, 144, 162, 180, 198, 216, 234, 252, 270, 288, 306, 324, and 342.

- All image files were displayed in the workspace to track the rotation.

- Using the **Paint Bucket** tool, all the images were filled with black, which was set to be the transparent color in the animation program.

- Many browsers do not recognize animations. The beginning and end GIFs in this animation are the original image.

- This animation should run at a medium speed.

- This animation can loop infinitely.

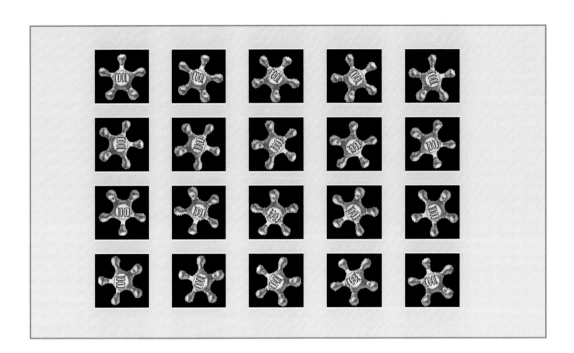

Working with Adobe Illustrator

7

Adobe Illustrator is a drawing program that produces vector graphics. You can make images from scratch or use and edit scanned, captured, or imported images. Illustrator is a superior art-editing program that includes many types of effects that you can apply to images—regardless of their source.

Illustrator allows you to copy, move, and paste images and selections and to undo an action using Edit menu commands. In addition, the user interface will also be familiar to those who run a Windows PC or a Macintosh. Illustrator's extensive help system also includes CD-based tutorials and demonstrations. Its *User Guide* and other manuals provide detailed information about Illustrator features.

Table 7.1 lists the file formats that Illustrator supports.

> **NOTE** In Windows, you can open files using the **File: Open** and **File: Open As** commands. The Macintosh version of Illustrator provides the **File: Open** command. Both versions save with the **File: Save**, **File: Save As**, and **File: Save a Copy**. With Windows and Macintosh computers, you can export files by choosing **File: Export**.

Table 7.1: Illustrator Supported File Formats

Format	Reads from	Saves to	Imports from	Exports to
Illustrator (*.PSD, *.PDD)	yes	yes	no	no
Illustrator EPS	yes	yes	no	no
Encapsulated PostScript (*.EPS)	yes	no	no	no
Acrobat Portable Document Format (*.PDF)	yes	yes	no	no
Amiga (*.IFF)	yes	no	no	no
ASCII	yes	no	no	no
BMP (*.BMP, *.RLE)	yes	no	no	yes
CMX	no	no	yes	no
Computer Graphics Metafile (*.CGM)	no	no	yes	no
CorelDRAW 5/6	no	no	yes	no
Filmstrip (*.FLM)	no	no	yes	no

Table 7.1: Illustrator Supported File Formats (continued)

Format	Reads from	Saves to	Imports from	Exports to
Freehand 4/5	no	no	yes	no
GIF89a (*.GIF)	yes	no	no	yes
JPEG (*.JPG)	yes	no	no	yes
Kodak Photo CD (*.PCD)	no	no	yes	no
Macintosh PICT	no	no	yes	no
MacPaint	no	no	yes	no
MS Word	yes	no	no	no
PCX (*.PCX)	yes	no	no	yes
Photoshop	yes	no	no	yes
Pixar (*.PXR)	yes	no	no	yes
PixelPaint	no	no	yes	no
PNG (*.PNG)	yes	no	no	yes
RTF	yes	no	no	no
Targa (*.TGA)	yes	no	no	yes
TIFF (*.TIF)	yes	no	no	yes
Windows Metafile (*.WMF)	no	no	yes	no
WordPerfect	no	no	yes	no

Illustrator also supports *plug-ins* (programs, utilities, or libraries that can add features to the current program).

SHORTCUT When you want to save an image to a GIF89a-compliant file, choose **File: Export** and choose the GIF89a format. In the GIF89a Options dialog box, clear the **Interlace** check box, if needed, accept all the other options, and click on **OK**.

STARTING ADOBE ILLUSTRATOR

To start Adobe Illustrator on a Windows computer, follow these steps:

1. Click on the **Start** button and select **Programs.** Windows opens the Programs menu.
2. Move the mouse pointer over Adobe. Windows opens a submenu.
3. Click on **Adobe Illustrator**. The Illustrator window (Figure 7.1) opens with a tool palette on the left side and three tool palettes on the right.

SHORTCUT If you have created a shortcut icon on your desktop for Illustrator, double-click on it to start the program.

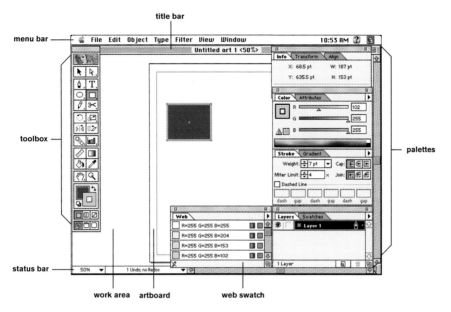

Figure 7.1 The Illustrator window showing the toolbox and four palettes, including a special palette with colors for the World Wide Web.

To start Adobe Illustrator on the Macintosh platform, open the Adobe Illustrator folder and double-click on the **Illustrator** icon.

THE ILLUSTRATOR WINDOW

The Illustrator window contains a variety of elements, many that are familiar to Windows and Macintosh users and some that require more explanation.

The Title Bar and Menu Bar

The Illustrator title bar and menu bar are standard elements. The title bar includes the name of the program, and the menu bar contains menus from which you select commands with which you can perform actions.

NOTE   Illustrator also contains context menus, which contain commands associated with objects on the desktop.

 To use a context menu, move the mouse pointer to an object, press and hold down the **Ctrl** key, click the mouse button, move the mouse pointer to the command, and click to select it.

To use a context menu, right-click on an object in the current window or a small arrow in palettes to open the menu, move the mouse pointer to the desired command, and left-click to select the command.

The Work Area

The Illustrator work area is the space below the title and menu bars, above the status bar at the bottom of the window, to the left of the toolbox, and to the right of the palettes. The work area can also contain image windows, if you have opened any image files.

You can work on more than one image file at a time. This is convenient when you want to use the colors from one image in another. When working on animations, you can open each frame, place them in order, and see the potential motion. You can also open the same image in more than one window. For example, you can show it at its actual size in one window and magnify or zoom in on it in another window. (For more information about zooming, refer to the "Changing the View of the Image" section later in the chapter.) When you change the image in one window, it automatically changes in the other. To open the current image in a second window, you can choose **Window: New Window.**

The Toolbox

The Illustrator toolbox is, by default, on the left side of the window. The toolbox contains several sections, which separate groups of tools by purpose.

 Click on this topmost button to display the opening splash screen from which you can click on a button (in the upper-left corner) to access the Adobe Internet site using your default Web browser, view your serial number, and see the names of those who worked on Illustrator. To close the splash screen, click on it.

The largest part of the toolbox is composed of many drawing and editing tools. Twelve toolbox buttons, which contain small arrows in their lower-right corners, open small palettes from which you can select currently hidden buttons to replace the default buttons permanently—until you replace them again.

To view the choices related to a particular button and select one, click and hold down the mouse button to view all the buttons. Then, slide the mouse pointer to the button to be selected and release the mouse button.

 Selection Tool–Click on this button (or press **V**) to move an image, *layer* (similar to an application of paint over a canvas or a sheet of acetate placed over an animation frame), or guide within the current window. For more information about using the **Selection** tool, see the "Selecting an Image" section later in the chapter. For more information about layers, see the "Working with Layers" section in Chapter 6.

Direct Selection Tool–Click on this button (or press **A** if the tool is displayed in the toolbox) to select or drag *anchor points* (the beginning or ending of a *path*, which is a very fine line or curve marking part of or comprising an object). The other tool on this palette is **Group Selection**. For more information about using the **Direct Selection** tool, see "Selecting an Image" later in the chapter.

Group Selection Tool–Click on this button (or press **A** if the tool is displayed in the toolbox) to select one or more objects or a group within a group, one at a time. (A *group* is a set of objects that have been made a set so that you can modify them as a single unit.) The other tool on this palette is **Direct Selection**. For more information about using the **Group Selection** tool, see "Selecting an Image" later in the chapter.

Pen Tool–Click on this button (or press **P** if the tool is displayed in the toolbox) to draw objects, which include anchor points and *end points*, which mark the ends of paths. The other tools on this palette are **Add Anchor Point**, **Delete Anchor Point**, and **Convert Direction Point**. For more information about using the **Pen** tool, see "Using the Pen Tools" later in the chapter.

Add Anchor Point Tool–Click on this button (or press **P** if the tool is displayed in the toolbox) and then move the mouse pointer to the path to add an anchor point to it. The other tools on this palette are the **Pen**, **Delete Anchor Point**, and **Convert Direction Point**. For more information about using the **Add Anchor Point** tool, see "Using the Pen Tools" later in the chapter.

Delete Anchor Point Tool–Click on this button (or press **P** if the tool is displayed in the toolbox) and then move the mouse pointer to an anchor point to remove it from a path. The other tools on this palette are the **Pen**, **Add Anchor Point**, and **Convert Direction Point**. For more information about using the **Delete Anchor Point** tool, see "Using the Pen Tools" later in the chapter.

Convert Direction Point Tool–Click on this button (or press **P** if the tool is displayed in the toolbox) and then move the mouse pointer to an anchor point on a curve to convert it to an angled anchor point. Click and drag to revert the angled anchor point. The other tools on this palette are the **Pen**, **Add Anchor Point**, and **Delete Anchor Point**. For more information about using the **Convert Direction Point** tool, see "Using the Pen Tools" later in the chapter.

Type Tool–Click on this button (or press **T** if the tool is displayed in the toolbox) and move the mouse pointer to the image to add text. The other tools on this palette are **Area Type**, **Path Type**, **Vertical Type**, **Vertical Area Type**, and **Vertical Path Type**. For more information about using the **Type** tool, see "Adding Text to an Image" later in the chapter.

Area Type Tool–Click on this button (or press **T** if the tool is displayed in the toolbox) and move the mouse pointer to a closed path to open the path and add text. The other tools on this palette are **Type**, **Path Type**, **Vertical Type**, **Vertical Area Type**, and the **Vertical Path Type**. For more information about using the **Area Type** tool, see "Adding Text to an Image" later in the chapter.

Path Type Tool–Click on this button (or press **T** if the tool is displayed in the toolbox) to convert a path to a type path and add text. The other tools on this palette are **Type**, **Area Type**, **Vertical Type**, **Vertical Area Type**, and **Vertical Path Type**. For more information about using the **Path Type** tool, see "Adding Text to an Image" later in the chapter.

Vertical Type Tool–Click on this button (or press **T** if the tool is displayed in the toolbox) to add vertically-aligned text. The other tools on this palette are **Type**, **Area Type**, **Path Type**, **Vertical Area Type**, and **Vertical Path Type**. For more information about using the **Vertical Type** tool, see "Adding Text to an Image" later in the chapter.

Vertical Area Type Tool–Click on this button (or press **T** if the tool is displayed in the toolbox) to a closed path to open the path and add vertically-aligned text. The other tools on this palette are **Type**, **Area Type**, **Path Type**, **Vertical Type**, and **Vertical Path Type**. For more information about using the **Vertical Area Type** tool, see "Adding Text to an Image" later in the chapter.

Vertical Path Type Tool–Click on this button (or press **T** if the tool is displayed in the toolbox) to convert a path to a type path and add vertically aligned text. The other tools on this palette are **Type**, **Area Type**, **Path Type**, **Vertical Type**, and **Vertical Area Type**. For more information about using the **Vertical Path Type** tool, see "Adding Text to an Image" later in the chapter.

Ellipse Tool–Click on this button (or press **N** if the tool is displayed in the toolbox) to draw an ellipse or circle starting from an edge. The other tools on this palette are **Centered Ellipse**, **Polygon**, **Star**, and **Spiral**. For more information about using the **Ellipse** tool, see "Using the Ellipse Tools" later in the chapter.

Centered Ellipse Tool–Click on this button (or press **N** if the tool is displayed in the toolbox) to draw an ellipse or circle starting from its center. The other tools on this palette are **Ellipse**, **Polygon**, **Star**, and **Spiral**. For more information about using the **Centered Ellipse** tool, see "Using the Ellipse Tools" later in the chapter.

Polygon Tool–Click on this button (or press **N** if the tool is displayed in the toolbox) to draw a polygon. The other tools on this palette are **Ellipse**, **Centered Ellipse**, **Star**, and **Spiral**. For more information about using the **Polygon** tool, see "Using the Polygon Tool" later in the chapter.

Star Tool–Click on this button (or press **N** if the tool is displayed in the toolbox) to draw a star. The other tools on this palette are **Ellipse**, **Centered Ellipse**, **Polygon**, and **Spiral**. For more information about using the **Star** tool, see "Using the Star Tool" later in the chapter.

Spiral Tool–Click on this button (or press **N** if the tool is displayed in the toolbox) to draw a spiral. The other tools on this palette are **Ellipse**, **Centered Ellipse**, **Polygon**, and **Star**. For more information about using the **Spiral** tool, see "Using the Spiral Tool" later in the chapter.

Rectangle Tool–Click on this button (or press **M** if the tool is displayed in the toolbox) to draw a rectangle or square starting from a corner. The other tools on this palette are **Rounded Rectangle**, **Centered Rectangle**, and **Centered Rounded Rectangle**. For more information about using the **Rectangle** tool, see "Using the Rectangle Tools" later in the chapter.

Rounded Rectangle Tool–Click on this button (or press **M** if the tool is displayed in the toolbox) to draw a rectangle or square starting from a corner. The other tools on this palette are **Rectangle**, **Centered Rectangle**, and **Centered Rounded Rectangle**. For more information about using the **Rounded Rectangle** tool, see "Using the Rectangle Tools" later in the chapter.

Centered Rectangle Tool–Click on this button (or press **M** if the tool is displayed in the toolbox) to draw a rectangle or square starting from its center. The other tools on this palette are **Rectangle**, **Rounded Rectangle**, and **Centered Rounded Rectangle**. For more information about using the Centered **Rectangle** tool, see "Using the Rectangle Tools" later in the chapter.

Centered Rounded Rectangle Tool–Click on this button (or press **M** if the tool is displayed in the toolbox) to draw a rectangle or square starting from its center. The other tools on this palette are **Rectangle**, **Centered Rectangle**, and **Centered Rounded Rectangle**. For more information about using the Centered Rounded Rectangle tool, see "Using the Rectangle Tools" later in the chapter.

Pencil Tool–Click on this button (or press **Y** if the tool is displayed in the toolbox) to draw on the image with the *stroke* (that is, the color of the brush stroke). The other tool on this palette is the **Paintbrush**. For more information about using the **Pencil**, see "Using the Pencil" later in the chapter.

Paintbrush Tool–Click on this button (or press **Y** if the tool is displayed in the toolbox) to paint on the image with the stroke color. The other tool on this palette is the **Pencil**. For more information about using the **Paintbrush**, see "Using the Paintbrush" later in the chapter.

Scissors Tool–Click on this button (or press **C** if the tool is displayed in the toolbox) to split a path into two paths. The other tool on this palette is the **Knife**.

Knife Tool–Click on this button (or press **C** if the tool is displayed in the toolbox) to cut through an object. The other tool on this palette is the **Scissors**.

Rotate Tool–Click on this button (or press **R** if the tool is displayed in the toolbox) to rotate the selected object. The other tool on this palette is **Twirl**. For more information about using the Rotate tool, see "Rotating a Selection" later in the chapter.

Twirl Tool–Click on this button (or press **R** if the tool is displayed in the toolbox) to rotate the selected object and blur its edges. The other tool on this palette is **Rotate**.

Scale Tool–Click on this button (or press **S** if the tool is displayed in the toolbox) to change the size, proportionally or nonproportionally, of the selected object. The other tool on this palette is **Reshape**. For more information about using the **Scale** tool, see "Scaling a Selection" later in the chapter.

Reshape Tool–Click on this button (or press **S** if the tool is displayed in the toolbox) to slightly change the selected path without affecting its overall shape. The other tool on this palette is **Scale**.

Reflect Tool–Click on this button (or press **O**) to flip an object from a user-defined center point. For more information about using the **Reflect** tool, see "Reflecting a Selection" later in the chapter.

Shear Tool–Click on this button (or press **W**) to skew an object from a user-defined center point. For more information about using the **Shear** tool, see "Shearing a Selection" later in the chapter.

Blend Tool–Click on this button (or press **B** if the tool is displayed in the toolbox) to blend the attributes of one object and another. The other tool on this palette is **Auto Trace**.

Auto Trace Tool–Click on this button (or press **B** if the tool is displayed in the toolbox) to have Illustrator automatically trace the outline of an image. The other tool on this palette is **Blend**.

Column Graph Tool–Click on this button (or press **J** if the tool is displayed in the toolbox) to insert a vertical bar graph on a page. This is equivalent to choosing **Object: Graphs: Type** and clicking on the **Column** button. The other tools on this palette are **Stacked Column Graph**, **Bar Graph**, **Stacked Bar Graph**, **Line Graph**, **Area Graph**, **Scatter Graph**, **Pie Graph**, and **Radar Graph**.

Stacked Column Graph Tool–Click on this button (or press **J** if the tool is displayed in the toolbox) to insert a vertical stacked bar graph on a page. This is equivalent to choosing **Object: Graphs: Type** and clicking on the **Stacked Column** button. The other tools on this palette are **Column Graph**, **Bar Graph**, **Stacked Bar Graph**, **Line Graph**, **Area Graph**, **Scatter Graph**, **Pie Graph**, and **Radar Graph**.

Bar Graph Tool–Click on this button (or press **J** if the tool is displayed in the toolbox) to insert a horizontal bar graph on a page. This is equivalent to choosing **Object: Graphs: Type** and clicking on the **Bar** button. The other tools on this palette are **Column Graph**, **Stacked Column Graph**, **Stacked Bar Graph**, **Line Graph**, **Area Graph**, **Scatter Graph**, **Pie Graph**, and **Radar Graph**.

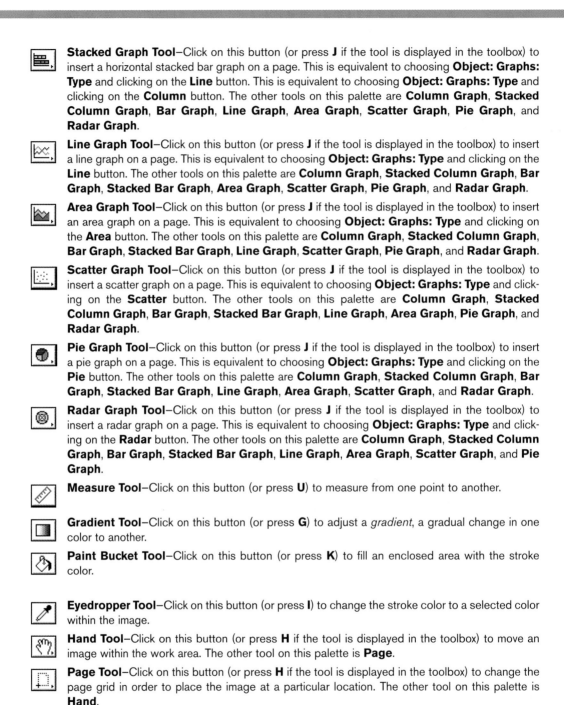

Stacked Graph Tool–Click on this button (or press **J** if the tool is displayed in the toolbox) to insert a horizontal stacked bar graph on a page. This is equivalent to choosing **Object: Graphs: Type** and clicking on the **Line** button. This is equivalent to choosing **Object: Graphs: Type** and clicking on the **Column** button. The other tools on this palette are **Column Graph**, **Stacked Column Graph**, **Bar Graph**, **Line Graph**, **Area Graph**, **Scatter Graph**, **Pie Graph**, and **Radar Graph**.

Line Graph Tool–Click on this button (or press **J** if the tool is displayed in the toolbox) to insert a line graph on a page. This is equivalent to choosing **Object: Graphs: Type** and clicking on the **Line** button. The other tools on this palette are **Column Graph**, **Stacked Column Graph**, **Bar Graph**, **Stacked Bar Graph**, **Area Graph**, **Scatter Graph**, **Pie Graph**, and **Radar Graph**.

Area Graph Tool–Click on this button (or press **J** if the tool is displayed in the toolbox) to insert an area graph on a page. This is equivalent to choosing **Object: Graphs: Type** and clicking on the **Area** button. The other tools on this palette are **Column Graph**, **Stacked Column Graph**, **Bar Graph**, **Stacked Bar Graph**, **Line Graph**, **Scatter Graph**, **Pie Graph**, and **Radar Graph**.

Scatter Graph Tool–Click on this button (or press **J** if the tool is displayed in the toolbox) to insert a scatter graph on a page. This is equivalent to choosing **Object: Graphs: Type** and clicking on the **Scatter** button. The other tools on this palette are **Column Graph**, **Stacked Column Graph**, **Bar Graph**, **Stacked Bar Graph**, **Line Graph**, **Area Graph**, **Pie Graph**, and **Radar Graph**.

Pie Graph Tool–Click on this button (or press **J** if the tool is displayed in the toolbox) to insert a pie graph on a page. This is equivalent to choosing **Object: Graphs: Type** and clicking on the **Pie** button. The other tools on this palette are **Column Graph**, **Stacked Column Graph**, **Bar Graph**, **Stacked Bar Graph**, **Line Graph**, **Area Graph**, **Scatter Graph**, and **Radar Graph**.

Radar Graph Tool–Click on this button (or press **J** if the tool is displayed in the toolbox) to insert a radar graph on a page. This is equivalent to choosing **Object: Graphs: Type** and clicking on the **Radar** button. The other tools on this palette are **Column Graph**, **Stacked Column Graph**, **Bar Graph**, **Stacked Bar Graph**, **Line Graph**, **Area Graph**, **Scatter Graph**, and **Pie Graph**.

Measure Tool–Click on this button (or press **U**) to measure from one point to another.

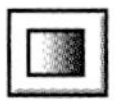

Gradient Tool–Click on this button (or press **G**) to adjust a *gradient*, a gradual change in one color to another.

Paint Bucket Tool–Click on this button (or press **K**) to fill an enclosed area with the stroke color.

Eyedropper Tool–Click on this button (or press **I**) to change the stroke color to a selected color within the image.

Hand Tool–Click on this button (or press **H** if the tool is displayed in the toolbox) to move an image within the work area. The other tool on this palette is **Page**.

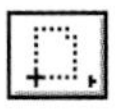

Page Tool–Click on this button (or press **H** if the tool is displayed in the toolbox) to change the page grid in order to place the image at a particular location. The other tool on this palette is **Hand**.

Zoom Tool–Click on this button or press **Z** to zoom in on the image.

The fill/stroke section (Figure 7.2) of the toolbox not only shows the current fill and stroke colors, *gradients* (that is, a gradual change from one color to another), or patterns but also contains tools with which you can manipulate the *fill* (that is, the background) and stroke.

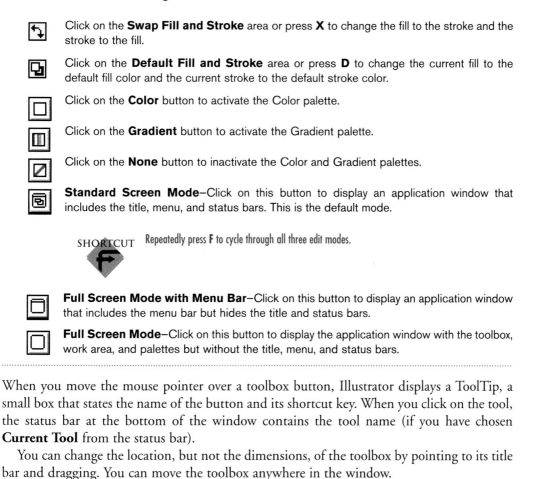

Figure 7.2 The fill/stroke section of the toolbox.

Click on the **Swap Fill and Stroke** area or press **X** to change the fill to the stroke and the stroke to the fill.

Click on the **Default Fill and Stroke** area or press **D** to change the current fill to the default fill color and the current stroke to the default stroke color.

Click on the **Color** button to activate the Color palette.

Click on the **Gradient** button to activate the Gradient palette.

Click on the **None** button to inactivate the Color and Gradient palettes.

Standard Screen Mode—Click on this button to display an application window that includes the title, menu, and status bars. This is the default mode.

SHORTCUT Repeatedly press **F** to cycle through all three edit modes.

Full Screen Mode with Menu Bar—Click on this button to display an application window that includes the menu bar but hides the title and status bars.

Full Screen Mode—Click on this button to display the application window with the toolbox, work area, and palettes but without the title, menu, and status bars.

When you move the mouse pointer over a toolbox button, Illustrator displays a ToolTip, a small box that states the name of the button and its shortcut key. When you click on the tool, the status bar at the bottom of the window contains the tool name (if you have chosen **Current Tool** from the status bar).

You can change the location, but not the dimensions, of the toolbox by pointing to its title bar and dragging. You can move the toolbox anywhere in the window.

You can hide or display the toolbox and all the palettes on the right side of the window by pressing the **Tab** key. To display the hidden toolbox and palettes, press the **Tab** key again.

You can hide the toolbox by choosing **Window: Hide Tools**. You can reveal a hidden toolbox by choosing **Window: Show Tools**.

The Illustrator Palettes

On the right side of the work area are three small windows that contain one, two, or three palettes each. Illustrator includes the following nine palettes:

The Info palette (Figure 7.3) displays the current coordinates of the mouse pointer, and other information, depending on the currently selected tool.

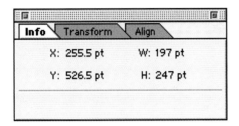

Figure 7.3 The Info palette.

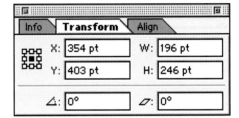

Figure 7.4 The Transform palette.

The Transform palette (Figure 7.4) provides information about the currently selected object: the current X-Y coordinates of the center of the object from bottom left corner of the *artboard* (the area of the work area in which you create and edit images), the width and height of the object, its angle of rotation, and its angle of skew. You can use this palette to modify the selected object.

The Align palette (Figure 7.5) enables you to align selected objects with each other and with the artboard. The Color palette (Figure 7.6) enables you to set the fill and stroke colors, gradients, or patterns. For more information, see the "Changing the Fill and Stroke Colors" section later in the chapter.

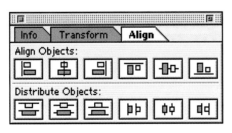

Figure 7.5 The Align palette.

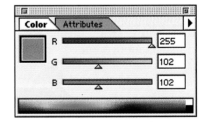

Figure 7.6 The Color palette.

The Attributes palette (Figure 7.7) contains options for printing images. This palette is not covered in this chapter.

The Stroke palette (Figure 7.8) enables you to specify stroke attributes. For more information, see the "Specifying Stroke and Line Attributes" section later in the chapter.

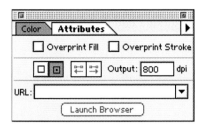

Figure 7.7 The Attributes palette.

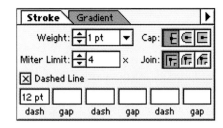

Figure 7.8 The Stroke palette.

The Gradient palette (Figure 7.9) contains options for modifying gradients. This palette is not covered in this chapter.

Use the Swatches palette (Figure 7.10) to specify fill and stroke colors, gradients, or patterns.

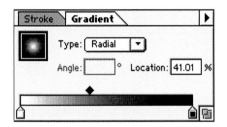

Figure 7.9 The Gradient palette.

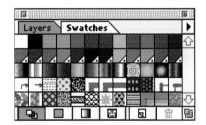

Figure 7.10 The default Swatches palette.

SHORTCUT

Illustrator provides a library of swatches, which includes System (Macintosh), System (Windows), and the 216-color Web swatch palette (Figure 7.13). To select the swatch that provides colors that are suitable for GIF animations, choose **Window: Swatch Libraries: Web**. For more information about the Web palette, see the "Using the Web Palette" section later in the chapter. To learn how to make the Web palette the default swatch and specify other Illustrator starting attributes, see the *User Guide*.

The Layers palette (Figure 7.11) enables you to edit particular elements of an image, including the fill, shadows behind the image, and the bits and pieces that make up the image itself. For more information, see the "Working with Layers" section in Chapter 6.

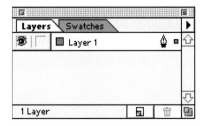

Figure 7.11 The Layers palette with one layer.

- Most palettes offer context menus. Simply click on the right-pointing arrow to open a menu of commands that are related to the palette.

- Some palettes have buttons arranged along the bottom margin. Click on a button to take a particular action, which is related to the palette. Buttons have associated Tool Tips.

- To display a particular palette, either click on its tab or choose a Show command from the Window menu. To hide a palette, choose a **Hide** command from the Window menu.

- You can hide or display the toolbox and all the palettes on the right side of the window by pressing the **Tab** key.

- You can hide or display the palettes without affecting the display of the toolbox by pressing **Shift+Tab**.

The Status Bar

A status bar (Figure 7.12), which displays Illustrator information, appears at the bottom of the window.

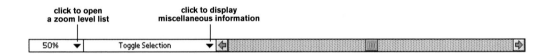

Figure 7.12 The Illustrator status bar.

The status bar is composed of two sections and a horizontal scroll bar.

At the left side of the status bar is the current percentage of zoom. You can zoom in or out a certain percentage by clicking on the downward-pointing arrow and selecting a level.

The next section displays one of four pieces of information: Current Tool, Date and Time, Free Memory, and the Number of Undos. Click on the downward-pointing arrow to select the type of information to be displayed.

- **Current Tool**—The name of the current tool.

- **Date and Time**—The day of the week, the date, and the time.

- **Free Memory**—In the Macintosh version, the percentage and amount of random-access memory (RAM) currently used by Illustrator. In the Windows version, the percentage and amount of virtual memory available to Illustrator.

- **Number of Undos**—The number of undos that can be redone; the number of redos that can be undone.

PREPARING TO CREATE AN IMAGE

Before you create an image, you may have to go through some steps, such as changing the stroke and fill colors, turning on a grid, and displaying the rulers. In addition, before you start working, you should learn how to change the view of an image, so that you can work on your image at the smallest level of detail or in its entirety.

Changing the Fill and Stroke Colors

Illustrator enables you to choose stroke and fill colors, gradients, or patterns in several ways—by clicking on a small section of the toolbox to selecting from a dialog box or palette.

 NOTE When you use a pattern or gradient for an image for the Web, you run the risk of having a browser misinterpret its colors—with poor results.

Switching Colors

You can return to the default fill colors or switch colors with a single click.

- To change the stroke color to the fill color and the fill color to the stroke color, click on **Switch Stroke and Fill** in the toolbox or press **X**. You can also click on the stroke or fill box to make it active.

- To change the stroke and fill colors to their default black and white, respectively, click on **Default Stroke and Fill** in the toolbox or press **D**.

Using the Web Palette

The best way to select the appropriate colors for GIF animations is to use the Web palette (Figure 7.13). To open the Web palette, choose **Window: Swatch Libraries: Web**. To select a color, follow these steps:

1. Open the Web palette.
2. Select the current stroke or fill color by pressing **X** or clicking on the stroke or fill box.
3. Select a color for the stroke or fill (whichever is active) by clicking on a color box in the Web palette. Illustrator applies the color change to the stroke or fill and to the Color palette.

WORKING WITH ILLUSTRATOR

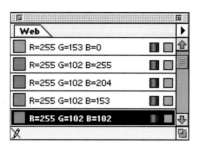

Figure 7.13 The Web palette.

Using a Color from an Image

You can select a new stroke or fill color from an open image file using the **Eyedropper** tool. To select a color, follow these steps:

1. Click on the **Eyedropper** tool or press **I**.
2. Select the current stroke or fill color by pressing **X** or clicking on the stroke or fill box.
3. To select a color for the stroke or fill (whichever is active), click on a color in the current image. Illustrator applies the color change to the stroke or fill and to the Color palette.

Showing the Grid

By default, Illustrator provides a hidden grid that controls the placement of image elements. When you add an element to an image, Illustrator "snaps" it to the grid. You can view the grid by choosing **View: Show Grid**, pressing **Ctrl+"** (Windows), or **Command+"** (Macintosh). To hide the grid, choose **View: Hide Grid,** or press **Ctrl+"** (Windows) or **Command+"** (Macintosh) again.

 Working with a grid in Illustrator allows you to align elements of an image. Because Illustrator is a vector graphics program, you will not be able to work at the pixel level as you can with programs that create bit maps.

You can specify grid options by following these steps:

1. Choose **File: Preferences Guides & Grid**. Illustrator opens the Guides & Grid section of the Preferences dialog box (Figure 7.14).

2. To choose a gridline color, either select from the Color drop-down list box or double-click on the color box and select options from a color picker dialog box.

3. To choose a gridline style, open the Style drop-down list box and make a selection.

4. To set space between gridlines, type a number and unit of measure in the Gridline Every text box.

5. To display heavier gridlines at regular intervals, type a number in the Subdivisions text box.

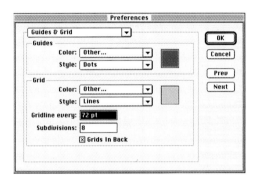

Figure 7.14 The Guides & Grid section of the Preferences dialog box.

NOTE Guides, which are not covered in this book, are lines that mark limits within a particular image window. So, if you want to line up several images, you can set guidelines to which the images will snap. Rulers must be turned on for the guides to work.

Turning on the Rulers

To measure all or part of an image, you can display vertical and horizontal rulers (Figure 7.15) within all the open image windows. When you turn on the rulers, they remain on display until you explicitly hide them—in this or a later Illustrator session. To display the rulers, choose **View: Show Rulers**, press **Ctrl+R** (Windows), or press **Command+R** (Macintosh). To hide the rulers, choose **View: Hide Rulers** or press **Ctrl+R** (Windows) or **Command+R** (Macintosh) again.

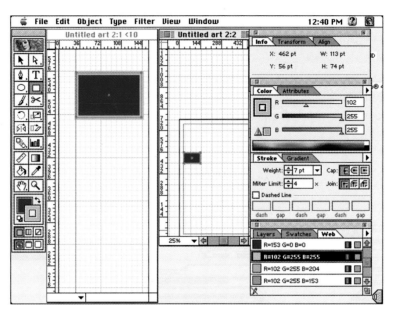

Figure 7.15 Two image windows with horizontal and vertical rulers showing points.

The rulers use the current unit of measure: points, picas, inches, millimeters, or centimeters. To change the unit of measure, choose **File: Preferences Units & Undo** and select an entry in the General drop-down list box.

NOTE   Because Illustrator uses points as the default unit of measure, carefully consider changing to a different unit.

Changing the View of an Image

When you view an image at its actual size, you may not be able to work on its details, or, conversely, you may not be able to see it completely—especially if it extends beyond the limits of your computer screen. Illustrator allows you to zoom in (that is, see the details) or zoom out (that is, see a greater part of a large composition). You can zoom in to 1,600% of the actual size; you can zoom out to 6.25% of the actual size.

Zooming In on an Image

You can zoom in using several methods:

♦ Choose **View: Zoom In**.

♦ Press **Ctrl++** (Windows) or **Command++** (Macintosh) repeatedly until the image looks as large as you want.

- Press **Ctrl+=** (Windows) or **Command+=** (Macintosh) repeatedly until the image looks as large as you want.
- Click on the **Zoom** tool or press **Z**. Drag the magnifying-glass mouse pointer to form a bounding box around the area on which you want to zoom in.
- Click on the **Zoom** tool or press **Z**. Then, move the magnifying-glass mouse pointer to the image, and click repeatedly until the image looks as large as you want.

 SHORTCUT   To activate the **Zoom In** tool:

Press **Ctrl+Spacebar.**

Press **Command+Spacebar.**

- Open the zoom level list box on the left side of the status bar and select a zoom level.

Zooming Out on an Image

You can zoom out using several methods:

- Choose **View: Zoom Out**.
- Press **Ctrl+-** (Windows) or **Command+-** (Macintosh) repeatedly until the image looks as small as you want.
- Click on the **Zoom** tool or press **Z**. Then, move the magnifying-glass mouse pointer to the image.
- Press and hold down the **Alt** key (Windows) or the **Option** key (Macintosh). Then, click repeatedly until the image looks as small as you want.

 SHORTCUT   To activate the **Zoom Out** tool:

Press **Ctrl+Alt+Spacebar.**

Press **Command+Option+Spacebar.**

- Open the zoom level list box on the left side of the status bar and select a zoom level.

Displaying an Image at 100%

You can display an image at its true size (that is, 100%) by taking one of the following actions:

- ◆ Double-click on the **Zoom** tool.
- ◆ Choose **View: Actual Size**, press **Ctrl+1** (Windows), or press **Command+1** (Macintosh).

Fitting an Image to the Application Window

You can adjust the view of an image to fit the application window. Illustrator is intelligent enough that when it carries out the command, it senses whether palettes are hidden or displayed. To fit an image to the window:

- ◆ Double-click on the **Hand** tool.
- ◆ Choose **View: Fit in Window**, press **Ctrl+0** (Windows), or press **Command+0** (Macintosh).

CREATING AN IMAGE—EXAMPLE 1

To create an image from scratch, click on one of the many Illustrator toolbox tools and start working.

Learning About the Toolbox Tools

The best way to learn about the tools with which you'll draw images is to use them. However, before you get started, it's a good idea to find out how these tools work and how to change their characteristics.

Using the Paintbrush

 Use the **Paintbrush** tool to paint blurry-edged strokes (using the default brush) with the stroke color. Every time you click on the **Paintbrush** tool, it acts as though you have added more paint to a paintbrush.

To use the **Paintbrush**, follow these steps:

1. Click on the **Paintbrush**.
2. Move the paintbrush mouse pointer to the image window and drag to "apply paint."

You can select attributes of the **Paintbrush** using the Paintbrush Options dialog box (Figure 7.16). To open the dialog box, double-click on the **Paintbrush**.

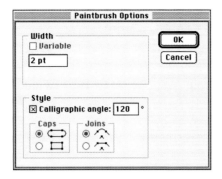

Figure 7.16 The Paintbrush Options dialog box.

The options in this dialog box are described below.

Width–In this text box, type the number, in points, for the width of the paintbrush stroke.

Variable–Check this check box if you use a pressure-sensitive drawing tablet with Illustrator. Otherwise, this option is not available.

Calligraphic–Check this check box to paint using varying widths on the upstroke and downstroke. When you check this check box, the Angle text box appears.

Angle–Type the number of degrees of rotation for a calligraphic paintbrush.

Caps–Click on an option button to specify rounded or squared caps (that is, the ends of lines and curves). This is not available if you have checked the Calligraphic check box.

Joins–Click on an option button to specify rounded or angled *joins* (that is, the places at which lines turn in other directions). This is not available if you have checked the Calligraphic check box.

Specifying Stroke and Line Attributes

The Stroke palette (Figure 7.17) provides stroke and line attributes using the **Pencil**, all the rectangles, the **Ellipse**, the **Polygon**, the **Star**, the **Spiral**, and the **Pen** tools.

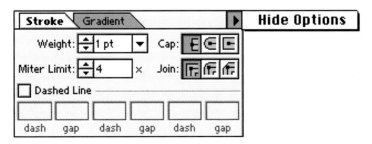

Figure 7.17 The filled-in Strokes palette with its menu.

The options in this palette are described below.

▶ Click on this button to open a shortcut menu with which you can close the palette except the Weight text/option box.

Weight–Type or select the width of the line from this text/option box. You can also click on the downward-pointing arrow on the right side of the text/option box to open a menu from which you can select the width.

Miter Limit–Type or select the angle of the line from *mitered* (that is, pointed) to *beveled* (that is, squared). This option is available only if you have clicked on the **Miter Join** button within the **Join** button set.

Dashed Line–Check this check box to define the attributes of a dashed line. Then, specify a pattern of dashes and gaps by typing values in the dash and gap text boxes, respectively.

Cap–Click on a button to specify a look for line ends: **Butt Cap** (squared ends), **Round Cap** (rounded ends), or **Projecting Cap** (squared ends that extend slightly beyond the end of the line).

Join–Click on a button to specify a look for the corners at which lines join: **Miter Join** (squared corners), **Round Join** (rounded corners), and **Bevel Join** (angled corners).

Using the Pencil

 Use the **Pencil** tool to draw sharp-edged strokes with the stroke color.

To use the **Pencil**, follow these steps:

1. Click on the **Pencil** tool.
2. Move the pencil mouse pointer to the image window and drag to insert pencil strokes, which are determined by the settings in the Stroke palette.
3. To erase part of the line that you just drew, press and hold down the **Ctrl** key (Windows) or the **Command** key (Macintosh), and drag back over the line.

Using the Rectangle Tools

With Illustrator, you can draw rectangles or squares with sharp or rounded corners starting at a corner or the center.

Use the **Rectangle** tool to draw a rectangle or square with square corners from the starting point of a corner.

Use the **Rounded Rectangle** tool to draw a rectangle or square with rounded corners with the starting point of a corner.

Use the **Centered Rectangle** tool to draw a rectangle or square with square corners starting from the center of the object.

Use the **Centered Rounded Rectangle** tool to draw a rectangle or square with rounded corners starting from the center of the object.

To draw a rectangle, click on one of the rectangle tools, move the mouse pointer to the drawing window, select a starting point, and drag the mouse from a corner or the center of the rectangle.

You can also use a rectangle tool and keyboard keys to draw particular types of rectangular objects:

◆ To draw a square from a center point, select a rectangle tool, press and hold down the **Shift** key, and drag the mouse.

◆ To draw a rectangle from a center point using the standard rectangle tool, press and hold down the **Alt** key (Windows) or the **Option** key (Macintosh) and drag the mouse.

You can draw a rectangle using specific dimensions. Simply follow these steps:

1. Select any rectangle tool.

2. Click on the work area at the desired location of the rectangle. Illustrator opens the Rectangle dialog box (Figure 7.18).

3. Type the width and height, in points, in the Width and Height text boxes.

4. Specify the amount of roundness of the corners by typing a value in the Corner Radius text box. The higher the value, the more rounded the corners are.

5. Click on **OK**. Illustrator inserts a rectangle from an edge or a center point, depending on the selected tool.

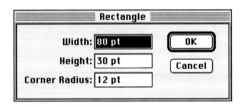

Figure 7.18 The filled-in Rectangle dialog box for a rounded rectangle.

Using the Ellipse Tools

With Illustrator, you can draw ellipses or circles starting at an edge or the center of the object.

Use the **Ellipse** tool to draw an ellipse or circle from the starting point of an edge.

Use the **Centered Ellipse** tool to draw an ellipse or circle starting from the center of the object.

To draw an ellipse or circle, click on an ellipse tool, move the mouse pointer to the drawing window, select a starting point, and drag the mouse.

You can also use an **Ellipse** tool and keyboard keys to draw particular types of elliptical objects:

◆ To draw a circle from a center point, press and hold down the **Shift** key and drag the mouse.

◆ To draw an ellipse from a center point using the standard Ellipse tool, press and hold down the **Alt** key (Windows) or the **Option** key (Macintosh) and drag the mouse.

You can draw an ellipse using specific dimensions. To do so, follow these steps:

1. Select either **Ellipse** tool.

2. Click on the work area at the desired location of the ellipse. Illustrator opens the Ellipse dialog box (Figure 7.19).

3. Type the width and height, in points, in the Width and Height text boxes.

4. Click on **OK.** Illustrator inserts an ellipse from an edge or a center point, depending on the selected tool.

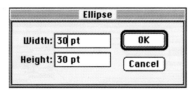

Figure 7.19 The filled-in Ellipse dialog box.

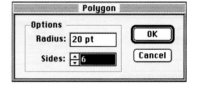

Figure 7.20 The filled-in Polygon dialog box for a six-sided object.

Using the Polygon Tool

To draw a symmetrical polygon, click on the **Polygon** tool, move the mouse pointer to the drawing window, select a starting point, and drag the mouse. You can rotate the polygon before you finish it by dragging the mouse pointer using a circular motion. You can drag the polygon to a new location before you finish it by pressing and holding down the **Spacebar** and dragging.

You can also use the **Polygon** tool and keyboard keys to affect the appearance of the polygon:

◆ To draw a polygon with edges at multiples of 45 degrees, press and hold down the **Shift** key and drag the mouse.

◆ To add a side to a polygon as you draw, press on the **Up** key.

◆ To remove a side from a polygon as you draw, press on the **Down** key.

You can draw a polygon using specific dimensions and number of sides. Simply follow these steps:

1. Select the **Polygon** tool.
2. Click on the work area at the desired location of the polygon. Illustrator opens the Polygon dialog box (Figure 7.20).
3. Type the radius, in points, in the Radius text box.
4. Specify the number of sides by typing or selecting a value from the Sides text/option box.
5. Click on **OK**. Illustrator inserts a polygon from the center point of the click.

Using the Star Tool

To draw a star, click on the **Star** tool, move the mouse pointer to the drawing window, select a starting point, and drag the mouse. You can rotate the star before you finish it by dragging the mouse pointer using a circular motion. You can drag the star to a new location before you finish it by pressing and holding down the **Spacebar** and dragging.

You can also use the **Star** tool and keyboard keys to affect the appearance of the star:

◆ To draw a star with edges at multiples of 45 degrees, press and hold down the **Shift** key and drag the mouse.

◆ To add a pointer to a star as you draw, press on the **Up** key.

◆ To remove a pointer from a star as you draw, press on the **Down** key.

You can draw a star using specific dimensions and number of points. Simply follow these steps:

1. Select the **Star** tool.
2. Click on the work area at the desired location of the star. Illustrator opens the Star dialog box (Figure 7.21).
3. Type the outer radius of the points of the star, in points, in the Radius 1 text box.
4. Type the inner radius of the points of the star, in points, in the Radius 2 text box.
5. Specify the number of points by typing or selecting a value from the Points text/option box.
6. Click on **OK**. Illustrator inserts a star from the center point of the click.

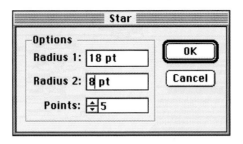

Figure 7.21 The filled-in Star dialog box.

Using the Spiral Tool

To draw a spiral, click on the **Spiral** tool, move the mouse pointer to the drawing window, select a starting point, and drag the mouse. You can rotate the spiral before you finish it by dragging the mouse pointer using a circular motion. You can drag the spiral to a new location before you finish it by pressing and holding down the **Spacebar** and dragging.

You can also use the **Spiral** tool and keyboard keys to affect the appearance of the spiral:

♦ To draw a spiral that curves at multiples of 45 degrees, press and hold down the **Shift** key and drag the mouse.

♦ To wind the spiral more tightly as you draw, press and hold down the **Up** key.

♦ To unwind the spiral as you draw, press and hold down the **Down** key.

You can draw a spiral using specific dimensions and number of points. Simply follow these steps:

1. Select the **Spiral** tool.
2. Click on the work area at the desired location of the star. Illustrator opens the Spiral dialog box (Figure 7.22).
3. Type the radius of the spiral, in points, in the Radius text box.
4. Type the decay of the spiral, in percent, in the Decay text box.
5. Specify the number of segments by typing or selecting a value from the Segments text/option box.
6. Click on a Style Option button to "Wind" the spiral counterclockwise or clockwise.
7. Click on **OK**. Illustrator inserts a spiral from the center point of the click.

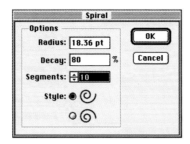

Figure 7.22 The filled-in Spiral dialog box.

Using the Pen Tools

Illustrator provides a set of unique drawing and editing tools with which you can draw and adjust very fine lines or curves.

Use the **Pen** to draw lines and curves that contain anchor points and end points. Illustrator marks the direction in which a line or curve is traveling by using direction lines and direction points.

◆ Illustrator marks direction points with filled circles.

◆ Selected anchor and end points are filled squares.

◆ Unselected anchor and end points are unfilled squares.

To use the **Pen**, follow these steps:

1. Click on the **Pen**.
2. Move the pen mouse pointer to the image and start drawing the path.
3. To draw a curved path segment, drag the mouse pointer. As you drag, Illustrator adds one or more direction lines.
4. To draw a straight path segment, click each time you want to change the direction of the path. Figure 7.23 shows an object that combines curved and straight lines.

To add an anchor point to the object, click on the **Add Anchor Point** tool, point to the location at which you'd like to add the anchor point, and click. Figure 7.24 shows the object with added anchor points.

To remove an anchor point from the object, click on the **Delete Anchor Point** tool, point to the anchor point that you'd like to remove, and click. Figure 7.25 shows the object with removed anchor points and a changed appearance.

To change an angled anchor point to a curved anchor point, click on the **Convert Direction Point** tool, point to the anchor point that you'd like to convert, click, and drag the anchor point to a new position. Figure 7.26 shows the object with a converted and moved anchor point.

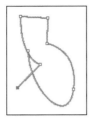

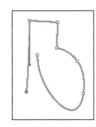

Figure 7.23
An object that combines curved and straight lines.

Figure 7.24
The object showing additional anchor points.

Figure 7.25
The object with fewer anchor points.

Figure 7.26
The object with a converted and moved anchor point.

NOTE Illustrator also provides menu commands with which you can further edit objects created and edited with the pen tools. Choose **Object: Path** and select subcommands to join, average, outline, offset, clean up, slice, and add anchor points.

Drawing an Image

To create an image, follow these steps:

1. Start Illustrator.

2. Choose **File: New**, press **Ctrl+N** (Windows), or press **Command+N** (Macintosh). Illustrator adds a blank page to the work area.

3. If needed, choose **Window: Swatch Libraries: Web**. Illustrator opens the Web swatch palette.

4. To reduce the size of the artboard for a smaller image, choose **File: Document Setup**, press **Ctrl+Shift+P** (Windows), or press **Command+Shift+P** (Macintosh). In the Document Setup dialog box (Figure 7.27), type new values in the Width and/or Height text boxes. (The minimum size is 144 × 144 points, which translates to 2 × 2 inches.) Click on **OK** .

5. Turn on the rulers by choosing **View: Show Rulers**, pressing **Ctrl+R** (Windows), or pressing **Command+R** (Macintosh).

SHORTCUT You can change the unit of measure by choosing **File: Preferences: Units & Undo**, choosing from the General drop-down list box, and clicking on **OK**.

6. If needed, select a fill color, stroke color, or both. For more information, refer to the "Changing the Fill and Stroke Colors" section earlier in the chapter.

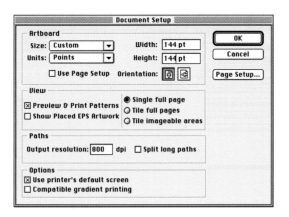

Figure 7.27 The Document Setup dialog box with a
144 × 144-point artboard, which is the minimum size.

7. To change the view of the drawing page, either zoom in or zoom out. For information about zooming, refer to the "Changing the View of an Image" section earlier in the chapter.

> **SHORTCUT** To start an image, it's a good idea to set a zoom level of 100% so that you can estimate the true size of the image. Then, you can zoom in when you insert new objects and edit the image.

8. Click on a drawing tool in the toolbox and create the first object in the image, making sure that you compare its size to the rulers.

9. Continue working on the image by repeating steps 6, 7, and 8, as needed.

10. To export the image as a GIF89a file, choose **File: Export**.

11. In the Export dialog box, fill in the file name and select **GIF89a**. Click on **Save**.

12. Fill in the GIF89a Options dialog box (Figure 7.28). Click on **OK**.

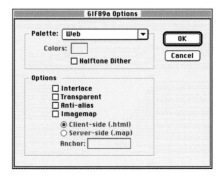

Figure 7.28 The GIF89a dialog box with options for a GIF image.

ABOUT THIS ANIMATION—RAINBOW STAR

starbow.gif 2K 21 × 20 Level: Easy

The rainbow star animation is a fixed star with a changing show of flashing lights in random colors.

◆ This animation is composed of nine images created in Illustrator and edited in Photoshop.

◆ All work is done at 100%.

◆ To create the original image, click on the Star tool and draw a star with approximately 0.5 inch radius.

◆ Apply the same fill and stroke color from the Web palette to the star.

◆ After an image is completed, export it to a GIF89a file. The original image remains in the work area.

◆ To create each of the remaining images, randomly apply a color from the Web palette and export the image to a GIF89a file.

◆ To make sure that colors don't repeat in succeeding images, it's a good idea to display all the images in the work area.

◆ Many browsers do not recognize animations. Each image in this animation can stand on its own.

◆ This animation loops forever.

◆ This animation looks better at a fast or medium speed.

MODIFYING AN IMAGE

After creating an image, you can modify it in several ways:

◆ Use selection tools to select part or all of an image.

◆ Use the Edit menu commands to copy, cut, paste, or delete part or all of an image.

◆ Use the transform commands on the Object menu commands to scale, rotate, skew, distort, or flip a selection.

◆ Use other Object menu commands to arrange, group, or ungroup objects within an image.

◆ Use Filter menu commands to apply innumerable special effects.

◆ Use Type menu commands to format or change the look of text.

Whenever you edit an image, it's a good idea to save it from time to time. This avoids your having to unnecessarily redo your work.

Selecting an Image

Sometimes you can work with an image without selecting it. For example, if you paint or draw on an image window, you don't need to make a selection. However, at other times, you must make a selection before working on an image. For example, if you want to copy, move, or remove an object, you must select it. Illustrator provides several selection tools.

The selection tools have several attributes in common:

- ◆ After you choose a selection tool, you can open a context menu, which contains commonly used commands.

- ◆ Illustrator surrounds a selection with anchor points, marks the center of the object, and adds end points to a line or curve.

- ◆ After you have made a selection, you can use Object menu commands to act on the selection. If you select text, you can use Text menu commands.

- ◆ You can drag a selection around the image window.

- ◆ One of the selection tool buttons has a small right-pointing arrow in its lower-right corner. This indicates the presence of another selection tool.

Selecting an Object

To select one or more objects within an image, Illustrator provides three selection tools: **Selection**, **Direct Selection**, and **Group Selection**.

To select an object or a layer in an object made up of two or more layers, click on the **Selection** tool.

To select anchor points or line or curve segments between anchor points, click on the **Direct Selection** tool.

To select a single object in a group or a single group within several groups, click on the **Group Selection** tool. Each click adds another object or group to the selection.

Selecting Several Objects at Once

To select several objects in an image, click on a selection tool and drag a bounding box around or through the objects that you want to select. Illustrator selects any image that is completely or partially within the bounding box.

To accumulate objects, click on the first object to select it, press and hold down the **Shift** key, and click on objects to add them to the selection. To remove an object from the selection, while holding down the **Shift** key, click on it again.

Selecting by Color or Style

◆ To select all the objects with color or style in common, you can choose **Edit: Select** and select a subcommand.

◆ To select all objects with the current paint style, choose **Edit: Select: Same Paint Style**.

◆ To select all objects with the current fill color, choose **Edit: Select: Same Fill Color**.

◆ To select all objects with the current stroke color, choose **Edit: Select: Same Stroke Color**.

◆ To select all objects with the current stroke weight, choose **Edit: Select: Same Stroke Weight**.

Inverting a Selection

To invert the selection (that is, select the unselected area and "unselect" the selected area), choose **Edit: Select: Inverse**. Illustrator draws a bounding box around the edges of the image window.

Selecting an Entire Image

To select all the objects and paths in an image, choose **Edit: Select All**, press **Ctrl+A** (Windows), or press **Command+A** (Macintosh).

Deselecting a Selection

To inactivate a selection, click away from the selection, choose **Edit: Deselect All**, press **Ctrl+Shift+A** (Windows), or press **Command+Shift+A** (Macintosh).

Moving a Selection or the Artboard

To move a selection, simply drag it to its new location.

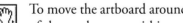 To move the artboard around the work area, click on the **Hand** tool, and drag any part of the work area—within or outside the artboard.

Copying, Cutting, and Pasting Selections

Most Windows- and Macintosh-based programs include an Edit menu that includes commands with which you can copy, cut, paste, and delete objects. In Illustrator, you can use Edit menu commands to work with selections.

Copying a Selection

To copy the current selection to the Clipboard, choose **Edit: Copy**, press **Ctrl+C** (Windows), or press **Command+C** (Macintosh). When you copy a selection, Illustrator leaves the orignal in place and places a copy in the Clipboard. If the **Copy** command is dimmed, you have not made a selection.

Cutting a Selection

To remove the current selection and place it in the Clipboard, choose **Edit: Cut**, press **Ctrl+X** (Windows), or press **Command+X** (Macintosh). If the **Cut** command is dimmed, you have not made a selection.

Pasting a Selection

You can paste selections (using Illustrator's three paste commands: **Paste**, **Paste in Front**, and **Paste in Back**. If the paste commands are dimmed, the Clipboard is empty.

◆ To paste a selection from the Clipboard into the current image, choose **Edit: Paste**, press **Ctrl+V** (Windows), or press **Command+V** (Macintosh).

◆ To paste a selection from the Clipboard in front of (that is, on top of) the current selection, choose **Edit: Paste in Front**, press **Ctrl+F** (Windows), or press **Command+F** (Macintosh).

◆ To paste a selection from the Clipboard behind (that is, underneath) the current selection, choose **Edit: Paste in Back**, press **Ctrl+B** (Windows), or press **Command+B** (Macintosh).

Deleting a Selection

To delete a selection permanently, either choose **Edit: Clear** or press the **Del** key. After you have deleted a selection, the only way to restore it is to choose **Edit: Undo**, press **Ctrl+Z** (Windows), or press **Command+Z** (Macintosh). If you have performed another action in the meantime, you may have to undo that before undoing the deletion.

Adding Text to an Image

Illustrator provides several tools with which you can add text to an image. To insert text, click on a type tool, click in the image at the starting location of the text, and start typing.

Illustrator's text tools are described below.

 Select the **Type** tool to add standard horizontally aligned text to an image.

Select the **Area Type** tool to open a closed path and add text. Note that the path must be at least as long as the text string will be.

Select the **Path Type** tool to add text that is aligned along a path. Note that the path must be at least as long as the text string will be.

 Select the **Vertical Type** tool to add standard vertically aligned text to an image.

 Select the **Vertical Area Type** tool to open a closed path and add vertically aligned text. Note that the path must be at least as long as the text string will be.

 Select the **Vertical Path Type** tool to add text that is vertically aligned along a path. Note that the path must be at least as long as the text string will be.

NOTE   If you want to select text, choose a selection tool and click on the text.

The Type menu provides many text tools that you can use to change the look of text in graphics for the World Wide Web:

◆ To select a new font for future text, choose **Type: Font** and choose from the cascading menu. Many fonts also provide text enhancement subcommands.

◆ To change the font size for future text, choose **Type: Size** and choose from the cascading menu. If you select **Other**, Illustrator opens the Character palette (Figure 7.29) from which you can choose a font, enhancement, and other attributes. You can also open the Character palette by choosing **Type: Character**.

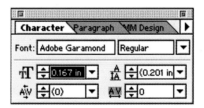

Figure 7.29 The Character palette.

TRANSFORMING A SELECTION—EXAMPLE 2

You can use the **Transform** command on the Object menu to change the look of a selected object. Using the **Transform** command and its subcommands, you can move, scale, rotate, shear, or reflect a selection.

Moving a Selection

You have already learned that you can move an object by selecting it, clicking on a selection tool, and dragging the selection around the work area. You can also use a dialog box to specify the position of an object in the work area or the distance it will move.

To move a selection using a transform subcommand, follow these steps:

1. Select one or more objects.

2. Choose **Object: Transform: Move**. Illustrator opens the Move dialog box (Figure 7.30).

3. To move the selection horizontally and/or vertically, type a value in the Horizontal text box, the Vertical text box, or both.

4. To move the selection a certain distance at a certain angle, type values in the Distance and Angle text boxes.

5. Click on **OK**. Illustrator moves the selection.

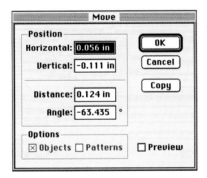

Figure 7.30 The Move dialog box.

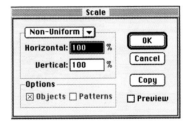

Figure 7.31 The Scale dialog box with Non-Uniform selected.

Scaling a Selection

You can scale an object using a toolbox tool or a transform subcommand.

To change the size, proportionally or nonproportionally, of a selected object using the **Scale** tool, follow these steps:

1. Click on the **Scale** tool. Illustrator marks the center of the object.

2. To change the center point of the object, drag the center mark.

3. To scale the object, click on a border and drag the mouse pointer. Illustrator shows the current size of the object with a blue border and changes the information in the Info palette.

To scale a selection using a transform subcommand, follow these steps:

1. Select one or more objects.
2. Choose **Object: Transform: Scale**. Illustrator opens the Scale dialog box (Figure 7.31).
3. To scale the selection proportionally, select **Uniform** from the drop-down list box. Then, fill in the percentage that you want to scale the object.
4. To scale the selection nonproportionally, select **Non-Uniform** from the drop-down list box. Then, fill in the horizontal and vertical percentages that you want to scale the object.
5. Click on **OK**. Illustrator transforms the selection.

Rotating a Selection

You can rotate an object using a toolbox tool or a transform subcommand.

To rotate a selected object using the **Rotate** tool, follow these steps:

1. Click on the **Rotate** tool. Illustrator marks the center of the object.
2. To change the center point of the object, drag the center mark.
3. To rotate the object, click on a border and drag the mouse pointer around the object. Illustrator shows the current rotation level of the object with a blue border and changes the information in the Info palette.

To rotate a selection using a transform subcommand, follow these steps:

1. Select one or more objects.
2. Choose **Object: Transform: Rotate**. Illustrator opens the Rotate dialog box (Figure 7.32).
3. In the Angle text box, type the number of degrees that you want to rotate the object.
4. Click on **OK**. Illustrator transforms the selection.

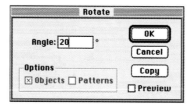

Figure 7.32 The Rotate dialog box.

Shearing a Selection

You can skew an object using a toolbox tool or a transform subcommand.

To skew a selected object using the Shear tool, follow these steps:

1. Click on the **Shear** tool. Illustrator marks the center of the object.

2. To change the center point of the object, drag the center mark.

3. To skew the object, click on a border and drag the mouse pointer to pull the border away or toward the center point. Illustrator shows the current level of skew with a blue border and changes the information in the Info palette.

To skew a selection using a transform subcommand, follow these steps:

1. Select one or more objects.

2. Choose **Object: Transform: Shear**. Illustrator opens the Shear dialog box (Figure 7.33).

3. In the Shear Angle text box, type the number of degrees that you want to skew the object.

4. In the Axis section, click on **Horizontal**, **Vertical**, or **Angle** to skew the object horizontally, vertically, or both horizontally and vertically, respectively.

5. Click on **OK**. Illustrator transforms the selection.

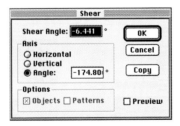

Figure 7.33 The Shear dialog box.

Reflecting a Selection

You can reflect (that is, flip) an object using a toolbox tool or a transform subcommand. To flip a selected object using the **Reflect** tool, follow these steps:

1. Click on the **Reflect** tool. Illustrator marks the center of the object.

2. To change the center point of the object, drag the center mark.

3. To flip the object, click on a border. Before you release the mouse button, Illustrator outlines the flipped object with a blue border and changes the information in the Info palette.

4. To rotate the flipped object, drag the mouse pointer around the object.

To flip a selection using a transform subcommand, follow these steps:

1. Select one or more objects.

2. Choose **Object: Transform: Reflect**. Illustrator opens the Reflect dialog box (Figure 7.34).

3. In the Axis section, click on **Horizontal**, **Vertical**, or **Angle** to flip the object horizontally, vertically, or both horizontally and vertically, respectively.

4. Click on **OK**. Illustrator transforms the selection.

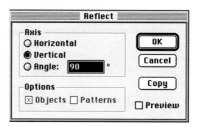

Figure 7.34 The Reflect dialog box.

Using the Transform Each Dialog Box

When you want to perform many transformations on a selection, use the Transform Each dialog box (Figure 7.35). Choose **Layer: Transform: Transform Each** to open this dialog box.

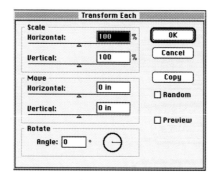

Figure 7.35 The Transform Each dialog box.

The sections in this dialog box are described below.

Scale–Slide the slider or type values in the Horizontal and/or Vertical text boxes to specify the amount that you want to increase or decrease the dimensions of the object as a percentage of its current size.

Move–Slide the slider or type values in the Horizontal and/or Vertical text boxes to specify the distance, in the current unit of measure, that you want to move the object horizontally and/or vertically.

Rotate–Drag the line around the circle or type the number of degrees that you want to rotate the object.

ABOUT THIS ANIMATION—SNAIL RULE

snail.gif 23K 600 × 50 Level: Medium

The snail rule animation features a snail that drags a rule across the page.

◆ This animation is composed of a snail on a white background. As the snail is dragged across the page, a blue rule increases in length. The animation is comprised of 24 frames.

◆ The snail's shell is a spiral filled with gold (255-204-0). The shell was rotated and skewed to lengthen it slightly. The snail's body (255-102-51) was drawn using the **Pencil** and **Paintbrush**. After moving the body in front of the shell, the shell is moved in front (**Object: Arrange: Bring to Front**), thereby hiding part of the body. Then, the entire image is selected and grouped (**Object: Group**).

◆ In the first file in the animation (**snail01**), the snail is selected (the **Selection** tool) and moved to the right side of the artboard. The image file is saved and then saved again as **snail02.**

◆ For each succeeding frame, the snail is selected and dragged toward the left, and a blue trail (51-102-153) is painted. It's important to make the stroke and fill the same color to avoid having a border.

◆ In the last two frames, when the snail is in the left side of the artboard, a smile is added (the **Pen** tool).

◆ Many browsers do not recognize animations. The first and last frames, although different, can be used as static images.

◆ After displaying the frames in the work area and touching up where needed, each file is exported to GIF89a format. Choose **File: Export** and select **GIF89a.**

◆ When you export files to GIF89a, Illustrator automatically crops each frame. This means that when you create the animation, you must change the *x-y* coordinates of each frame. The first frame has a position of 550,0; the last frame is located at 25,0. When edited in Photoshop, all images were adjusted to the same size.

◆ This animation was created using GifBuilder using the frame optimization feature. It was edited in Photoshop and reanimated using GIF Construction Set.

◆ This animation runs once.

◆ This animation should be set at a relatively fast speed.

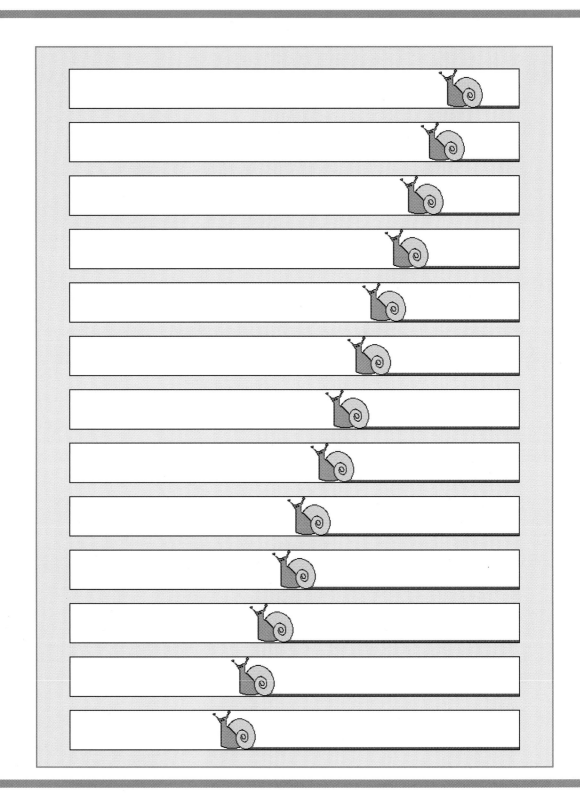

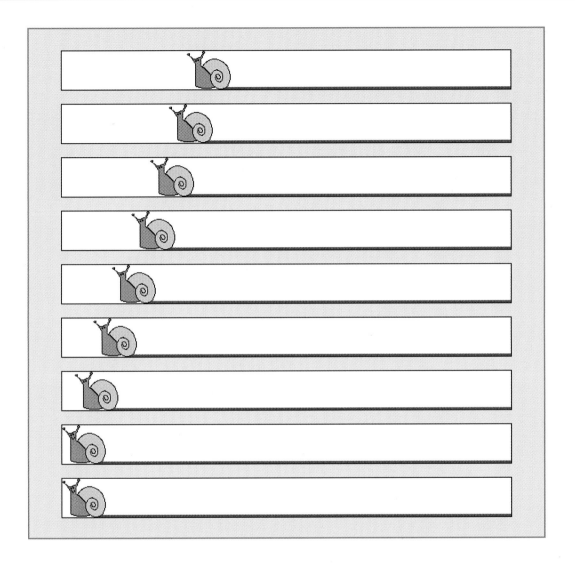

APPLYING SPECIAL EFFECTS

The Filter menu contains many commands with which you can apply artistic effects. Some work very well in images for the World Wide Web. To apply an effect, select a command and a subcommand. Then, you will probably have to choose options from a dialog box. As you might expect, the image determines both your choice of commands and the results of the effects.

SHORTCUT If you don't like the look of an effect generated by a command, choose **Edit: Undo**, press **Ctrl+Z** (Windows), or press **Command+Z** (Macintosh). To be completely safe, make a copy of the image file and look at the results on the copy, thereby preserving the look of the original image.

Illustrator provides the following special-effects commands that can produce positive changes to files that will be exported to the GIF89a format:

Distort–Use these subcommands and dialog boxes to skew and otherwise change the dimensions and corner angles of the image.

Ink Pen–Use these subcommands and dialog boxes to apply texture to an image. Be careful to keep the original colors.

Stylize–Use these subcommands and dialog boxes to apply effects within the image. Note that you can add a drop shadow to an image by choosing the **Drop Shadow** subcommand.

Working with
CorelDRAW

CorelDRAW is a sophisticated, full-featured drawing program that produces vector graphics. (For a description or vector graphics, see Chapter 1.) It is bundled in a suite of other applications, including the Corel PHOTO-PAINT paint program, with which you can create and edit bit maps; the CorelDREAM 3D three-dimensional illustration program; and other programs and utilities. This chapter covers CorelDRAW and CorelSCAN, a scanning utility.

With CorelDRAW, you can make images from scratch or use and edit scanned, captured, or imported images. CorelDRAW includes many types of effects that you can apply to any and all images—regardless of their source.

CorelDRAW allows you to copy, move, and paste images and selections and to undo an action using Edit menu commands. CorelDRAW's help system includes the CorelTUTOR (in the Windows version only) instructions as well as Hints, context-sensitive tips. Its user manuals provide information about CorelDRAW's features and the other programs in the suite.

Table 8.1 lists the file formats that CorelDRAW reads from, saves to, imports from, and exports to.

In the table, Windows file formats are represented by W; Macintosh formats are represented by M.

Table 8.1 CorelDRAW-Supported File Formats

Format	Reads from	Saves to	Imports from	Exports to
Adobe Illustrator (.AI)	Yes (W)	Yes (W)	Yes (W,M)	Yes (W,M)
Adobe Photoshop	No	No	Yes (M)	Yes (M)
ANSI Text (.TXT)	No	No	Yes (W)	Yes (W)
ASCII (.TXT)	No	No	Yes (M)	Yes (M)
AutoCAD Drawing File (DWG)	No	No	Yes (M)	No
AutoCAD Drawing Interchange (DXF)	No	No	Yes (M)	Yes (M)

Table 8.1 CorelDRAW-Supported File Formats (continued)

Format	Reads from	Saves to	Imports from	Exports to
CompuServe Bitmap (.GIF)	No	No	Yes (W,M)	Yes (W,M) (and to Internet -ready format (W))
Computer Graphics Metafile (CGM)	No	No	Yes (M)	Yes (M)
Corel Barista (.HTM)	No	Yes (W)	No	Yes (W) (and to Internet- ready format)
Corel PHOTO-PAINT Image (.CPT)	No	No	Yes (W)	Yes (W)
Corel Presentation Exchange (.CMX)	Yes (W,M)	Yes (W,M)	Yes (W,M)	Yes (W,M)
Corel WordPerfect (.WP7)	No	No	Yes (W)	Yes (W)
Corel WordPerfect Graphic (.WPG)	Yes (W)	Yes (W)	Yes (W)	Yes (W)
CorelDRAW (.CDR)	Yes (W,M)	Yes (W,M)	Yes (W,M)	No (W)
CorelDRAW Template (.CDT)	Yes (W,M)	Yes (W,M)	No	No
Encapsulated PostScript (.EPS)	No	No	Yes (W,M)	Yes (W,M)
Enhanced Windows Metafile (.EMF)	Yes (W)	Yes (W)	Yes (W)	Yes (W)
GEM File (GEM)	No	No	Yes (M)	Yes (M)
GEM Paint File (IMG)	No	No	Yes (M)	No
GIF Animation (.GIF)	No	No	Yes (W)	No
HPGL Plotter File (PLT)	No	No	Yes (M)	Yes (M)
JPEG Bitmaps (.JPG)	No	No	Yes (W,M)	Yes (W,M) and to Internet-ready format (W)
Kodak Photo-CD Image (PCD)	No	No	Yes (M)	No
Lotus Pic (PIC)	No	No	Yes (M)	No
Macintosh PICT	No	No	Yes (M)	Yes (M)
MacPaint Bitmap (MAC)	No	No	Yes (M)	Yes (M)
Microsoft Resource Interchange File Format (RIFF)	No	No	Yes (M)	No
MS Word for Windows (.DOC)	No	No	Yes (W)	Yes (W)
PaintBrush (PCX)	No	No	Yes (M)	Yes (M)
Pattern File (.PAT)	Yes (W,M)	Yes (W,M)	No	No
PICT Resource (PCR)	No	No	Yes (M)	Yes (M)
PixelPaint (PPT)	No	No	Yes (M)	No
PostScript Interpreted (.PS, .PRN, .EPS)	Yes (W)	No	Yes (W,M)	No
QuickTime Movie (MOV)	No	No	Yes (M)	No
Rich Text Format (.RTF)	No	No	Yes (W,M)	Yes (W)
Scitex CT Bitmap (SCT)	No	No	Yes (M)	No

Table 8.1 CorelDRAW-Supported File Formats (continued)

Format	Reads from	Saves to	Imports from	Exports to
Garga Bitmap (TGA)	No	No	Yes (M)	Yes (M)
TIFF Bitmap (.TIF)	No	No	Yes (W,M)	Yes (W,M)
True Type Font (.TTF)	No	No	No	Yes (W)
Wavelet Compressed Bitmap (.WI)	No	No	Yes (W)	Yes (W)
Windows Bitmap (.BMP)	No	No	Yes (W,M)	Yes (W,M)
Windows Metafile (.WMF)	Yes (W)	Yes (W)	Yes (W,M)	Yes (W,M)
WordPerfect Graphics (WPG)	No	No	Yes (M)	Yes (M)

◆ To open a vector file, choose **File: Open** or press **Ctrl+O** (in the Windows version) or **Command+O** (in the Macintosh version).

◆ To save a vector file, choose **File: Save**, choose **File: Save As**, press **Ctrl+S** (Windows) or press **Command+S** (Macintosh).

◆ To import a bit-mapped file, choose **File: Import**, press **Ctrl+I** (Windows), or press **Command+I** (Macintosh).

◆ To export a bit-mapped file, choose **File: Export** or press **Ctrl+H** (Windows) or **Command+E** (Macintosh).

◆ To export a file to an Internet-ready format in Windows only, choose **File: Publish to Internet**.

NOTE In Windows, you can add or remove file types to be imported from or exported to. In the Import or Export dialog box, click on the **File Types** button. Then, fill in the File Types dialog box.

STARTING CORELDRAW

To start CorelDRAW on a Windows computer, follow these steps:

1. Click on the **Start** button and select **Programs**. Windows opens the Programs menu.

2. Move the mouse pointer over CorelDRAW. Windows opens a submenu.

3. Click on **CorelDRAW**. The CorelDRAW window (Figure 8.1) opens with a tool palette on the left side and three tool palettes on the right.

SHORTCUT If you have created a shortcut icon on your desktop for CorelDRAW, double-click on it to start the program.

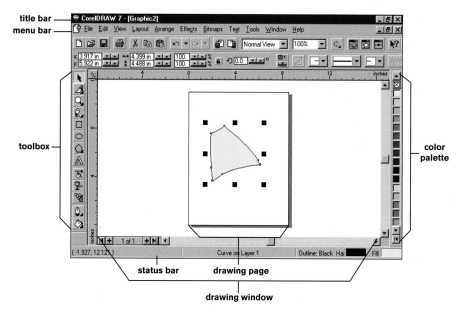

Figure 8.1 The CorelDRAW window with an object in the drawing window.

To start CorelDRAW under the Macintosh platform, open the Corel folder, and double-click on the **CorelDRAW** icon.

THE CORELDRAW WINDOW

When you start CorelDRAW, a Welcome dialog box appears. You can start or open a graphic, use the CorelTUTOR (in Windows only), or find out what's new. You can also clear the check mark from the check box to display the CorelDRAW window in the future without opening this dialog box first.

The CorelDRAW window contains a variety of elements, many familiar to Windows and Macintosh users and some that require more explanation.

The Title Bar and Menu Bar

The CorelDRAW title bar and menu bar are standard elements. In Windows, the title bar includes the name of the program; in both the Windows and Macintosh versions, the menu bar contains menus from which you select commands with which you can perform actions. CorelDRAW also contains *context menus*, which contain commands associated with objects on the desktop. To use a context menu, right-click on an object in the current window (in Windows), press and hold down the **Ctrl** key and click on an object (in Macintosh), or click on a small arrow in palettes to open the menu. Then, move the mouse pointer to the desired command and click to select the command.

The Standard Toolbar

Below the menu bar is the standard toolbar, with standard editing buttons on the left, and some buttons and other elements that are unique to CorelDRAW on the right.

New—Click on this button to start a new image. This is equivalent to choosing **File: New** (Windows) or **File: New: Document** (Macintosh) or pressing **Ctrl+N** (Windows) or **Command+N** (Macintosh).

Open—Click on this button to open an existing image file. This is equivalent to choosing **File: Open**, pressing **Ctrl+O** (Windows), or pressing **Command+O** (Macintosh).

Save—Click on this button to save the current file. This is equivalent to choosing **File: Save** (or pressing **Ctrl+S** in Windows or **Command+S** on the Macintosh) or choosing **File: Save As** (or pressing **F12** in Windows) if you are saving a new file.

Print—Click on this button to print the current file. This is equivalent to choosing **File: Print**, pressing **Ctrl+P** (Windows), or pressing **Command+P** (Macintosh).

Cut—Click on this button to remove the current selection and place it in the Clipboard. This is equivalent to choosing **Edit: Cut**, pressing **Ctrl+X** (Windows), or pressing **Command+X** (Macintosh). If this button is dimmed, you have not selected an object. For more information about selecting and cutting, see the "Modifying an Image" section later in this chapter.

Copy—Click on this button to copy the current selection into the Clipboard. This is equivalent to choosing **Edit: Copy**, pressing **Ctrl+C** (Windows), or pressing **Command+C** (Macintosh). If this button is dimmed, you have not selected an object. For more information about selecting and copying, see the "Modifying an Image" section later in this chapter.

Paste—Click on this button to paste the contents of the Clipboard at the current location in the image. This is equivalent to choosing **Edit: Paste**, pressing **Ctrl+V** (Windows), or pressing **Command+V** (Macintosh). If this button is dimmed, the Clipboard is empty. For more information about pasting a selection, see the "Modifying an Image" section later in this chapter.

Undo—Click on this button to undo the most recent action. This is equivalent to choosing **Edit: Undo**, pressing **Ctrl+Z** (Windows), or pressing **Command+Z** (Macintosh). If this button is dimmed, you have not performed an action, you can't undo the action, or you have already performed one undo.

Redo—Click on this button to redo the most recent undo. This is equivalent to choosing **Edit: Redo**, pressing **Ctrl+Shift+Z** (Windows), or pressing **Command+Option+Z** (Macintosh). If this button is dimmed, you have not performed an undo.

Import—Click on this button to open the Import dialog box. This is equivalent to choosing **File: Import**, pressing **Ctrl+I** (Windows), or pressing **Command+I** (Macintosh).

Export—Click on this button to open the Export dialog box. This is equivalent to choosing **File: Export**, pressing **Ctrl+H** (Windows), or pressing **Command+E** (Macintosh).

View Quality–Open this drop-down list box to select the look of the image: for Windows, **Simple Wireframe**, **Wireframe**, **Draft View**, or **Normal View** (the default); for Macintosh, **Wireframe**, **Full-Screen Preview**, or **Preview Selected Only**. This is equivalent to choosing one of the top three or four commands on the View menu.

Zoom Levels–Open this drop-down list box–on the Windows standard toolbar only–to change the size of the current image onscreen. (This does not change the actual dimensions of the image.) This is equivalent to choosing **View: View Manager**, choosing **View: Roll-Ups: View Manager**, or pressing **Ctrl+F2** and choosing from the View Manager *roll-up* (a dialog box that rolls down from its title bar). You can also right-click on any toolbar and choose **Zoom** to display the Zoom toolbar. You will learn more about zooming and its effects in the "Zooming an Image" section later in this chapter.

NOTE

To access the View Manager on a Macintosh computer, choose **View: Toolbars: Roll-Ups**. When the Roll-Ups toolbar appears, click on the **View Manager Roll-Up** button.

Application Launcher–Click on this button–on the Windows standard toolbar only–to open a menu from which you can start another Corel application. This menu lists only those applications that are currently installed on your computer.

Scrapbook Roll-Up–Click on this button–on the Windows standard toolbar only–to open the Scrapbook roll-up from which you can control the look of an image's border and interior and from which you can import objects to be inserted into the image. This is equivalent to choosing View: Roll-Ups: Tools: Scrapbook.

Symbols Roll-Up–Click on this button to open a roll-up from which you can select elements from symbol fonts installed on your computer. This is equivalent to choosing **View: Roll-Ups: Tools: Symbols** (Windows), choosing **Tools: Symbols** (Macintosh), pressing **Ctrl+F11** (Windows), or pressing **Command+Shift+J** (Macintosh).

Script and Preset Roll-Up–Click on this button to open a roll-up from which you can select *scripts* (that is, macros) and *presets* (that is, predefined image attributes). In the Windows version, this is equivalent to choosing **View: Roll-Ups: Tools: Script** and **Preset Manager**.

What's This Help–Click on this button and then click on an object onscreen to display context-sensitive help about that object or the help window. This is equivalent to choosing **Help What's This?** or pressing **Shift+F1**. To "deselect" context-sensitive help, press **Esc**.

CorelTUTOR–Click on this button–which is available in the Windows version only–to start a CorelDRAW tutorial. This is equivalent to choosing **Help: CorelTUTOR**.

Learning More About Toolbars

CorelDRAW button bars, such as the standard toolbar, the toolbox, and its associated property bar (both described in the section called "The Toolbox and Property Bars"), have certain common characteristics. Note that the Macintosh version does not include property bars.

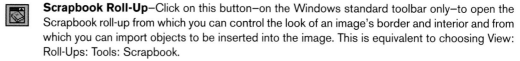

- When you move the mouse pointer over a toolbar button in the Windows version, CorelDRAW displays a ToolTip, a small yellow box that states the name of the button and, in the status bar at the bottom of the window, an explanation of the button. In the Macintosh version, the name of the button and a brief description appear in the status bar.

- You can change the location of a toolbar by pointing to an area above, below, or next to a button and dragging.

- You can move a toolbar to any part of the window. If you move a toolbar away from the top, left or right side, or bottom, it floats (Figure 8.2).

- You can drag a floating toolbar around by its title bar or any area away from a button.

- In the Windows version, you can change the size of a floating toolbar by pointing to an edge and, when the mouse pointer changes to a double-pointed arrow, dragging the edge. In the Macintosh version, point to the small black square in the lower-right corner of the toolbar and drag to resize. Release the mouse button when the toolbar is the desired size. In Windows, double-click on the floating toolbar to anchor it to its default position below the menu bar or toolbar above it. In Windows, double-click on the fixed toolbar to float it at its last position and shape. Note that you can also move a fixed toolbar to the left or the right.

Figure 8.2 The floating toolbox.

Hiding and Displaying Toolbars

Sometimes, particularly when working on a large or magnified picture, it's easier to edit or draw in a work area temporarily cleared of toolbars. To hide or display one or more toolbars follow these steps:

1. Choose **View: ToolBars** (Windows) or **View: ToolBars: ToolBars** (Macintosh). CorelDRAW opens the Toolbars dialog box (Figure 8.3).

2. To display a toolbar, place a check mark in the check box preceding its name.

3. To hide a toolbar, clear the check box preceding its name.

4. Click on **OK**.

Figure 8.3 The Toolbars dialog box.

 SHORTCUT In Windows, you can hide or display the property bar by choosing **View: Property Bar**. The Macintosh version does not provide property bars.

The Toolbox and Property Bars

The CorelDRAW toolbox is, by default, on the left side of the window. The toolbox contains many drawing and editing tools. Six toolbox buttons, which contain small arrows in their lower-right corners, indicate that you can open a *flyout*, a small palette from which you can select currently hidden buttons to replace the default button permanently—until you replace it again. In the Windows version, when you click on a button, the context-sensitive property bar displays related options. The Macintosh version does not include property bars. Figure 8.4 shows the No Selection property bar, which is the default when there is no image onscreen or you have not selected an object.

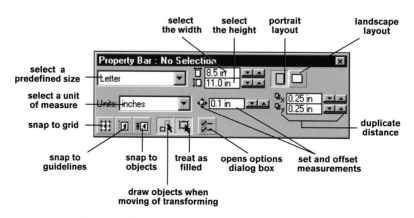

Figure 8.4 The floating, resized No Selection property bar.

CorelDRAW toolbox tools and their associated property bars described below.

 Pick Tool–Click on this button to select, move, or resize a selected image. To "deselect" a selection, either right-click away from the selection or press **Esc**. The associated Windows-version property bar is Curve or Connector.

 Shape Tool–Click on this button (which is known as the Node Edit tool in the Macintosh version) and optionally select it from the flyout, which also includes the Knife and Eraser tools, to change the shape of an image or an object, such as a rectangle, ellipse, line, text, or bit map. The associated Windows-version property bar is Edit Curve, Polygon, and Envelope.

 Knife Tool–Click on this button and select it from the flyout, which also includes the **Shape** and **Eraser** tools, to cut an object. The associated Windows-version property bar is the **Knife, Eraser and Natural Pen** tool (see Figure 8.15).

 Eraser Tool–Click on this button and select it from the flyout, which also includes the **Shape** and **Knife** tools, to erase part of an object without erasing part of an associated closed path. The **Eraser** tool does not erase in the same way that eraser tools in other art programs erase: Use this tool to split objects.

 Zoom Tool–Click on this button and select it from the flyout, which also includes the **Pan** tool (or the **Panning** tool in the Macintosh version), to zoom in on the image. The associated Windows-version property bar is the **Zoom Tool** (see Figure 8.13). You'll learn more about zooming in the "Zooming an Image" section later in this chapter.

 Pan Tool–Click on this button and select it from the flyout, which also includes the **Zoom** tool, to move an image around the current window. For more information about using the **Pan** (or **Panning**) tool, see the "Moving a Selection" section later in this chapter.

 Freehand Tool–Click on this button and select it from the flyout, which also includes the **Bezier**, **Natural Pen** (in the Windows version only), **Dimension** (which is immediately below on its own flyout in the Macintosh toolbox), and **Connector Line** (which is on the Dimension flyout in the Macintosh toolbox) tools, to draw a freehand line in any direction. The associated Windows-version property bar is Curve or Connector (see Figure 8.14). For more information about using the Freehand tool, see "Using the Freehand Tool" later in this chapter.

 Bezier Tool–Click on this button and select it from the flyout, which also includes the **Freehand** tool (and other in the Windows version), to draw a Bezier curve. The associated Windows-version property bar is Curve or Connector. For more information about the **Bezier** tool, see "Using the Bezier Tool" later in this chapter.

Natural Pen Tool—Click on this Windows-version button and select it from the flyout, which also includes the **Freehand**, **Bezier**, **Dimension**, and **Connector Line** tools, to draw a free-hand line or curve using a selected pen point. The associated Windows-version property bar is Knife, Eraser and Natural Pen Tool (see Figure 8.15). For more information about the **Natural Pen** tool, see "Using the Natural Pen Tool" later in this chapter.

Dimension Tool—Click on this button and select it from the flyout, which also includes the **Freehand**, **Bezier**, **Natural Pen**, and **Connector Line** tools in the Windows version and other dimension tools in the Macintosh version, to draw a *dimension line*, which incorporates measurement lines into a drawing (such as engineering or architectural) for accuracy. The associated Windows-version property bar is Dimension or Call Out.

Connector Line Tool—Click on this button and select it from the flyout, which also includes the **Freehand**, **Bezier**, **Natural Pen**, and **Dimension** tools in the Windows version and other dimension tools in the Macintosh version, to connect two objects in the image.

Rectangle Tool—Click on this button to draw a rectangle or square. The associated property bar is Rectangle (see Figure 8.16). For more information about the **Rectangle** tool, see "Using the Rectangle Tool" later in this chapter.

Ellipse Tool—Click on this button to draw an ellipse or circle. The associated property bar is Ellipse (see Figure 8.17). For more information about the **Ellipse** tool, see "Using the Ellipse Tool" later in this chapter.

Polygon Tool—Click on this button and select it from the flyout, which also includes the **Spiral** and **Graph Paper** (or **Grids** in the Macintosh version) tools, to draw a polygon. The associated Windows-version property bar is Symmetrical Polygon (see Figure 8.18). For more information about the **Polygon** tool, see "Using the Polygon Tool" later in this chapter.

Spiral Tool—Click on this button and select it from the flyout, which also includes the **Polygon** and **Graph Paper** tools, to draw a spiral. The associated Windows-version property bar is Graph Paper (or Grids) and Spiral Tool (see Figure 8.19). For more information about the **Spiral** tool, see "Using the Spiral Tool" later in this chapter.

Graph Paper Tool—Click on this button, which is known as Grids in the Macintosh version, and select it from the flyout, which also includes the **Polygon** and **Spiral** tools, to draw an object with rows and columns. The associated Windows-version property bar is Graph Paper and Spiral Tool. For more information about the **Graph Paper** tool, see "Using the Graph Paper (Grids) Tool" later in this chapter.

Text Tool—Click on this button to add text to the image. The associated Windows-version property bar is Editing Text (see Figure 8.20). For more information about the **Text** tool, see "Using the Text Tool" later in this chapter.

NOTE: In the Macintosh version, the **Text** tool is located on a flyout, which also includes the **Paragraph Text** tool, which is not covered in this book.

Interactive Fill Tool—Click on this button to fill the interior of the image with color, pattern, or texture. The associated Windows-version property bar is Interactive Uniform (Model Color) Fill.

Interactive Transparency Tool—Click on this button, which is available only in the Windows version, to fill the interior of the image with a transparent color, pattern, or texture. The associated property bar is Interactive Fountain Transparency.

Interactive Blend Tool—Click on this button, which is available only in the Windows version, to blend objects, gradually changing from the characteristics of the first to the last. The associated property bar is Blend.

 NOTE You can perform some blending using the Blend roll-up, which is available in both versions of CorelDRAW. However, when you blend the end result may be a color that is not in the 216-color palette.

 Outline Pen Dialog—Click on this button to specify characteristics of the *outline pen*, which is the pen with which you create the borders of objects. For more information about the outline tools, see the "Modifying an Image" section later in this chapter.

 NOTE To use the Outline tool flyout, press and hold down the mouse button, move the mouse pointer to the desired button, and release the mouse button. The selected tool does not replace the **Outline** tool in the toolbox.

 Outline Color Dialog—Click on this button to specify color characteristics of outlines.

 Pen Roll-Up—Click on this button to open the Pen roll-up with which you can specify line attributes.

 No Outline—Click on this button to remove the border from selected objects.

 Hairline Outline—Click on this button to add a hairline (1/4-point) border to selected objects.

 1/2 Point Outline—Click on this Windows-only button to add a 1/2-point border to selected objects.

 2 Point Outline (Thin)—Click on this button to add a 2-point border to selected objects.

 8 Point Outline (Medium)—Click on this button to add an 8-point border to selected objects.

 16 Point Outline (Medium-Thick)—Click on this button to add a 16-point border to selected objects.

 24 Point Outline (Thick)—Click on this button to add a 24-point border to selected objects.

 NOTE The Macintosh version also provides the **Color Roll-Up**, **Outline Pen**, **White Outline Color**, and **Black Outline Color** buttons.

 Fill Tool—Click on this button to open the Fill tool flyout from which you can fill selected objects with color, patterns, or textures and change fill attributes. Note that the selected tool does not replace the **Fill** tool in the toolbox. For more information about selecting colors and color options, see the "Selecting Color Options" section later in this chapter.

Fill Color Dialog–Click on this button to specify colors and other options for *uniform* (that is, solid one-color) fills.

 Fountain Fill Dialog–Click on this button, known as Fountain Fill in the Macintosh version, to specify colors and other options for *fountain* (that is, a two-color gradient) fills.

 Pattern Fill Dialog–Click on this Windows-version button to specify colors and other options for fills using patterns.

 Texture Fill Dialog–Click on this button, known as Texture Fill in the Macintosh version, to specify colors and other options for fills using textures.

 PostScript Fill Dialog–Click on this button, known as **PostScript Fill** in the Macintosh version, to specify colors and other options for fills using textures and patterns written in the PostScript language.

 No Fill–Click on this button to remove the fill from the selected object.

 Color Roll-Up–Click on this button to open the Color roll-up with which you can specify color options. For more information, see the "About the Color Roll-Up" section later in this chapter.

 Special Fill Roll-Up–Click on this button to open the Special Fill roll-up with which you can specify special fountain, pattern, or texture fills.

The Macintosh version also provides the **White Fill**, **Black Fill**, **Two-Color Bitmap Pattern**, **Vector Pattern**, and **Full-Color Bitmap Pattern** buttons.

The Drawing Window and the Drawing Page

The drawing window is the entire area below the standard toolbar, to the right of the toolbox, and above the status bar at the bottom of the window. The work space includes the drawing page, which by default is located in the center of the drawing window; a vertical and horizontal scrollbar; and page navigation and insertion tools.

You can see only a small part of the drawing window on your computer screen; the drawing window extends beyond all sides of the drawing page. The lower-left corner of the drawing page represents the center of the drawing window.

You can use the drawing window to hold objects that you don't plan—at least for now—to include in the current image or objects on which you have tested effects, colors, and so on; simply drag these objects onto the area outside the drawing page to move them out of the image.

CorelDRAW allows you to open more than one window in the drawing window area. In multiple windows, you can display images from different or the same files. For example, you can display two images to obtain colors or characteristics from one to use in the other. Or, you can view the same image at different sizes to see both the details and the overall look. To add a window containing a different image, choose **File: Open** to open an existing image or **File: New** to create a new image. To open a new window for the image already onscreen, choose **Window: New Window**. Then, select **Window: Cascade** to display one window behind the other with both title bars showing, **Window: Tile Horizontally** to display one window above the other, or **Window: Tile Vertically** to display the windows side by side. To close a window in the Windows version, click on the **Close** button (the *X* in the upper-right corner of the window). To close a window in the Macintosh version, click on the **Close** box in the upper-left corner of the window. To maximize the remaining window, click on the **Maximize** button in the upper-right corner of the window. Another way to maximize the remaining window, to fill in the empty space left by a closed or minimized window, is to choose **Window: Tile Horizontally** or **Window: Tile Vertically**.

Changing the Size of the Drawing Page

When you're working on Web graphics, which are almost always small, it's a good idea to reduce the size of the drawing page. This allows you to work in greater detail and automatically scale the rulers so that you can better judge image size and dimensions. To change the size of the drawing page for the current image, follow these steps:

1. Choose **Layout: Page Setup** (Windows) or **Layout: Document Layout (Macintosh)**. CorelDRAW opens the Page Setup dialog box (Figure 8.5).

2. From the drop-down list box to the right of the Width text/list box, select a unit of measure.

3. In the Width text/list box, type or select a new value.

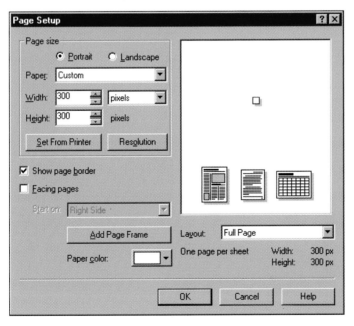

Figure 8.5 The Page Setup dialog box with its default settings.

4. In the Width text/list box, type or select a new value.

5. Click on **OK**. Figure 8.6 shows the resized drawing page in the center of the drawing window. Notice the rescaled rulers.

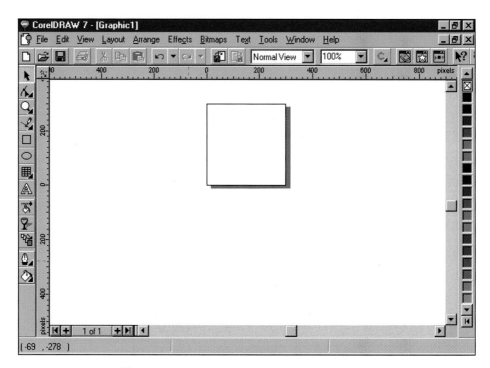

Figure 8.6 A resized drawing page and rescaled rulers.

About CorelDRAW Roll-Ups

As you have already learned, roll-ups are dialog boxes with which you can change attributes for drawing and editing features. In the Macintosh version, a roll-up is a standard dialog box. However, in the Windows version, you can decrease the size of the roll-up so that only its title bar is onscreen. This means that you can keep several roll-ups in the drawing window ready to use. Figure 8.7 shows four roll-ups, one open and three closed.

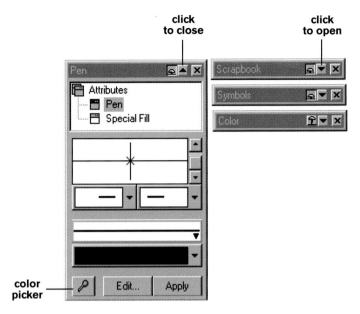

Figure 8.7 Four roll-ups, one open and three closed.

To display a roll-up:

Choose **View: Roll-Ups** and select a subcommand. Choose **View: Toolbars**, check the **Roll-Ups** check box, and click on **OK**. Then, click on a toolbar button.

Choose **View: Toolbars Roll-Ups** to open the Roll-Ups toolbar. Then, click on a toolbar button. Choose **View: Toolbars: Toolbars**, check the **Roll-Ups** check box, and click on **OK**. Then, click on a toolbar button.

You can perform additional actions in Windows:

- To roll down (that is, open) a roll-up, click on the downward-pointing arrow.
- To roll up (that is, close) a roll-up, click on the upward-pointing arrow.
- To close a roll-up automatically after using it, click on the **Autoclose** button so that it does not look as though it is pressed down.
- To keep a roll-up open after using it, click on the **Autoclose** button so that it looks as though it is pressed down.

- To close all roll-ups on the screen, right-click immediately below the title bar of any roll-up and choose **Close All** from the menu. To remove a roll-up from the screen, click on the **Close** button.

- To display a help window for a roll-up, right-click immediately below its title bar and choose **Help**.

- To display all roll-ups on the left and/or right side of the screen, right-click immediately below the title bar of a roll-up and choose **Arrange All**.

- To display the current roll-up on the left or right side of the screen, right-click immediately below its title bar and choose **Arrange**.

- To add a roll-up to another roll-up or a group of roll-ups, open all the affected roll-ups, select one, press and hold down **Alt**, and drag it to another. CorelDRAW adds the roll-up to the group and adds its name to the group list. Repeat this until all are grouped.

- You can specify the default alignment of roll-ups and can define new groups of roll-ups by choosing **Tools: Customize**, clicking on the **Roll-Ups** tab, and selecting options from the Roll-Ups section of the Customize dialog box. If you need assistance, click on the Help button in the lower-right corner.

- To "ungroup" a grouped roll-up temporarily, right-click immediately below the title bar and select **Group List**.

- To "ungroup" the current roll-up from its group permanently, right-click immediately below the title bar and select **Ungroup**.

You'll learn more about selected roll-ups as you continue reading this chapter.

The Color Palette

The color palette on the right side of the drawing window in the Windows version or at the bottom of the window in the Macintosh version enables you to set outline (that is, border) and fill (that is, interior) colors of objects. By default, the color palette displays only one column of color boxes to allow for more working space in the drawing window. You can also float and resize the color palette so that you can all the colors at once.

The default palette includes buttons with which you can display particular colors.

 Click on the left-pointing arrow to display four columns of color boxes and a horizontal scroll bar that you can use to display additional columns. Click on the button in the upper-left corner to return to a one-column display. Note that certain actions, such as minimizing, restoring, or maximizing the application window, automatically close the larger palette.

SHORTCUT In the Windows version, you can display a specific number of columns in the color palette permanently. Choose **Tools: Customize**, click on the color palette, and change the number (from 1 to 7) in the Maximum Number of Rows While Docked text/list box. Note that every column that you add removes space from the drawing window.

 Click on the upward-pointing arrow in the Windows version or the left-pointing arrow in the Macintosh version to display colors toward the top of the palette—unless the top is onscreen.

 Click on the downward-pointing arrow in the Windows version or the right-pointing arrow in the Macintosh version to display colors toward the bottom of the palette—unless the bottom is onscreen.

For more information about CorelDRAW colors, see the "Selecting Color Options" section later in this chapter.

The Status Bar

A status bar (Figures 8.8 and 8.9), which displays CorelDRAW information, appears at the bottom of the window.

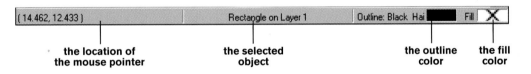

Figure 8.8 The CorelDRAW status bar in the Windows version.

Figure 8.9 An example of the status bar in the Macintosh version.

The status bar is composed of three (Windows) or four (Macintosh) sections.

◆ The current coordinates of the mouse pointer.

◆ The name and other information about the current object.

◆ Additional information about the selected object (Macintosh version).

◆ Two boxes—one showing the current outline color and the other the current fill color. If the selected object is not filled, the Fill box contains a large *X*.

To hide or display the status bar, choose **View: Status Bar**.

PREPARING TO CREATE AN IMAGE

Before you create an image, you may have to go through some steps, such as changing the outline and fill colors, turning on the grid, and displaying the rulers. In addition, before you start working, you should learn how to change the view of an image, so that you can work on your image at a detailed level or in its entirety.

Selecting Color Options

Most art programs have many color options. CorelDRAW is no exception. In this section, you will learn about the Color roll-up, find out how to select a color palette, change the outline and fill colors from the default black and white, and select a color from the current image.

About the Color Roll-Up

You can select a variety of color options, including a color palette, the outline color, and the fill color from within the Color roll-up (Figure 8.10).

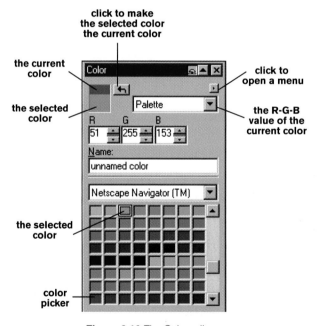

Figure 8.10 The Color roll-up.

The Color roll-up contains these elements:

- ◆ The color box in the upper-left corner shows the current outline or fill color in the top half and the currently selected color, which may replace the outline or fill color, in the bottom half.

- Click on this button to replace the current color with the selected color.
- Click on this button to open a drop-down menu from which you can select several color options.
- From the drop-down list box in the top part of the roll-up, select the type of color system or model that you will use. For Web graphics and animations, choose **Palette**.
- From the text/list boxes, type or select color values to select custom colors.
- Use the Name text box to name the selected color.
- From the drop-down list box, select the palette. This option is not available if you have not chosen **Palette** from the topmost drop-down list box. For Web graphics and animations, it's best to choose either Netscape Navigator or Microsoft Internet Explorer in the Windows version or Uniform Colors in the Macintosh version. For more information and other ways to select a color palette, see the next section, "Selecting a Color Palette."
- From the large box, click on a color box to select it.
- In the Windows version, click on the color picker and click on an object to select its color. CorelDRAW inserts the color in the bottom part of the color box.
- In the Macintosh version, click on an object to select its color, and click on the **Update From** button. (This button is also available in the Special Fill roll-up.)
- Click on the **Fill** button to make the color in the bottom part of the color box the new fill color.
- Click on the **Outline** button to make the color in the bottom part of the color box the new outline color.

Selecting a Color Palette

As you have learned in prior chapters, it is very important to select the appropriate color palette for Web images and animations. In the Windows version, CorelDRAW provides palettes for both the Netscape Navigator and Microsoft Internet Explorer browsers. Each palette contains the same 216 colors, but they are arranged differently.

There are several ways to select an appropriate color palettes:

- Choose **View: Color Palette** and select either **Netscape Navigator** or **Microsoft Internet Explorer** in the Windows version or **Uniform Colors**, which is the closest match, in the Macintosh version.
- In the Windows version, choose **View: Roll-Ups: Color**. In the Color roll-up, choose **Palette**, and select either **Netscape Navigator** or **Microsoft Internet Explorer**.
- In the Macintosh version, if the Roll-Ups toolbar is hidden, choose **View: Toolbars: Roll-ups.** Then, click on the **Color Roll-Up** button on the Roll-Ups toolbar, choose **Palette**, and select **Uniform Colors**.

♦ In the Macintosh version, if the Roll-Ups toolbar is hidden, choose **View: Toolbars: Toolbars**. Check the **Roll-Ups** check box. Then, click on the **Color Roll-Up** button on the Roll-Ups toolbar, choose **Palette**, and select **Uniform Colors**.

♦ Click on the **Fill** tool and click on the **Color Roll-Up** button. In the Color roll-up, choose **Palette** and select either **Netscape Navigator** or **Microsoft Internet Explorer** (Windows) or **Uniform Colors** (Macintosh).

Changing the Outline and Fill Colors

As you have already learned, you can select outline and fill colors using the Color roll-up. You can also choose from the color palette in the drawing window. To select outline and fill colors, follow these steps:

1. Find the appropriate color box by scrolling around the color palette.

2. To choose the outline color in the Windows version, right-click on the desired color. In the Macintosh version, press and hold down the Ctrl key and click on the desired color. If an image is in the drawing page, CorelDRAW changes the outline color. If the drawing page is empty, the Outline Color dialog box (Figure 8.11) appears.

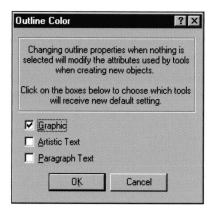

Figure 8.11 The Outline Color dialog box.

3. To set the new outline color as the default for graphics, artistic text, and/or paragraph text, check the appropriate text boxes. Then, click on **OK**.

4. To choose the fill color, left-click on the desired color. If an image is in the drawing page, CorelDRAW changes the fill color. If the drawing page is empty, CorelDRAW opens the Uniform Fill dialog box, which is identical to the Outline Color dialog box.

Selecting a Color from an Image

You can select a new outline or fill color from the current image by using the color picker (Windows) or the **Update From** button (Macintosh) in the Color roll-up. To select a color, follow these steps:

1. If needed, move the Color roll-up so that you'll have a clear view of the image.
2. Open the Color roll-up. (Note that you can move the Color roll-up after you open it.)
3. Click on the color picker or the **Update From** button.
4. Click on a color in the current image.
5. To make the color the new fill color, click on the **Fill** button (Windows) or **Apply Fill** button (Macintosh).
6. To make the color the new outline color, click on the **Outline** button (Windows) or **Apply Outline** button (Macintosh).

Showing the Grid

By default, CorelDRAW provides a hidden grid that can control the placement of borders of objects. As you create an object, you move the mouse pointer over intersections of horizontal and vertical grid lines. If you have activated the snap-to-grid feature, as you move the pointer over an intersection, CorelDRAW "snaps" it to the grid. You can either let the border rest on the grid or continue to move it. In the Windows version, you can view or hide the grid by choosing **View: Grid**. In the Macintosh version, you can view or hide the grid by choosing **Layout: Grid and Ruler Setup**, clicking on the **Grid** tab, and checking the **Show Grid** check box.

To activate the snap-to-grid feature, do one of the following:

- Click on the **Snap to Grid** button in the No Selection property bar.
- Choose **Layout: Snap to Grid**.
- Press **Ctrl+Y** (Windows), or press **Command+Option+H** (Macintosh).
- Choose **Layout: Grid and Ruler Setup**. Click on the **Grid** tab and place a check mark in the **Snap to Grid** check box.

NOTE

Guides, which are not covered in this book, are lines that mark limits within a particular image window. So, if you want to line up several images, you can set guidelines to which the images will snap.

Turning on the Rulers

To measure all or part of an image, you can display vertical and horizontal rulers (Figure 8.12) within all the open image windows. When you turn on the rulers, they remain on display until you explicitly hide them—in this or a future CorelDRAW session. To display the rulers, choose **View: Rulers**. To hide the rulers, choose **View: Rulers** again. To display or hide rulers in the Macintosh version, you can also press **Command+Option+R**.

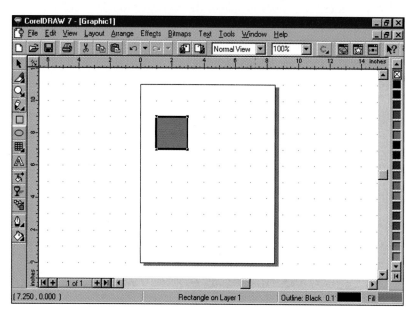

Figure 8.12 An image window with horizontal and vertical rulers and a rectangle snapped to the grid.

The rulers use the current unit of measure: inches, centimeters, points, or picas, and many more. To change the unit of measure, follow these steps:

1. Choose **Layout: Grid and Ruler Setup**. CorelDRAW opens the Grid & Ruler Setup dialog box.

2. Click on the **Ruler** tab, if needed.

3. Make a selection from the Horizontal drop-down list box. In the Windows version, CorelDRAW changes the unit of measure for both horizontal and vertical rulers.

4. If you are using the Macintosh version, make a selection from the Vertical drop-down list box.

5. Click on **OK**.

Zooming an Image

When you view an image at its actual size, you may not be able to work on its details, or, conversely, you may not be able to see it completely—especially if it extends beyond the limits of your computer screen. CorelDRAW allows you to zoom in (that is, see the details) or zoom out (that is, see a greater part of a large image). You can zoom in up to 405,651% of the actual size; you can zoom out to 1% of the actual size.

CorelDRAW provides many zoom tools in the standard toolbar, toolbox, the Zoom Tool property bar (Windows), the Zoom toolbar, and the View Manager roll-up, all shown in Figure 8.13.

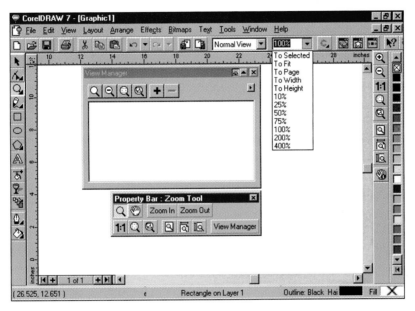

Figure 8.13 CorelDRAW zoom tools.

◆ To open the Windows version Zoom Tool property bar, click on the **Zoom** tool in the toolbox. If the property bar is still hidden, choose **View: Property Bar**.

◆ To open the Zoom toolbar (Windows), right-click on the toolbar and select **Zoom** from the menu; or choose **View: Toolbars**, check the **Zoom** checkbox, and click on **OK**.

◆ To open the Zoom toolbar(Macintosh), press and hold down the **Ctrl** key, click on the toolbar, and select **Zoom** from the menu; or choose **View: Toolbars: Zoom**; or choose **View: Toolbars: Toolbars**, check the **Zoom** checkbox, and click on **OK**.

◆ To open the View Manager roll-up, choose **View: View Manager**, choose **View: Roll-Ups View Manager**, or press **Ctrl+F2**.

◆ To open the context menu in the Windows version, click on the **Zoom** tool in the toolbox and right-click in the drawing window.

◆ To choose from the Zoom Levels text box/drop-down list box on the standard toolbar in the Windows version, click on a zoom level.

SHORTCUT   If you want to zoom in to a particular value in the Windows version, simply type it in the Zoom Levels text box/drop-down list box.

CorelDRAW zoom tools are described below.

 Zoom In–To zoom in, click on this button and repeatedly click the magnifying-glass mouse pointer in the drawing window. The Windows-version context menu equivalents are the **Zoom In** command or the **Zoom** command and subcommand with a value greater than the current value. The Zoom Levels text box/drop-down list box equivalent is a value greater than the current level. This is a View Manager roll-up button.

 Zoom In–To zoom in, click on this button and repeatedly click the magnifying-glass mouse pointer in the drawing window. The Windows-version context menu equivalents are the **Zoom In** command or the **Zoom** command and subcommand with a value greater than the current value. The Zoom Levels text box/drop-down list box equivalent is a value greater than the current level. This is a Zoom toolbar button.

 Zoom In–To zoom in, repeatedly click on this button. The Windows-version context menu equivalents are the **Zoom In** command or the **Zoom** command and subcommand with a value greater than the current value. In the Windows version, the Zoom Levels text box/drop-down list box equivalent is a value greater than the current level. This is in the Windows-version Zoom Tool property bar.

 Zoom Out–To zoom out, repeatedly click on this button or repeatedly press **F3**. The Windows-version context menu equivalents are the **Zoom Out** command or the **Zoom** command and subcommand with a value less than the current value. The Zoom Levels text box/drop-down list box equivalent is a value less than the current level. This is in the Zoom toolbar and View Manager roll-up.

 Zoom Out–To zoom out, repeatedly click on this button or repeatedly press **F3** (Windows version only). The Windows-version context menu equivalents are the **Zoom Out** command or the **Zoom** command and subcommand with a value less than the current value. The Windows-version Zoom Levels text box/drop-down list box equivalent is a value less than the current level. This is in the Windows-version Zoom Toolbar property bar.

 Zoom Actual Size–To return the image to its actual size, click on this button. The Windows-version context menu equivalent is **Zoom 1:1**. There is no Zoom Levels text box/drop-down list box equivalent. This is in the Windows-version Zoom Tool property bar and the Zoom toolbar.

NOTE You can also choose **View: Full-Screen Preview** or press **F9** to view an image at full size. When you select this command, CorelDRAW removes all elements from the screen.

Zoom to Selected—To center selected objects in the drawing window, click on this button or press **Shift+F2**. The Windows-version context menu equivalent is **Zoom to Selection**. The Windows-version Zoom Levels text box/drop-down list box equivalent is **To Selected**. This is in the Windows-version Zoom Tool property bar, Zoom toolbar, and View Manager roll-up.

Zoom to All Objects—To center all objects in the drawing window, click on this button. There are no context menu or Zoom Levels text box/drop-down list box equivalents. This is in the Windows-version Zoom Tool property bar, Zoom toolbar, and View Manager roll-up.

Zoom to Page—To center all objects in the center of the drawing page, click on this button or press **Shift+F4**. The Windows-version context menu equivalent is **Zoom to Page**. The Windows-version Zoom Levels text box/drop-down list box equivalent is **To Page**. This is in the Windows-version Zoom Tool property bar and the Zoom toolbar.

Zoom to Page Width—To zoom in on the width of the drawing page, click on this button in the Windows version. The context menu equivalent is **Zoom to Width**. The Zoom Levels text box/drop-down list box equivalent is **To Width**. This is in the Windows version Zoom Tool property bar and the Zoom toolbar.

Zoom to Page Height—To zoom in on the height of the drawing page, click on this button in the Windows version. The context menu equivalent is Zoom to Height. The Zoom Levels text box/drop-down list box equivalent is **To Height**. This is in the Windows version Zoom Tool property bar and the Zoom toolbar.

You can save particular zoom levels for the current image file. Click on this button in the View Manager roll-up.

To delete a saved zoom level from the View Manager roll-up, select it and click on this button.

Fitting an Image to the Application Window

You can adjust the view of an image to fit the application window. To fit an image to the window. select one of the following:

- ◆ Click on the **Zoom** tool, right-click in the drawing window, and select **Zoom to Fit**.
- ◆ Press **F4**.
- ◆ Select **To Fit** from the Windows version Zoom Levels text box/drop-down list box.

CREATING AN IMAGE—EXAMPLE 1

To create an image from scratch, click on a toolbox tool and start working.

Using the Drawing Tools

The best way to learn about the tools with which you'll draw images is to use them. However, before you get started, it's a good idea to find out how these tools work and how to change their characteristics.

Using the Freehand Tool

Click on the **Freehand** tool or optionally select it from the flyout, to draw a freehand line in any direction. Start the line by clicking and holding down the mouse button and dragging. In the Windows version, while continuing to hold down the mouse button and holding down the **Shift** key and moving back over the drawn line, you can erase part of the freehand line. To stop drawing a line, release the left mouse button.

In the Windows version, you can control characteristics of the **Freehand** tool or the current freehand object using the Curve or Connector property bar (Figure 8.14).

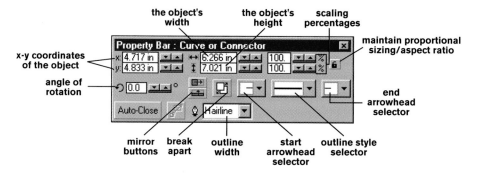

Figure 8.14 The floating, resized Curve or Connector property bar.

Using the Bezier Tool

Click on the **Bezier** tool or optionally select it from the flyout to draw a *Bezier curve*, a smooth arc that CorelDRAW calculates using mathematical formulas. To draw a Bezier curve, progressively click on points that will make up the curve. To stop drawing, either click on another tool or press the **Spacebar**.

In the Windows version, you can control characteristics of the **Bezier** tool or the current Bezier curve using the Curve or Connector property bar.

Using the Natural Pen Tool

Click on the **Natural Pen** tool, which is available only in the Windows version or optionally select it from the flyout to draw a freehand line or curve using a selected pen point. Start a line or curve by clicking and holding down the left mouse button and dragging. To stop drawing a line, release the left mouse button.

You can control characteristics of the **Natural Pen** tool and the current line or curve using the Knife, Eraser and Natural Pen Tool property bar (Figure 8.15).

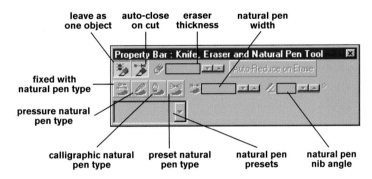

Figure 8.15 The floating, resized Knife, Eraser and Natural Pen Tool property bar.

Using the Rectangle Tool

Click on the **Rectangle** tool to draw a rectangle or square. To draw a rectangle, move the mouse pointer to the drawing window, select a starting point, and drag the mouse.

To draw a square, press and hold down the **Ctrl** key and drag the mouse.

To draw a square, press and hold down the **Shift** key and drag the mouse.

In the Windows version, you can control characteristics of the **Rectangle** tool and the current rectangle using the Rectangle property bar (Figure 8.16).

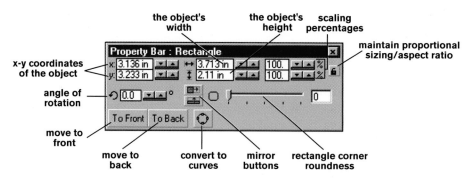

Figure 8.16 The floating, resized Rectangle property bar.

Using the Ellipse Tool

Click on the **Ellipse** tool to draw an ellipse or circle. To draw an ellipse, move the mouse pointer to the drawing window, select a starting point, and drag the mouse.

To draw a circle, press and hold down the **Ctrl** key and drag the mouse.

To draw a circle, press and hold down the **Shift** key and drag the mouse.

In the Windows version, you can control characteristics of the **Ellipse** tool and the current ellipse using the Ellipse property bar (Figure 8.17).

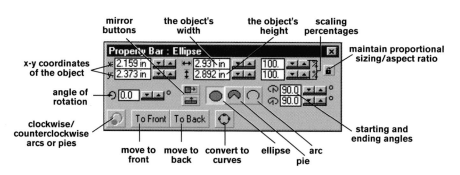

Figure 8.17 The floating, resized Ellipse property bar.

Using the Polygon Tool

Click on the **Polygon** tool to draw a polygon. To draw a polygon, move the mouse pointer to the drawing window, select a starting point, and drag the mouse.

To draw a symmetrical polygon, press and hold down the **Ctrl** key and drag the mouse.

To draw a symmetrical polygon, press and hold down the **Shift** key and drag the mouse.

In the Windows version, you can control characteristics of the **Polygon** tool and the current polygon using the Symmetrical Polygon property bar (Figure 8.18).

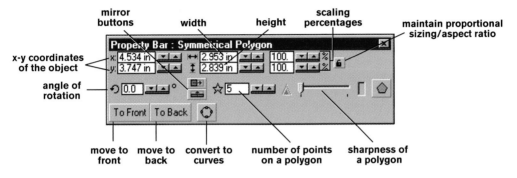

Figure 8.18 The floating, resized Symmetrical Polygon property bar.

Using the Spiral Tool

Click on the **Spiral** tool to draw a spiral. To draw a spiral, move the mouse pointer to the drawing window, select a starting point, and drag the mouse.

In the Windows version, you can control characteristics of the **Spiral** tool and the current spiral using the Graphic Paper and Spiral Tool property bar (Figure 8.19).

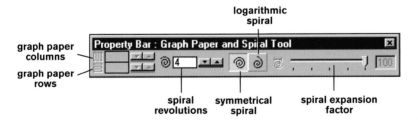

Figure 8.19 The floating, resized Graph Paper and Spiral Tool property bar.

Using the Graph Paper (Grids) Tool

Click on the **Graph Paper** tool (or in the Macintosh version, the **Grids** tool) to draw a rectangular object with rows and columns. To draw a rectangular graph-paper object, move the mouse pointer to the drawing window, select a starting point, and drag the mouse.

To draw a square graph-paper object, press and hold down the **Ctrl** key and drag the mouse.

To draw a square graph-paper object, press and hold down the **Shift** key and drag the mouse.

In the Windows version, you can control characteristics of the **Graph Paper** tool and the current graph-paper object using the Graphic Paper and Spiral Tool property bar.

The Text Tool

Click on the **Text** tool to add *artistic text* (that is, a short text string) to the image.

In the Windows version, you can control characteristics of the **Text** tool and the current text using the Editing Text property bar (Figure 8.20).

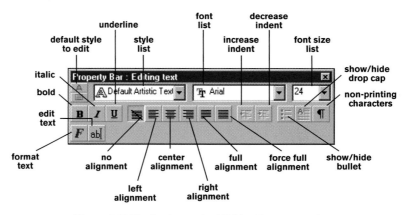

Figure 8.20 The floating, resized Editing Text property bar.

Drawing an Image

To create an image, follow these steps:

1. Start CorelDRAW.

2. Click on the **New** button, choose **File: New** (Windows), choose **File: New: Document** (Macintosh), press **Ctrl+N** (Windows), or press **Command+N** (Macintosh). CorelDRAW opens a new drawing page and drawing window.

3. If needed, select the Netscape Navigator or Microsoft Internet Explorer palette in the Windows version or the Uniform Colors palette in the Macintosh version. For more information, refer to the "Selecting a Color Palette" section earlier in this chapter.

4. If needed, select a outline color, fill color, or both. For more information, refer to the "Changing the Outline and Fill Colors" section earlier in this chapter.

5. To change the view of the drawing page, either zoom in or zoom out. For information about zooming, refer to the "Zooming an Image" section earlier in this chapter.

> **SHORTCUT** To start an image, it's a good idea to set a zoom level of 100% so that you can estimate the true size of the image. Then, you can zoom in when you insert new objects and edit the image.

6. Click on a drawing tool in the toolbox and create the first object in the image, making sure that you compare its size to the rulers.

7. Continue working on the image by repeating steps 4–6, as needed.

8. To export the image as a GIF file, choose **File: Export**, press **Ctrl+H** (Windows), or press **Command+E** (Macintosh).

9. In the Export dialog box, fill in the filename and select **CompuServe Bitmap** (GIF). Click on **Export**.

10. Fill in the Bitmap Export dialog box (Figure 8.21). Click on **OK**.

11. Fill in the Gif89a Options dialog box (Figure 8.22) in the Windows version or the GIF Options dialog box in the Macintosh version. Click on **OK**.

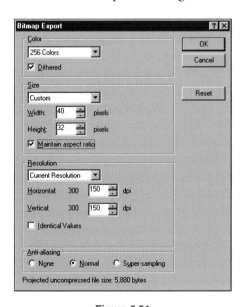

Figure 8.21
The Bitmap Export dialog box with options for a GIF image.

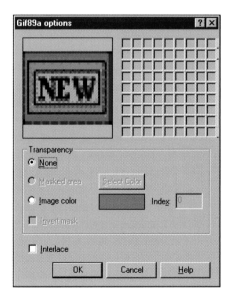

Figure 8.22
The Gif89a Options dialog box.

ABOUT THIS ANIMATION—ORANGE-RED-YELLOW NEW

orynew.gif 7K 40 × 32 Level: Easy

The orange-red-yellow new animation alternates the display of two images.

- ◆ This animation is composed of two images created in CorelDRAW.
- ◆ The original image's first rectangle, which is red, forms the outer dimensions. The first rectangle was drawn at a 100% zoom level.
- ◆ The second orange rectangle is centered on top of the first, and the third yellow rectangle rests on the second. To add these images accurately, the zoom level was set to 400%.
- ◆ Use the **Text** tool to insert and format the text in the middle of the smallest rectangle.
- ◆ To format the text, choose **Format: Text** or press **Ctrl+T**. To move the text within the image, click on it and drag. To resize the text, drag the handles surrounding the text block.
- ◆ After an image is completed, save it (for example, **orynew1**) and save it again as the basis for the final image (**orynew2**) in the series.
- ◆ Reverse the colors in the second image.
- ◆ Many browsers do not recognize animations. Each image in this animation can stand alone.
- ◆ This animation loops infinitely.
- ◆ This animation looks better at a medium speed.

MODIFYING AN IMAGE

After creating an image, you can modify it in several ways:

- ◆ Use the **Pick** tool to select one or more objects in an image. Then, move the objects or use the handles marking the border to resize or change the dimensions.
- ◆ Use the Edit menu commands to copy, cut, paste, duplicate, clone, or delete part or all of an image.
- ◆ Use the transform commands on the Arrange menu commands to position, rotate, scale and mirror, size, or skew a selection.
- ◆ Use various roll-ups to apply other special effects.
- ◆ Use Text menu commands to edit or change the look of selected text objects.
- ◆ Use effects commands to apply innumerable special effects. These commands are not covered in this book.

◆ In the Windows version of CorelDRAW, convert the image to a bit map. Then, use Bitmaps menu commands to apply effects.

 NOTE Whenever you edit an image, it's a good idea to save it from time to time. This avoids your having to unnecessarily redo your work.

Selecting Objects

Sometimes you can work with an image without selecting any of the objects in it. For example, if you add an object to an image or change an object's outline or fill colors, you might not have to make a selection. However, most of the time, you must make a selection before working on an object. For example, if you want to copy, move, or remove an object from an image, you must select it. CorelDRAW provides two means of selecting objects: the **Pick** tool and the **Select All** command.

◆ To select a single object, click on the **Pick** tool. CorelDRAW selects the object, and the status bar shows information about the selected object. If you want to select another object in the image, click on it.

◆ To add an object to the selection, make sure that the **Pick** tool is still selected, and press and hold down the **Shift** key. Then, click on the new selection. The status bar shows the number of selected objects.

◆ To select all the objects in the drawing page and drawing window, either choose **Edit: Select All** or double-click on the **Pick** tool. The status bar shows the number of selected objects.

CorelDRAW provides the following selection features:

◆ After you have made a selection, CorelDRAW surrounds it with an invisible bounding box with visible handles at each corner and in the middle of each side (Figure 8.23). The program also adds *end points*, which mark the beginnings and ends of curves and lines, and *anchor points*, which indicate the location of a change in the direction (such as a corner) in the outline of an object.

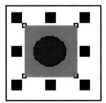

Figure 8.23 A selected rectangle with eight handles and four anchor points.

◆ If you click again on the selection, CorelDRAW changes the handles (Figure 8.24) so that you can rotate and/or skew the object. Click repeatedly to switch between the sets of handles.

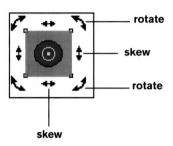

Figure 8.24 A selected rectangle with rotate and skew handles.

◆ After you have made a selection, you can use menu commands to act on the object and apply effects. You can select from the menu bar, or move the mouse pointer to the object and right-click (Windows) or press the **Ctrl** key and click (Macintosh) to open a context menu from which you can select commonly used editing commands.

◆ You can drag a selection around the drawing page and drawing window. When you drag a selection, CorelDRAW indicates its current position with a bounding box (Figure 8.25). The selection doesn't actually move until you have released the left mouse button. You can change the selection in other ways, as described in the following sections.

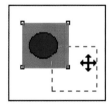

Figure 8.25 A rectangular object being moved.

◆ To "deselect" a selection, click on a location outside the selection.

Copying, Pasting, Cutting, and Deleting Selections

CorelDRAW features an Edit menu that includes commands with which you can copy, cut, paste, delete, duplicate, and clone objects.

Copying a Selection

To copy the current selection to the Clipboard, choose **Edit: Copy**, press **Ctrl+C** (Windows), or press **Command+C** (Macintosh). When you copy a selection, CorelDRAW leaves the selection in place and places a copy in the Clipboard. If the **Copy** command is dimmed, you have not made a selection.

Cutting a Selection

To remove the current selection and place it in the Clipboard, choose **Edit: Cut**, press **Ctrl+X** (Windows), or press **Command+X** (Macintosh). If the **Cut** command is dimmed, you have not made a selection.

 WARNING When you make a selection, CorelDRAW "undims" the **Copy** and **Cut** commands. This does not mean that the selection is automatically copied to the Clipboard. To copy or cut a selection, you must explicitly choose **Edit: Copy** or **Edit: Cut**.

Pasting a Selection

To paste a selection from the Clipboard into the current image, choose **Edit: Paste**, press **Ctrl+V** (Windows), or press **Command+V** (Macintosh). When you paste a selection, CorelDRAW places it on top of the selection. If the **Paste** command is dimmed, the Clipboard is empty.

Duplicating a Selection

You can paste a selection into the current image without using the Clipboard. Choose **Edit: Duplicate**, press **Ctrl+D** (Windows), or press **Command+D** (Macintosh). CorelDRAW duplicates the object on top of the selection but offsets it slightly toward the upper-right corner of the drawing window (Figure 8.26).

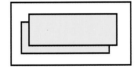

Figure 8.26 A selection and its duplicate.

Cloning a Selection

Cloning is another method of duplicating a selection. Cloning takes the duplication process an additional step: the selection is not only duplicated but the selection and the clone are linked. Then, when you change the original object, the clone automatically changes.

However, when you modify the clone, the original does not reflect the change and that and related attributes are no longer linked. To clone a selection, choose **Edit: Clone**.

Deleting a Selection

To delete a selection permanently, either choose **Edit: Clear** or press the **Del** key. After you have deleted a selection, the only way to restore it is to choose **Edit: Undo**, press **Ctrl+Z** (Windows), or press **Command+Z** (Macintosh). However, if you have performed another action after the deletion, you will have to undo that action before undoing the deletion.

Grouping and Ungrouping Selections

Grouping and ungrouping allow you to unite an image because you want to keep its present appearance or to adjust it as a whole. For example, to move an image made up of many objects, it doesn't make sense to move one object at a time—particularly if you have spent a great deal of time placing the objects within the image. To move an entire image, select all the objects and groups that you have formed in the past by choosing **Edit: Select All** or pressing **Command+A** (Macintosh). Then, group the selected objects by choosing **Arrange: Group**, pressing **Ctrl+G** (Windows), or pressing **Command+G** (Macintosh). CorelDRAW surrounds the group with handles. Drag the image to its new location. Finally, ungroup the group (if needed) into its individual objects by choosing **Arrange: Ungroup**, pressing **Ctrl+U** (Windows), or pressing **Command+U** (Macintosh). To ungroup both the current group and groups that you have formed before in the Windows version, choose **Arrange: Ungroup All**.

TRANSFORMING A SELECTION

Remember that when you make a selection, you can click one more time to display rotate and skew handles. You can either use the handles to transform the appearance of a selection or you can choose **Arrange: Transform** and use the subcommands in the Windows version or select options in the Transform roll-up in the Macintosh version. The following sections describe the actions of each of the transform commands or options.

 NOTE In the Windows version, you can use the property bars to transform a selected type of object (for example, rectangle, ellipse, and so on). For information about using the property bars, see Figures 8.14 through 8.20 in the "Using the Drawing Tools" section earlier in this chapter.

Moving a Selection

You can move an object by using the mouse or issuing a menu command and selecting options from a roll-up.

To use the mouse to move an object, follow these steps:

1. Select the object.
2. Move the mouse pointer to the area within the selection.
3. Drag the selection around the drawing page or the drawing window.

Choose **Arrange: Transform: Position** (Windows), choose **Arrange: Transform** and select **Position** from the drop-down list box (Macintosh), press **Alt+F7** (Windows), or press **Option+F7** (Macintosh) to open the Position roll-up (Figure 8.27) with which you can specify values for a move.

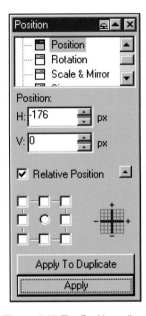

Figure 8.27 The Position roll-up.

Rotating a Selection

You can rotate an object by using the mouse or issuing a menu command and selecting options from a roll-up.

To use the mouse to rotate an object, follow these steps:

1. Select the object.
2. Click on the selection again to display rotate and skew handles (see Figure 8.24).
3. To change the center of the rotation, drag the circular handle in the middle of the selection.

4. To rotate the selection, drag one of the double-pointed curved arrows at the corners of the selection. CorelDRAW shows the progress of the rotation by changing the angle of a bounding box surrounding the selection.

Choose **Arrange: Transform: Rotate** (Windows), choose **Arrange: Transform** and select **Rotation** from the drop-down list box (Macintosh), press **Alt+F8** (Windows), or press **Option+F8** (Macintosh) to open the Rotation roll-up (Figure 8.28) with which you can specify values for a rotation.

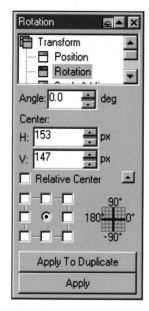

Figure 8.28 The extended Rotation roll-up.

Skewing a Selection

You can skew an object by using the mouse or issuing a menu command and selecting options from a roll-up.

To use the mouse to skew an object, follow these steps:

1. Select the object.
2. Click on the selection to display rotate and skew handles (see Figure 8.24).
3. To skew the selection horizontally, drag one of the double-pointed straight arrows at the top and bottom of the selection to the left or right. CorelDRAW shows the current skew by changing the angle of a bounding box surrounding the selection.

4. To skew the selection vertically, drag one of the double-pointed straight arrows at the left and right sides of the selection toward the top or bottom of the drawing window. CorelDRAW shows the current skew by changing the angle of a bounding box surrounding the selection.

Choose **Arrange: Transform: Skew** (Windows), choose **Arrange: Transform** and select **Skew** from the drop-down list box (Macintosh), press **Alt+F11** (Windows), or press **Option+F11** (Macintosh) to open the Skew roll-up (Figure 8.29) with which you can specify values for skewing the selection.

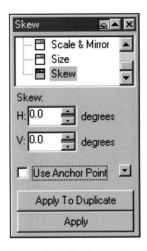

Figure 8.29 The Skew roll-up.

Scaling a Selection

You can scale an object by issuing a menu command and selecting options from a roll-up.

 NOTE You can also change the dimensions of an object by specifying measurements for height, width, or both. To do this, choose **Layer: Transform: Size** or press **Alt+F10** and fill in the Size roll-up.

Choose **Arrange: Transform: Scale and Mirror** (Windows), choose **Arrange: Transform** and select **Scale & Mirror** from the drop-down list box (Macintosh), press **Alt+F9** (Windows), or press **Option+F9** (Macintosh) to open the Scale & Mirror roll-up (Figure 8.30) with which you can specify values for scaling the selection.

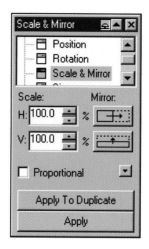

Figure 8.30 The Scale & Mirror roll-up.

Mirroring a Selection

You can mirror, or flip, an object by issuing a menu command and selecting options from a roll-up.

Choose **Arrange: Transform: Scale and Mirror** (Windows), choose **Arrange: Transform** and select **Scale & Mirror** from the drop-down list box (Macintosh), press **Alt+F9** (Windows), or press **Option+F9** (Macintosh) to open the Scale & Mirror roll-up with which you can specify values for mirroring the selection.

Sizing a Selection

You can change the dimensions of an object by using the mouse or issuing a menu command and selecting options from a roll-up.

To use the mouse to size an object, follow these steps:

1. Select the object.

2. Click on the selection to display rectangular handles at the corners and midpoints of the selection (see Figure 8.23).

3. To size the selection but keep it in proportion, drag a corner handle diagonally away or toward the center of the object. CorelDRAW shows the current dimensions of the object with a bounding box.

4. To size a side of the selection without keeping it in proportion, drag a midpoint handle away or toward the center of the object. CorelDRAW shows the current dimensions of the object with a bounding box.

Choose **Arrange: Transform Size** (Windows), choose **Arrange: Transform** and select **Size** from the drop-down list box (Macintosh), press **Alt+F10** (Windows), or press **Option+F10** (Macintosh) to open the Size roll-up (Figure 8.31) with which you can set particular values for the height and/or width of the selection.

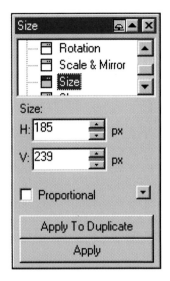

Figure 8.31 The Size roll-up.

CONVERTING TO A BIT MAP—EXAMPLE 2

As you have learned, a GIF file is a bit map. CorelDRAW provides two ways of converting to the bit-mapped file format. In the Windows version, you can convert an object or grouped objects to a bit map within CorelDRAW, and in both versions, you can export the entire image to a GIF file in which it is converted.

NOTE
If you open a bit map in CorelDRAW, the program converts the file to a CorelDRAW document. Therefore, this should be the last action you take on a particular file.

Sometimes, you can avoid having the conversion process drastically change objects or images by converting to a bit map. To do this in the Windows version, make a selection and choose **Bitmaps: Convert to Bitmap**. The current property bar (if property bars are turned on) becomes the Bitmap or OLE Object property bar.

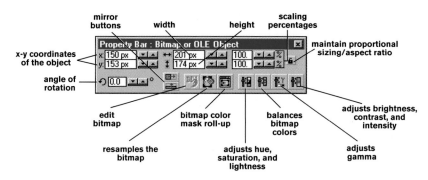

Figure 8.32 The Bitmap or OLE Object property bar.

To apply color to a bit map and to make certain commands available, choose **Bitmaps: RGB Color (24-bit)**.

After the selection is a bit map and has been converted to RGB color, most or all other Bitmaps menu commands become available.

Table 8.2 describes the actions of each of the Bitmaps menu commands that apply to creating Web images. Each command has an associated dialog box with which you can adjust and preview the effects on a particular bit map. The best way to see how these commands work is to experiment with them on the images that you create.

Table 8.2 Bitmaps Menu Commands and Their Actions in the CorelDRAW Windows Version

Command	Actions
Bitmaps: Resample	Changes the bit map size using a selected unit of measure, or changes the resolution.
Bitmaps: 2D Effects: Edge Detect	Changes the appearance of the bit map's outline and background.
Bitmaps: 2D Effects: Offset	Slightly changes the location of the bit map—horizontally and/or vertically—on the drawing page.
Bitmaps: 2D Effects: Pixelate	Adds dots to a bit map, which can result in a blurring effect.
Bitmaps: 2D Effects: Swirl	Rotates the bit map at a set angle and direction.
Bitmaps: 2D Effects: Wet Paint	Applies the look of wet paint, which can result in a smeared or blurry look.
Bitmaps: 3D Effects: 3D Rotate	Rotates a bit map as if it were on a turntable.
Bitmaps: 3D Effects: Emboss	Applies an embossed finish using depth and direction settings.
Bitmaps: 3D Effects: Page Curl	Curls a corner of the bit map at a particular orientation, width, and/or height.
Bitmaps: 3D Effects: Perspective	Changes the perspective of the bit map symmetrically (**Perspective**) or asymmetrically (**Shear**).
Bitmaps: 3D Effects: Pinch Punch	Reduces or increases the size of the middle of the bit map.
Bitmaps: 3D Effects: Map to Object	Changes the shape of the bit map, spherically or cylindrically, by a specified percentage.
Bitmaps: Blur: Gaussian	Applies different levels of blur to the bit map.

Table 8.2 Bitmaps Menu Commands and Their Actions in the CorelDRAW Windows Version (continued)

Command	Actions
Bitmaps: Blur: Motion	Applies a motion blur to the bit map using settings for speed and direction.
Bitmaps: Blur: Smooth	Blurs the interior of the bit map by a set percentage.
Bitmaps: Noise: Add Noise	Inserts dots within the bit map and the bounding box surrounding it.
Bitmaps: Noise: Remove Noise	Removes a certain number of dots from within the bit map.
Bitmaps: Sharpness Sharpen	Sharpens the edges of the bit map. You can consider sharpness to be the opposite of blur.
Bitmaps: Sharpness Unsharpen Mask	Sharpens some of the edges and areas within the bit map.
Bitmaps: Artistic Glass Block	Changes the bit map so that it appears as though you are looking through a glass block to see it.
Bitmaps: Artistic Impressionist	Applies scattered dots of a specified size to the bit map.
Bitmaps: Artistic Vignette	Inserts an oval frame with sharp or faded edges around the bit map.
Bitmaps: Color Transform Psychedelic	Applies random colors to the bit map and the area within the bounding box.
Bitmaps: Color Transform Solarize	Adjusts the level of black and white (as in a photographic negative) within the bit map.

ABOUT THIS ANIMATION—SQUARE-SQUARE

squsquar.gif 2491K 32 × 32 Level: Easy

This animation is a square within a square. The outer square rotates counterclockwise and changes sizes. The inner square rotates clockwise. The rotations were done using the rotation handles to generate a random effect.

- ◆ This animation is composed of four images.
- ◆ A red rectangle is created.
- ◆ A yellow rectangle is created and is rotated 45 degrees. Its size is adjusted to touch all four sides of the red rectangle. The first image is saved.
- ◆ In the second image, each of the rectangles is selected separately and rotated a random number of degrees. The image is saved.
- ◆ Each of the rectangles in the second image is rotated. The image is saved as the third file.
- ◆ The fourth file is rotated in the same way.
- ◆ Many browsers do not recognize animations. For these browsers, the first file (**squsqu01**) begins and ends the animation.
- ◆ This animation is looped infinitely.
- ◆ Each file but the first and last has a time delay of 6/100ths of a second. The first is delayed for 1/100th, and the last for 3/100th. This adjusts for having the first and last images the same file.

SCANNING AND ANIMATING AN IMAGE— EXAMPLE 3

If you have access to a scanner, you open the door to many possibilities: You can use images from a variety of sources: photographs, magazines, catalogs, and so on, as a starting point for unique animations. CorelSCAN provides features that allow you to improve the quality of the scan.

To scan an image, follow these steps:

1. Choose **File: Acquire** from CorelSCAN. After a few seconds, CorelDRAW starts CorelSCAN.

    NOTE CorelSCAN is not part of the standard CorelDRAW installation. To install CorelSCAN, you must choose **Custom Installation**.

2. Click on **Setup Scanner and Processing Options**. Then, click on **Scan**. Click on **Next**.

3. Select your scanner from the drop-down list box, and either select your scanner software (**Yes**) or CorelSCAN (**No**). Then, click on **Next**.

4. If you choose CorelSCAN, answer the prompts in the following dialog boxes. CorelSCAN tests your computer for graphic resolution.

5. If you choose your scanner software, scan the picture. CorelSCAN asks you about the image, including its destination, color, resolution, and dimensions. Based on your answers, you have the option to clean up the scanned image. CorelSCAN completes the scan.

6. Return to CorelDRAW.

ABOUT THIS ANIMATION—ACCORDION

accordn.gif 4031K 75 × 36 Level: Easy

The accordion is a scanned grayscale clip art picture.

- ◆ This animation is composed of five GIFs; the first is repeated at the middle and at the end.
- ◆ The first image was scanned in from a copyright-free book of clip art, adjusted for size, and converted to a bit map.
- ◆ The second and fourth images were stretched and skewed.
- ◆ Each image was surrounded by a black and gold picture frame drawn to avoid setting a transparent color. The accordian has an interior and background of white, which would result in transparent pixels within the image. Painting a background color that would become transparent would be a very difficult task; sometimes there is no set border for the image.
- ◆ The first, third, and fifth frames are identical.
- ◆ Many browsers do not recognize animations. The beginning and end GIFs in this animation are the original image.
- ◆ This animation should run at a medium speed.
- ◆ This animation can loop infinitely.

Working with GifBuilder

GifBuilder is a drag-and-drop animation utility for Macintosh computers. Developed by Yves Piguet, GifBuilder is a *freeware* program; that is, it is free for anyone to download and use. With GifBuilder, you can animate GIF, PICT, and TIFF files as well as Photoshop images.

NOTE You can convert QuickTime movies, PICS, FilmStrips, and Photoshop layers to animations by choosing **File: Convert** and then choosing the file to convert.

To create an animation, start GifBuilder and drag each frame into a window. Then, edit the animation by choosing menu commands and selecting options.

GifBuilder supports the GIF89a standard, enables you to animate an unlimited number of frames, provides five palettes, and allows you to create custom palettes. With GifBuilder, you can set transparency, looping, and time delays as well as offsets, and you can specify the method of replacing the contents of one frame with the next.

ABOUT THE FRAMES WINDOW

The Frames window eventually contains every frame of an animation, which makes it easy to edit either single frames or the animation as a whole. Figure 9.1 illustrates the desktop with GifBuilder active, the first frame dragged into the Frames window, and all the image files that will comprise the animation.

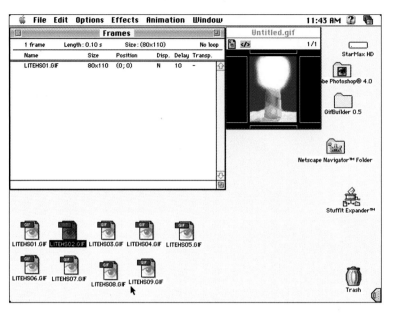

Figure 9.1 The desktop showing the Frames window, the animation window, and the art files.

The Frames window is composed of two sections: The one-row top contains information about the animation, and the remaining part shows the details of each frame in the animation.

The top row, from left to right, shows:

◆ The number of frames (that is, the number of images in the animation)

◆ The total time, in seconds, that the animation runs once, from the first frame to the end

◆ The dimensions (that is, the size of the image), which you can set by choosing **Options: Image Size** and filling in the dialog box.

◆ The number of times that the animation will loop (that is, play more than once)

The remaining columnar part of the window contains the following information:

◆ **Name**—This column lists the names of the frames in the animation.

◆ **Size**—This column shows the size of each frame, in pixels, with the width followed by the height. All frames do not have to have the same dimensions.

◆ **Position**—This column shows the position of the frame. The default position is 0,0, which means that the frame will be 0 pixels from the top and 0 pixels from the left edge of the animation. To change the position (that is, offset) of the frame, choose **Options: Frame Position** and fill in the dialog box.

ABOUT THIS ANIMATION—THE LIGHTHOUSE

litehous.gif 10K 80 x 110 Level: Medium

The lighthouse consists of a revolving light on a static base. This animation proves that you can use colors from the 216-color palette to add shadows and highlights.

- This animation is composed of nine GIFs, one repeated.
- The images are drawn in Adobe Illustrator and edited in Adobe Photoshop; the animation is created using GifBuilder.
- The body of the lighthouse is painted once, blue is added as the future transparent color.
- The borders between the lighthouse and blue are touched up pixel by pixel. Any mix of blue and the lighthouse colors results in an unwanted blue halo.
- After completing the lighthouse and transparent color, make nine copies of the file.
- Between the roof of the lighthouse and its body, add blobs of white paint. The borders between the "light beam" and blue must be touched up to avoid a blue halo.
- Each image shows a slow movement of the light beam toward the back. When the opposite beam should appear, add a small blob.
- When the beam points toward you, increase its size and add a yellow ring for emphasis.
- To build the animation, start at a head-on beam. Add frames showing the revolving light. The next to last frame is a repeat of the head-on beam, followed by the large beam.
- Set the animation to loop infinitely.
- This animation works best at a relatively high speed.

NOTE Offsetting is useful when animating a small image against a larger static background. (For more information about this type of animation, refer to the "Animating Part of an Image" section in Chapter 2.)

- **Disp**—This column indicates the disposal method; that is, the way in which the current frame replaces the previous one. To specify a disposal method, choose **Options: Disposal Method** and select a method from the submenu. For more information, see the "Disposing of a Frame" section later in this chapter.

◆ **Delay**—This column lists the interframe delay, which is the time between the display of one frame and the display of the next. To change the interframe delay, choose **Options: Interframe Delay** and fill in the dialog box. For more information, see the "Setting the Interframe Delay" section later in this chapter.

◆ **Trans**—This column indicates whether your animation has a transparent color. Unless each frame in the animation is rectangular, specifying transparency is critical. To set transparency, choose **Options: Transparent Background** and select a subcommand. For more information, see the "Specifying a Transparent Color" section later in this chapter.

GETTING READY TO ANIMATE

Before you start GifBuilder, it's a good idea to arrange all your image file icons in a small area of the desktop. Then, when you start the program, you'll be able to work without constantly rearranging or moving files around your desktop.

STARTING GIFBUILDER

 To start GifBuilder, open the GifBuilder folder and double-click on the **GifBuilder** icon. The menu bar and the empty Frames window open.

 NOTE When you need to edit an animation, plan on using the same program that you used to create the animation. Otherwise, small incompatibilities between animation programs may result in your spending unnecessary time in additional editing.

Creating an Animation

To animate a series of images in GifBuilder, follow these steps:

1. Start the program. GifBuilder opens an empty frame window and preview window.

 NOTE If the Frames window does not open, choose **Window: Frames Window**. If the Preview window does not open, choose **Window: Preview Window**.

2. Drag an image file into the Frames window. GifBuilder displays a line of information about the frame in the Frames window and shows the image in the Preview window.

 NOTE You can also add a file by choosing **File: Add Frame** or pressing **Command+K** and selecting from the resulting dialog box.

3. Continue adding image files in the order in which you want them to appear in the animation.

4. To change the order of a frame, drag it up or down until it is in the desired position. GifBuilder shows the current position with a horizontal line.

5. To test-run the animation from the first frame through the last, choose **Animation: Start**. You can do this at any time. The Animation menu also allows you to run the animation one frame at a time, pause it, and continue it.

 WARNING   Don't save the animation until you have selected all the options for it. If you save, you may not be able to perform all the edits that you would like.

EDITING AN ANIMATION

Creating an animation is just the beginning of the process. You can edit an animation one frame at a time, every frame, or a range of frames:

◆ To edit a single frame, select it and choose a menu command.

◆ To select the entire animation for editing, choose **Edit: Select All** or press **Command+A**.

◆ To select a range of frames, click on the first frame in the range, hold down the **Shift** key, and click on the last frame in the range.

Choosing a Color Palette

If you use the 216-color palette in your art program, you should ensure that you are using the proper palette by following these steps:

1. Select one or more frames.

2. Choose **Options: Colors** and select a subcommand:

◆ **System Palette**—The standard Macintosh system palette.

◆ **Gray Shades**—A 256-color gray scale palette.

◆ **Best Palette**—The colors used in the selected frames.

◆ **6×6×6**—The 216-color Netscape palette. This is the best choice.

Specifying a Transparent Color

Even though you may have set a transparent color in your art program, GifBuilder will not recognize this setting. If you want to define a transparent color, you'll have to do so in GifBuilder. To specify a color that will become transparent, follow these steps:

1. Select one or more frames.
2. Choose **Options: Transparent Background** and select a subcommand:
   - ◆ **No**—You will have no transparent color.
   - ◆ **White**—White is the transparent color.
   - ◆ **Based on First Pixel**—The color of the pixel in the upper- left corner of the frame is the transparent color. If the image within the frame is surrounded by a color, choose this option.
   - ◆ **Other**—This opens a color picker dialog box from which you can choose a transparent color using HSL or RGB values.

SHORTCUT To open the color picker dialog box, double-click on the Transp. column in the Frames window.

The Transp. column contains characters that indicate your transparent color choice.

- ◆ A dash (-) indicates no transparent color.
- ◆ W indicates white.
- ◆ 1 indicates the first pixel.
- ◆ A color box shows the transparent color chosen from the color picker dialog box.

Disposing of a Frame

The disposal method controls the look of each succeeding frame in an animation. When you select a transparent color and choose an inappropriate disposal method, unwanted parts of an image can remain in the image that follows.

To control frame disposal, follow these steps:

1. Select one or more frames.
2. Choose **Options: Disposal Method** and select a subcommand:
   - ◆ **Unspecified**—This subcommand replaces the entire current frame with the entire following frame. This is a good choice for frames for which you have not set transparent colors.
   - ◆ **Do Not Dispose**—This subcommand, the default, displays all the pixels that are not replaced by pixels in the following frame. The left-over pixels show through the transparent areas of the frame.
   - ◆ **Restore to Background**—This subcommand enables the background color of the Web page to show through the transparent parts of the current frame. This is a good choice for frames with transparent areas.
   - ◆ **Restore to Previous**—This subcommand displays the previous image.

The Disp. column contains characters that indicate your transparent color choice.

- ◆ U indicates **Unspecified**.
- ◆ N indicates **Do Not Dispose**.
- ◆ B indicates **Restore to Background**.
- ◆ P indicates **Restore to Previous**.

SHORTCUT To change the disposal method, select one or more frames and double-click to cycle through the choices.

Setting the Interframe Delay

To control the speed at which one frame follows another, follow these steps:

1. Select one or more frames.
2. Choose **Options: Interframe Delay** and select options from a dialog box:
   - ◆ Click on the **As Fast as Possible** option button to run at top speed.
   - ◆ In the text box, type a number representing one-hundredths of a second. For example, type 1 to set a speed of 1/100ths of a second, a very fast speed.

The Delay column contains the value that you entered in the text box, or a dash (-) if you selected **As Fast as Possible**.

SHORTCUT To open the dialog box in which you set the interframe delay, double-click on the Delay column in the Frames window.

ABOUT THIS ANIMATION—DEBORAH'S MOON

debmoon.gif 7K 85 x 85 Level: Medium)

Deborah's moon shows phases of the moon and ends with a profile of the man in the moon. As the moon grows larger, the sky and stars become brighter. The moon seems to rotate through its phases. The frames of this animation were created by hand by a landscape artist, were scanned into the computer, and painted and edited in Photoshop.

- ◆ This animation is composed of seven GIFs.
- ◆ The paper frames of the animation were scanned in as a single strip, cut, and pasted into individual images.
- ◆ The first frame (debmoon1) uses the darkest blue (0-0-51) from the 216-color palette. The stars are made completely white, pixel by pixel.
- ◆ The second frame (debmoon2) has a semi-transparent wash of blue to slightly dim the stars.
- ◆ The sky in the third frame (debmoon3) is the next lighter blue (0-0-102). Another wash of semi-transparent blue fades the stars further.

- ◆ The fourth and fifth frames keep the same sky color and the stars continue to fade.
- ◆ With the sixth frame, the stars are gone and a pale yellow (255-255-204) is applied to the moon.
- ◆ The last frame adds more yellow (255-255-102) to the moon.
- ◆ This animation should loop infinitely.
- ◆ The animation works best at a medium speed.

Looping an Animation

To loop an animation, follow these steps:

1. Choose **Options: Loop**. GifBuilder opens a dialog box.
2. To have the animation run once, click on the **No** option button.
3. To loop the animation endlessly, click on **Forever**.
4. To specify the number of times that the animation should loop, type a value in the text box.
5. Click on **OK**.

Optimizing an Animation

Before you save an animation, you can have GifBuilder optimize the animation. Simply choose **Options: Frame Optimization** any time before you save.

When you have GifBuilder optimize an animation, it will analyze each frame and remove pixels whose colors are duplicated in subsequent frames in an animation. So, the result will be smaller files, which means animations that load more quickly. For example, in a test animation, an unoptimized file was 29,921 bytes, and the optimized version was 20,740 bytes. Figure 9.2 shows a saved, optimized animation file in the Frames window.

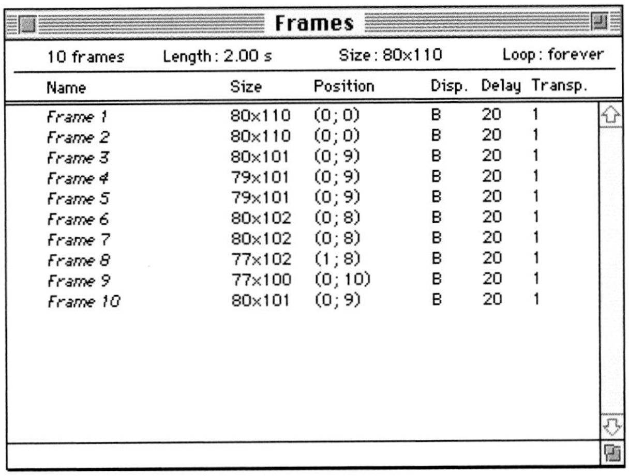

Frames

10 frames | Length: 2.00 s | Size: 80x110 | Loop: forever

Name	Size	Position	Disp.	Delay	Transp.
Frame 1	80x110	(0; 0)	B	20	1
Frame 2	80x110	(0; 0)	B	20	1
Frame 3	80x101	(0; 9)	B	20	1
Frame 4	79x101	(0; 9)	B	20	1
Frame 5	79x101	(0; 9)	B	20	1
Frame 6	80x102	(0; 8)	B	20	1
Frame 7	80x102	(0; 8)	B	20	1
Frame 8	77x102	(1; 8)	B	20	1
Frame 9	77x100	(0; 10)	B	20	1
Frame 10	80x101	(0; 9)	B	20	1

Figure 9.2 A saved, optimized animation file.

CREATING AN IMG TAG AUTOMATICALLY

You can have GifBuilder create an HTML statement for an animation. Simply choose **Edit: Copy HTML Image Tag**. GifBuilder copies a statement such as this:

```
<img src="litehous.gif" width=80 height=100>
```

to the Clipboard. Then, paste the statement into your HTML document.

An Incomplete History of Animation

Animation creates the illusion of motion through a series of changing images, each in a single *frame*. Using different techniques, such as drawing or painting on celluloid or photographing paper cutouts, puppets, or clay, animation artists have entertained and educated audiences since the early eighteenth century.

Today's animation techniques started many centuries ago in three different locations: Greece, Egypt, and China. Whether later scientists knew about the early discoveries of Aristotle, Ptolemy of Alexandria, or an unknown inventor in China is doubtful.

THE PERSISTENCE OF VISION

The basis for animation is the persistence of vision, a concept that resulted from the study of both light and the behavior and anatomy of the eye, as well as discoveries in 130 A.D. by Ptolemy and in 1824 by Peter Mark Roget. The *persistence of vision* is the retention of an image on the eye's retina after the image has been removed altogether or replaced by another image.

The retina retains a picture of an image for 0.1 second before processing the following image. So, if a series of images flashes by at a certain speed—at least 10 frames per second—the brain interprets the series as a single moving image. If the speed is too slow, the brain identifies each image, thus losing the concept of motion. However, if the speed is too fast, the effect is gone; the result is a blur. According to many studies, the retina must sense the break between the end of one image and the beginning of the next for the effect to take place.

Some psychologists dispute the importance of persistence of vision. Instead, they believe a better explanation is the *positive afterimage*, in which the brain retains the color and brightness of an image such as a light after it has been turned off or removed.

ANIMATION DEVICES

To illustrate the persistence of vision, Roget invented the *thaumatrope*, named by combining the Greek words *thaumato*, which means miracle or wonder, and *trope*, which means turning. A thaumatrope is a card or disk with a different picture on each side. When you attach strings to the left and right sides of the disk and spin the thaumatrope, the two pictures seem to merge.

The *phenakistoscope* was designed in 1831 or 1832 by Joseph Antoine Ferdinand Plateau, a Belgian physicist and mathematician. The phenakistoscope (from the Greek words *phenak*, which means cheat, and *scope*, which means instrument for viewing) is a disk with a series of images, hence the first film strip. When you rotate the disk, the images merge and appear to move, thereby cheating the eye. Many regard the phenakistoscope as the true parent of motion pictures.

 NOTE The Optisches Spielzeug oder wie die Bilder laufen lernten page (**http://www.rfl.de/fuesslin/ e_os.htm**) provides several illustrations of animation devices.

The *zoetrope* (from the Greek word zoe, meaning life), invented by Pierre Desvignes in 1834 (after having been invented in China in 180 A.D.), has two very contrasting names: the wheel of the devil and the wheel of life. The zoetrope is a drum that contains a long strip of paper around the bottom inside perimeter and a series of slits around the top perimeter. When you spin the zoetrope and view through the slits, you can see motion.

The close relative of the zoetrope, the *praxinoscope* (from the Greek word *praxi*, meaning action), was patented by Charles-Emile Reynaud in 1877. The praxinoscope has a shorter cylinder than the zoetrope and a set of mirrors around the center rather than slits. When you spin the praxinoscope and look at the mirror, you can see a moving image.

Imagine a strip of images for a zoetrope or praxinoscope cut into individual pictures, compiled into a booklet, and stapled at the top. When you riffle the pages, the images on the pictures seem to be moving. In effect, you have created a *flip-book*, another motion device.

All these early animation-viewing devices were human-powered, so the effect of motion depended strictly on the speed at which they moved.

 NOTE Ruth Hayes is an animator who is well-known for her flip-books. On her How to Make a Zoetrope page (**http://www.halcyon.com/rhayes/html/zoe2.html**), she gives comprehensive directions on making a zoetrope with modern materials. Her home page, Random Motion (**http://www.halcyon. com/rhayes/**), displays an animated flip-book, zoetrope, and movie projector.

PHOTOGRAPHY AND MOVEMENT

In the early nineteenth century, Nicéphore Niépce started experimenting with photography. In 1816 he had captured an image by exposing it for 8 hours, and by 1826 or 1827 he had taken what was considered to be the first true photograph. In 1829 Louis-Jacques Daguerre joined Niépce in his studies of photography, and by 1839 had commercialized the daguerrotype, a photographic exposure on silver.

Eadweard Muybridge, born Edward James Muggeridge in England, was known for his photographs of the Yosemite Valley and for inventing the automated camera shutter. With camera automation came the ability to study humans and animals in motion. In 1873, Leland Stanford, the former governor of California and a race-horse owner, hired Muybridge to study the movement of horses in order to improve his breeding program. Eventually, Muybridge adapted his motion photographs to the zoetrope. Figures A.1 and A.2 show examples of Muybridge's work.

Figure A.1 Two series of horse photographs by Muybridge.

Figure A.2 Muybridge's study of a running man, done around 1879.

EXPERIMENTS WITH MOTION PICTURES

In 1883 William Kennedy Laurie Dickson, an English engineer and amateur photographer, emigrated to the United States to work for Thomas Edison. During 1888 Edison charged Dickson with researching the possibility of making motion pictures. To gather information, Dickson interviewed Eadweard Muybridge, other motion photographers, and other photography experts.

During the same period, in 1884 George Eastman developed roll paper photographic "film," and in 1888 he produced the Kodak Brownie, the first portable camera for amateur photographers. The paper film proved to be too fragile. Dickson encouraged Eastman to contact Hannibal Goodwin, who had just invented celluloid film.

By November 1890 Dickson had constructed a camera and had made a short experimental motion picture using transparent celluloid roll film that Eastman was now manufacturing. Edison then assigned a team to work on the *kinetoscope*, with which a single individual could view a motion picture.

The coin-operated kinetoscope (from the Greek *kineto*, meaning movable) was patented by Edison in 1891. It used a sprocket system to move 50 feet of 35 millimeter film in an endless loop that an individual could watch, in a magnified version, through a peephole. In 1893 Edison opened the first film studio, the Black Maria, in a tarpaper shack in West Orange, New Jersey. By 1894 kinetoscope parlors were located in New York and Europe.

After seeing the kinetoscope in action, several inventors started developing film projectors for groups rather than individuals. The most prominent were the Lumière brothers, Louis and Auguste, who ran a photographic supplies factory in Lyons, France. Their hand-cranked lightweight cinématographe, introduced in 1895, was an instant success. The Lumières went on to produce many films, primarily from real life—the first documentaries.

Dickson encouraged Edison to buy the Vitascope camera and projector, which were based on the Phantascope projector, invented by Charles Francis Jenkins and Thomas Armat. Although audiences continued to pay for kinetoscope (and competing single-user projectors) peepshows into the early twentieth century, the era of group audiences and lengthier motion pictures had arrived.

THE EARLY FILMS

During the development of the first projectors, any motion picture attracted an audience. For example, the Lumières produced a series of films showing common events, such as workers leaving a factory and a gardener watering a lawn. Edison's early productions showed circus acts, dancing girls, and actors performing dramatic pieces. Edwin Porter joined Edison in 1897 and, a few years later, produced the classic silent films *The Life of an American Fireman* (1902) and *The Great Train Robbery* (1903) for the Edison studio.

In 1896 Georges Méliès, a French magician, produced the first of about 500 films. One of his first motion pictures used special effects to show his shoes walking across the floor and his clothes disappearing. Other Méliès films covered subjects such as Cinderella, Cleopatra, Hamlet, and even the Dreyfus trial. One of his best known works is *A Trip to the Moon* (*Le Voyage Dans La Lune*) which he made in 1902. It combined actors, drawings, animation, and other special effects. Figures A.3 and A.4 show two images from *A Trip to the Moon*.

Figure A.3 An image of the sun from *A Trip to the Moon*.

Figure A.4 The man in the moon with an embedded rocket.

EARLY CARTOONS AND THEIR MAKERS

The innovator and magician Méliès truly fit into the early age of film animation, which included inventors, comic strip artists, and entrepreneurs.

James Stuart Blackton

James Stuart Blackton is considered the first true animator. In 1900 he added animated smoke to a scene, and in 1906 he produced the first completely animated cartoon, the *Humorous Phases of a Funny Face*.

Winsor McCay

Newspaper comic strip artists, such as Winsor McCay, quickly became interested in animated movies. McCay, who started as a graphic artist, later drew political cartoons and other illustrations for the *Cincinnati Times Star*. McCay started drawing the *Little Nemo* (Figure A.5) comic strip around the turn of the century. While touring the United States as a vaudeville caricaturist, McCay met James Stuart Blackton. Based on conversations with Blackton and a child's flip-book, McCay created a 4,000-frame, hand-colored Little Nemo film between 1908 and 1911.

Figure A.5 Winsor McCay based his first animated film on his comic strip character Little Nemo.

In 1912 he released *The Story of a Mosquito*, and in 1914, the 10,000-frame *Gertie the Dinosaur*. In 1917 he introduced *The Sinking of the Lusitania*, which had 25,000 frames.

Max Fleischer and the Fleischer Studios

Max Fleischer also began as a newspaper cartoonist. In 1915 J. R. Bray, an animation pioneer, hired Fleischer to make instructional films. Fleischer and his brother Dave founded the Fleischer Studios, whose earliest character Koko the Clown starred in *Out of the Inkwell* (1915) and other cartoon films. The Fleischer Studios created Betty Boop in 1930 and Popeye in 1936.

Max Fleischer also experimented with many animation techniques. He invented rotoscoping, with which an animator draws or paints over live-action frames that are projected onto a drawing table. Used for the first time in *Out of the Inkwell*, rotoscoping continues today in features such as *Who Framed Roger Rabbit* (1988) and *Beauty and the Beast* (1991). He also was a pioneer in three-dimensional effects.

Otto Messmer

Under the name of Master Tom, Felix the Cat appeared in his first cartoon late in 1919. Felix was the first cartoon to be featured in a comic strip, reversing the usual trend. Pat Sullivan produced the series, but the Sullivan employee Otto Messmer originated the character and animated the Felix cartoons. Felix was the first cartoon character to be heavily merchandised. When sound films became popular, the series faltered; the studio's attempts at adding sound fell short of the *synchronized sound* (a recording on a disk was synchronized with the images in the film) used by The Disney Brothers Studio.

Walt Disney

By 1920 Hollywood studios employed 20,000 people, and 35 million movie tickets sold each week. During that year, Walt Disney, while working at the Kansas City (Missouri) Film Ad Service, sold his first animated film. Early in 1921 Disney made the first of a series of short comedy animated and live-action films. In 1923 he started the *Alice* series, in which a real girl lived in a cartoon world and moved to Los Angeles.

Disney came into the limelight with *Steamboat Willie* (1928), which was animated by Ub Iwerks and starred Mickey Mouse and Minnie Mouse. *Steamboat Willie* used a synchronized musical score written by Carl Stalling, later famous for his work on Warner Brothers cartoons.

Disney was well known for his innovations. He was the first to use a *storyboard* to lay out a complete story before starting animation. He also kept up with the latest technologies in color and sound and insisted that his animators study motion. And although the artistry of Disney films was sometimes questioned, the personalities of his characters always shone through.

Today the company, now Walt Disney Productions, is an innovator in computer animation and other technologies as well as in marketing its products.

The Warner Brothers and Leon Schlesinger

The four Warner brothers started as film distributors in 1903. By 1913 they turned to film production. Sam Warner, the leader, invested in the Vitaphone synchronized sound system and introduced synchronized sound in the film *Don Juan* (1926). In 1927 the studio produced *The Jazz Singer*, the first film with spoken dialogue.

In 1929 Rudy Ising and Hugh Harmon, who started at Disney, approached Leon Schlesinger, who had helped finance *The Jazz Singer*, with the idea of a cartoon series that would compete against Disney's Silly Symphonies and use a voice soundtrack, an improvement over Disney's synchronized sound. The next year, Schlesinger, Ising, and Harmon along with Isadore (Friz) Freleng, the head animator, and Rollin Hamilton, an animator, began Looney Tunes, Warner Brothers' cartoon division.

After Ising and Harmon left, Schlesinger attracted such animators as Chuck Jones, Bob Clampett, Tex Avery, Frank Tashlin, and Robert McKimson; the musical director Carl Stalling; and Mel Blanc, the voice of 90% of the Looney Tunes characters. Until 1940 the group worked in the "Termite Terrace," a small building at the studio.

Through the years, the Warner group created many innovative and sometimes artistic cartoons and introduced characters such as Bugs Bunny, Porky Pig, and Daffy Duck. Schlesinger left Warner Brothers in 1944. The Looney Tunes division closed in 1962.

EXPERIMENTAL ANIMATION

During the same time that many animators were creating popular cartoons for mass audiences, others experimented with animation as a serious art form.

The first experimental animator-artist was Emile Cohl, who like Winsor McCay was a caricaturist and comic strip artist and like Méliès was a magician. In addition, he began as a jeweler's apprentice and served in the French military. Cohl made his first animated film, *Fantasmagorie*, in 1908 at the Gaumont movie studio.

Through the years, artists have experimented with all types of media (paper cutouts, puppets, a variety of objects, clay, melted wax, and even insects) and many techniques (combining actors and cartoons, stopping and even rewinding film, painting images directly on film or on glass, tinting film, and stirring oil), covering many subjects—from daily life to the wildest fantasies.

Occasionally, experimental animators have crossed the line from art for art's sake to commerce or from commerce to art. For example, John Hubley, who started at Disney and worked on *Snow White* (1939) and *Bambi* (1942), left for United Productions of America (UPA). As chief director, he encouraged the animators to create modern, minimalist characters and background instead of the realistic look of popular cartoons. Oskar Fischinger was a German artist who went in the other direction. After Hitler came to power, he left his animation company in Frankfurt and moved to Hollywood where he worked for Paramount, MGM, and Disney—with mixed results. He quarreled with management over both artistry and payments. Finally, in the mid 1940s, he painted oils and only rarely created animated advertisements.

Appendix B surveys the animation techniques used to develop popular cartoons, experimental animation, and animated GIFs.

Traditional Animation Techniques

Animation is the presentation of a series of still pictures at a certain rate of speed—usually 24 pictures, or frames, per second. Over many years, animators have developed several animation techniques, most of which you can apply to your GIF animation work on the computer. This appendix includes a brief discussion of each technique.

DRAWING AND PAINTING ON CELS

Many of the true animation pioneers, such as Winsor McCay and Emile Cohl, drew with pen and ink or painted on paper or *cels*, frames of celluloid. In the original animated movies, each frame was a complete drawing: the movable character or object in the foreground and the more static background scene. Each film was made up of many cels—there were approximately 24 frames for each second of film. To create 1 minute of action, an animator had to draw 1,440 pictures, a time-consuming activity. For example, Winsor McCay's very short 1911 cartoon, based on his *Little Nemo* comic strip, comprised 4,000 drawings and took 3 years to complete. McCay's 1914 cartoon, *Gertie the Dinosaur*, was made up of 10,000 drawings. As cartoons got longer, they required many more drawings. For example, the 1937 feature-length Disney cartoon *Snow White and the Seven Dwarfs* was comprised of about 477,000 drawings. Obviously, Disney did not spend more than 350 person-years (based on McCay's *Little Nemo* schedule) to create *Snow White*.

To streamline animation, in 1914 John R. Bray started experimenting with separating the components of each frame. He developed the following three-step process:

1. He painted the background, which was hand-copied onto many sheets of tracing paper.
2. He drew the foreground animation on opaque paper.
3. He layered the tracing paper background on top of the opaque paper foreground to create the entire frame.

Bray and his colleague Earl Hurd further refined the system by drawing the foreground animation on celluloid, which was both transparent and stronger than paper.

Today, those who create animated films using hand-drawn cels split up the work even more. Experienced animators draw the most important foreground animations, and junior animators, also known as *in-betweeners*, draw the less important animations in between. Other animators specialize in drawing backgrounds.

Often, the frames are made up of a few component pictures: the background, characters or objects that move less than the main character or object, and the main character or object, which moves the most. Animators even change the position of some of the background pictures to show movement. For example, to show a primary character running toward the right, they may move the background a little to the left with each frame. Some animators separate drawings with panes of glass to create a three-dimensional effect.

STOP-MOTION ANIMATION

Stop-motion animation, which has been in existence at least as long as painting and drawing on cels, is the posing and filming of a variety of objects—from live humans to dead insects to scale models—one frame at a time. Several early filmmakers, including Arthur Melbourne-Cooper, James Stuart Blackton, and Georges Méliès, worked in stop-motion.

Posing humans for stop-motion animation is known as *pixillation*. Instead of moving at their regular speed or at their usual gait, the humans are posed to show some movement. For example, a fixed camera can shoot 24 frames of a human posed in 24 distinct locations in a room, such as at a doorway, by a window, in the middle of the room, at another window, in a corner, and so on. The result is a 1-second film that shows the human jumping around the room at an impossible pace. If the camera shoots two or three duplicate frames per position, the human moves a little more slowly but still behaves much differently than a human walking, jumping, or running around the room in a live-action film. The Beatles' film *A Hard Day's Night* contains fine examples of pixillation.

Another stop-action technique is time-lapse photography, in which a fixed camera shoots a frame every few minutes, hours, or days. The most common time-lapse effects show seeds sprouting into seedlings, clouds racing by the camera, or automobiles moving along a multilane highway. Some of the first examples of time-lapse photography were Edwin S. Porter's 1901 Edison film *Pan-American Exposition by Night* and *Star Theater*, which shows the demolition of a Manhattan building.

Unlike cel animation, stop-motion animation is three-dimensional. Animators pose three-dimensional objects on sets—usually miniature—that are much like theater sets.

The first major use of stop-motion animation was in the 1933 full-length feature film *King Kong*, which combined stop-motion animation with live-action. Recent stop-motion films include Tim Burton's 1993 Disney film *Nightmare Before Christmas* and the 1996 Disney film *James and the Giant Peach*—both of which relied on computers to control the stop-motion effects.

Puppet and Clay Animation

Those who animate puppets and clay represent an important segment of stop-motion animation. For each frame of an animated film, these animators pose and shoot one or more movable characters in miniature sets. To indicate movement or emotion, animators resculpt arms, legs, and heads, which is time-consuming, or pop replacement limbs and heads into place.

Renowned puppet and clay animators include George Pal, the inventor of the replacement system; Art Clokey, who created the television character Gumby; and Will Vinton, who invented

Claymation™ for both film and advertisements. The British animator, Nick Park, has produced Oscar-winning films starring Wallace, a bumbling detective, and Gromit, his intelligent and long-suffering dog. Each half-hour Wallace and Gromit film takes at least two years from start to finish.

Go-Motion Animation

When the action in a live-action film speeds up, frames actually blur and the brain expects to see blurred images. Because stop-motion animation, like other animation, simulates movement, there is no blur.

To correct the lack of blur, Phil Tippett, a stop-motion and special-effects guru, developed go-motion, which adds motion blur to an animation. The first film in which go-motion was used was *Dragonslayer*, the 1981 Walt Disney/Paramount film.

ON-FILM ANIMATION

Earlier in this appendix, you learned that many of the first animators drew or painted frame by frame and then shot the completed frames. In contrast, using on-film animation, an animator works directly on the film, which has already been developed or will never be developed.

Scratching, Drawing, and Painting on Film

Although it was first used in the 1930s, scratching, drawing, and painting on film is one of the newer forms of animation. In on-film animation, the animator scratches the film with a tool, draws on it using pen and ink or marker pens, paints directly on it, or even applies ink with a small rubber stamp. When the last frame is complete, the film is ready to be shown.

Coloring and Tinting

In the early days of animation, before color film came on the scene, many animators used tinting, toning, and hand-tinting to add color to their films. Animators *tinted* a film by dipping it in a dye solution that applied color to the white areas of the film. They *toned* a film by dipping it in a solution that added color to the emulsion (i.e., the black areas) of the film. Animators *hand-tinted* films by painting directly on each frame. Experienced professionals could work with all three processes on a film, resulting in a mix of colors.

ART UNDER THE CAMERA

Under-the-camera animation is probably more closely related to painting on canvas and other classical painting techniques than any other form of animation. An under-the-camera animator works with one frame at a time, using paint or colored oil, cutouts, jointed figures, or the pinscreen. The animator creates an image on a horizontal surface and shoots the completed work with a camera that is fixed above the work—hence, under the camera. For the next frame, the animator creates a new work in the work area (thus replacing the previous image) and shoots a new photograph. So, at any one time, there is only one piece of artwork, which is gone forever when the animator replaces it with the next frame.

One of the most famous under-the-camera works is Lotte Reiniger's 1926 feature-length animated film *The Adventures of Prince Ahmed* (*Die Abenteur des Prinzen Achmed*), which used paper cutouts.

Oil Wiping

In oil-wiping animation, a rarely used under-the-camera technique, a tray filled with several colored oils that do not mix is stirred with a tool or finger to make interesting patterns, which are shot with a fixed camera over the tray. The animator pours colored oils into the tray and stirs the oils, photographing frames as the combination of oils is pleasing to the eye.

Pinscreen Animation

Developed by Alexandre Alexeieff and Claire Parker in the 1930s, pinscreen animation, an under-the-camera technique, uses tens of thousands or hundreds of thousands of pins inserted in a white board to create a three-dimensional white-gray-black animation. The animator moves pins to create a picture. If the animator pulls a pin away from the board so that it extends its full length, the effect is black; the pin "throws" a black shadow onto the white board. If he or she pushes a pin so that it is flush with the board, the effect is white; there is no shadow. Pins adjusted between those two extremes produce various gray effects that become darker as a pin's shadow lengthens. When the pins are adjusted properly, the animator shoots a frame with a fixed camera and starts adjusting the pinscreen for the next frame. As you might expect, pinscreen animation is a very time-consuming process, and frames that must be reshot are very difficult to reconstruct.

ROTOSCOPING

Rotoscoping is a process of tracing over three-dimensional live-action shots to create a two-dimensional animation. Using rotoscoping, the animator does not have to be a master of anatomy or movement. He or she shoots a live-action sequence and then projects it, one frame at a time, as a guide for drawing or painting on cels. The cartoonist Max Fleischer invented rotoscoping and used it extensively in his *Out of the Inkwell* series, which started in 1915. The Fleischer Studio also used rotoscoping to create its Betty Boop series, which ran from 1930 to 1939. Disney also used rotoscoping in its animated films.

THE OPTICAL PRINTER

The optical printer, which, for the most part, has been replaced by the computer, is a camera that shoots frames from projected films, combining several films into one. Animators use optical cameras to combine animations with live-action, to change the speed of film to slow or fast, or to create special effects such as Superman superimposed over a city scene.

As the projector runs, the operator of the optical printer shoots the projected film, eliminating or adding frames, changing the size and appearance of the projected film, and combining images.

COMPUTER ANIMATION

The advent of microcomputers changed animation techniques in two ways: it improved the quality of individual drawings and accurately generates characters and animations. Using today's sophisticated drawing programs, an animator can apply special effects with a few mouse clicks. It's easy to make a copy of a drawing, to make subtle changes to the copy to indicate movement, and to save the edited drawing as a new file. By repeating that process, an animator can quickly create a series of frames. With a computer animation system, an animator can draw the first and last frames and let the computer fill in the rest. Or, an animator can draw a model of a character and let the animation system add the details, such as colors, shadows, and automated movement.

A Timeline of Animation and Related Subjects

This appendix lists events in the history of animation and both related and unrelated occurrences along the way.

c340 B.C.—Aristotle (384–322), in *Parva Naturalia*, states his observations about the principles of light and motion aftereffects.

c130 A.D.—Claudius Ptolemaeus (c90–168), known as Ptolemy, the Greek astronomer and geographer, discovers the persistence of vision.

180—In China, an unknown invents a zoetrope.

1451—The German goldsmith and printer Johannes Gutenberg (1400–1468) prints a German poem on his printing press using his discovery, movable type.

1604—The German astronomer Johan Kepler (1571–1630) explains the optics of the eye.

1611—Kepler develops the projection theory of stereoscopic vision.

1625—Christoph Scheiner (1573–1650), who discovered sunspots, observes the retinal image.

1676—The Danish astronomer Olaus Roemer (1644–1710) measures the speed of light.

1709—Professor István Simándi of Hungary creates a projector to educate using animations.

1727—Scientists discover that silver nitrate darkens when exposed to light.

1816—The French chemist and inventor Joseph Nicéphore Niépce (1765–1833) captures a photographic image with an 8-hour exposure.

1816—Sir David Brewster (1781–1868), a Scottish physicist, invents the kaleidoscope. Later, he improved the stereoscope (see 1833) by adding refracting lenses.

1824—Peter Mark Roget (1779–1869), a physician and creator of *Roget's Thesaurus*, presents a paper on the persistence of vision to the British Royal Society and demonstrates this effect with his thaumatrope.

1825—The Czech physiologist Jan Evangelista Purkinje (1787–1869) describes motion aftereffect. It is said that Aristotle and Lucretius also described it.

1826—Niépce makes the first photograph using a *camera obscura*, a small room with a built-in lens, and a metal plate made of pewter.

1829—The French painter and inventor Louis-Jacques Mandé Daguerre (1789–1851) and Niépce agree to study photography together.

1831—The Belgian physicist Joseph Antoine Ferdinand Plateau (1801–1883) invents the phenakistoscope. Plateau is known for damaging his eyesight by looking at the sun. He was blind by 1840.

1833—The English physicist and inventor Sir Charles Wheatstone (1802–1875) invents the stereoscope, a device with which an individual views two pictures simultaneously. This results in a three-dimensional effect. Wheatstone also invented the concertina.

1833—The English mathematician Charles Babbage (1792–1871) invents the analytical engine, the predecessor of the digital computer.

1837—Daguerre captures a photographic image in 20 minutes.

1837—Wheatstone and Sir William Fothergill Cooke (1806–1879) patent the electric telegraph.

1839—Daguerre commercializes the daguerrotype, using silver-plated copper sheets treated with iodine vapor.

1839—The English physicist and inventor William Henry Fox Talbot (1800–1877) prints multiple photographs from paper negatives on silver chloride-coated paper, using the calotype method.

1843—The English writer and mathematician Augusta Ada, Countess of Lovelace (1815–1852), publishes the *Sketch of the Analytical Engine*, her notes explaining a computer.

1844—Talbot published *Pencil of Nature*, the first book illustrated with photographs.

1844—The American inventor and artist Samuel Finley Breese Morse (1791–1872) sends the first telegraph message between Baltimore and Washington.

1846—The German optician and industrialist Carl Zeiss (1816–1888) begins manufacturing camera lenses.

1851—In England, Talbot takes the first flash photograph using an electric spark.

1855—The English chemist and inventor Alexander Parkes (1813–1890) invents xylonite, a form of celluloid.

1859—The first wide-angled lens is produced.

1861—The American inventor Coleman Sellers (1827–1907) patents the kinematoscope, which flashes a series of photographs on a screen.

1861—The first color photographic process was developed.

1861—In the United States, the first transcontinental telegraph system begins.

1865—The German physiologist and psychologist Ewald Hering (1834–1918) and the German physiologist and physicist Hermann Ludwig Ferdinand von Helmholtz (1821–1894) perform the first measurements of stereoscopic acuity.

1866—English-born American Edweard Muybridge (1830–1904) becomes a professional photographer.

1867—Étienne Jules Marey (1830–1903), the French scientist and inventor, starts studying animal motion.

1869—The French inventor and poet, Émile Hortensius Charles Cros (1842–1888) publishes his theory of three-color photography.

1871—The American inventor Thomas Alva Edison (1847–1931) creates the stock ticker.

1872—Leland Stanford (1824–1893) commissions Muybridge to study the motion of horses. He finally is successful in 1877 because he has to wait until then for faster speed photography.

1876—The Scottish professor Alexander Graham Bell (1847–1922) patents the telephone, beating the American Elisha Gray (1835–1901), the manufacturer of telegraph equipment and founder of Western Electric, and his challenge in the U.S. Supreme Court.

1877—Cros invents the paléophone, a phonograph.

1877—The French inventor Charles-Emile Reynaud (1844–1918) patents the praxinoscope.

1877—Edison invents the gramophone (a phonograph) and the carbon microphone.

1878—The English inventor, chemist, and physicist Sir William Crookes (1832–1919) develops the cathode ray tube, a vacuum tube that is the predecessor of television.

1879—Edison invents the incandescent light bulb.

1880—Muybridge designs the zoopraxiscope, a version of the zoetrope, to show his animal motion photographs.

1880—The first photographs appear in newspapers.

1882—Marey produces the first single multi-image camera, the chronophotographic gun camera, which takes a series of 12 small photographs in 1 second.

1883—Edison discovers the Edison effect, or thermionic emission, the basis of broadcast tubes.

1884—In Germany, Paul Nipkow (1860–1940) invents an early version of television, a mechanical scanning disc.

1884—George Eastman (1854–1932) develops paper photographic roll film.

1886—Edison hires Reginald Aubrey Fessenden (1866–1932) as his chief chemist.

1887—Hannibal Goodwin (1822–1900), an Episcopalian minister living in New Jersey, invents celluloid film.

1888—German-born American inventor Émile Berliner (1851–1928) demonstrates a flat disc gramophone record.

1888—Eastman introduces the box camera, which uses his paper roll film.

1888—Edison charges William Kennedy Laurie Dickson (1860–1937) with researching the possibility of making motion pictures.

1889—Eastman develops flexible roll film using a nitro-cellulose base.

1890—Dickson constructs a camera and makes a short experimental motion picture using transparent celluloid roll film. Edison assigns a team to work on the kinetoscope.

1890—In England, William Friese-Greene (1855–1921) builds the kinematograph camera and projector, which use celluloid film.

1891—Edison patents the coin-operated Kinetoscope, a hand-cranked projector for individual viewers.

1892—Eastman starts the Eastman Kodak Company.

1893—In West Orange, New Jersey, Edison opens the first film studio, the Black Maria, a tarpaper shack that rotates on tracks in order to use the sun for illumination.

1893—In Chicago, Muybridge opens the Zoopraxographical Hall, a theater in which to show his motion pictures.

1894—Kinetoscope parlors open in New York and Europe.

1895—Émile Berliner develops a method of making several shellac copies of a record from a master record. In 1915, he invents acoustic tile.

1895—Auguste Marie Louis Nicolas Lumière (1862–1954) and Louis Jean Lumière (1864–1948) create the Cinématographe, a hand-cranked projector weighing less than 20 pounds. On December 28, the Lumière brothers give their first public showing at the Grand Café, Boulevard des Capucines, Paris. The design of the theater is adapted from Reynaud's Theatre Optique.

1895—The Lumières release their first motion picture, *La Sortie des Usines Lumière*.

1895—Dickson, with E. B. Koopman, Henry N. Marvin, and Herman Casler, founds the American Mutoscope and Biograph Company, known later as American Biograph or Biograph.

1896—In England, Guglielmo Marconi (1874–1937) patents wireless telegraphy.

1896—Dickson patents the American Biograph camera and projector.

1896—Charles Francis Jenkins and Thomas Armat design the Phantascope projector for group showings. Edison buys the system and names it the Vitascope.

1896—James Stuart Blackton (1875–1941), with Albert E. Smith, founds the Vitagraph film studio. Warner Brothers buys Vitagraph in 1925.

1896—Charles Pathé (1863–1957) founds Pathé Frères with his brother Émile.

1897—A fire in the Bazar de la Charité theater kills 140.

1897—Itinerant exhibitors buy projectors and films and go on the road.

1897—Edwin Stanton Porter (1870–1941), soon to be called the father of the story film, joins Edison's company. He works for Edison until 1909.

1897—The French magician Georges Méliès (1861–1938) constructs a film studio at his residence.

1899—The Danish engineer Valdemar Poulsen (1869–1942) records sound magnetically. In 1900, he patents the Telegraphone wire recording system, the predecessor to the magnetic tape recorder.

1899—The American Marconi Company, the predecessor to RCA, is started.

1899—The Englishman Arthur Melbourne-Cooper animates matches in the stop-action film *Matches: An Appeal*.

1900—Eastman Kodak introduces its Brownie camera.

1900—Blackton makes *The Enchanted Drawing*, a combination of live-action and animation, for Edison.

1900—Color and sound film is demonstrated at the Paris Exposition.

1901—Edison opens a film studio at East 21st Street in Manhattan.

1901—Porter uses time-lapse photography to film the *Pan-American Exposition by Night*.

1901—A newsreel shows Queen Victoria's funeral.

1901—Marconi sends wireless signals across the Atlantic Ocean.

1901—Fessenden starts experimenting with voice transmission. He later invented amplitude modulation (that is, AM).

1902—The U.S. Supreme Court decides that Edison did not invent the motion picture but had combined the discoveries of other inventors.

1902—Méliès releases *A Trip to the Moon*, a 14-minute film with 30 scenes.

1902—Pathé acquires the Lumière patents and opens a studio in Vincennes.

1903—Porter releases the 6-minute film *Life of an American Fireman* and the 12-minute film *The Great Train Robbery*, which is comprised of 14 separate shots.

1903—American Biograph opens an indoor studio on East 14th Street in Manhattan.

1904—Winsor Zezic McCay (1867–1934), a comic strip artist, produces the cartoon *Dreams of a Rarebit Fiend* for Edison.

1904—The comic book is introduced.

1904—Over 8,000 nickelodeons (movie theaters) are open in the United States.

1905—Pathé uses machines to apply color to black-and-white films.

1906—Fessenden broadcasts the first American radio program from Brant Rock, Massachusetts.

1906—The American physicist and inventor Lee de Forest (1873–1961), the father of radio, invents the Audion, the three-element vacuum tube known today as the triode.

1906—Blackton releases his animated film, *Humorous Phases of a Funny Face*.

1907—David Wark Griffith (1875–1948) begins work as a motion picture actor.

1907—The first film company arrives in Los Angeles.

1907—Late in the year, Chicago starts censoring movies.

1907—De Forest starts the first regular radio broadcasts.

1908—About 20 film companies are in existence.

1908—Melbourne-Cooper animates toys in the stop-action film *Dreams of Toyland*.

1908—Emile Cohl (1857–1938), a French caricaturist, comic strip artist, and magician produces *Fantasmagorie*, a frame-by-frame animated film.

1908—McCay, the producer of the *Little Nemo* comic strip, starts work on his first Little Nemo animated film, completed in 1911 and composed of 4,000 drawings.

1908—The Motion Picture Patents Company (MPPC) pools the 16 most significant film patents. The company closes in 1918 after many court battles.

1908—American Biograph hires Griffith.

1909—Pathé starts producing newsreels in France. The next year, the company introduces newsreels in the United States.

1909—Vitagraph releases *The Life of Moses*, a five-reel live-action film.

1910—American Biograph starts winter filming in Los Angeles.

1910—There are now about 13,000 theaters in the United States with sales of 26 million tickets per week at about seven cents per ticket. The average show consists of three 10-minute reels.

1910—John R. Bray (1879–1978) produces *The Dachsund and the Sausage*, the first animated film to tell a story.

1911—Mack Sennett (1884–1960) produces his first Keystone Kops comedy.

1911—Pathé starts distributing Méliès' films.

1912—Movie cameras with motors replace hand-cranked cameras.

1912—McCay adapts *The Newlyweds and Their Baby*, the George McManus comic strip, into the first animated series.

1912—Edison produces the first talking motion pictures.

1912—Warner Brothers, Fox, and Universal start operations.

1913—The first serial, *The Adventures of Kathlyn*, is released.

1914—Charlie Chaplin (1889–1977) introduces his tramp character.

1914—McCay releases the *Gertie the Trained Dinosaur* cartoon, which has 10,000 drawings.

1914—Bray starts experimenting with separate static background and animated foreground frames. He joins with Earl Hurd to refine the system, eventually drawing the foreground animations on transparent celluloid.

1914—Pathé produces the serial, *The Perils of Pauline*.

1914—The 3,300-seat Strand Theater opens in Manhattan.

1914—Frederick Eugene Ives (1856–1937), the inventor of the photographic halftone process, experiments with natural colors for motion pictures.

1915—Griffith releases the 159-minute-long *Birth of a Nation*.

1915—Austrian-born American Max Fleischer (1883–1972), with his brother Dave (1894–1979), releases *Out of the Inkwell*, the first animated film to use his invention, rotoscoping. The Fleischer brothers also created sing-along cartoons with bouncing balls to indicate the proper place in the lyrics.

1915—More than 60% of American movie production takes place in Hollywood. The industry now employs 15,000 workers.

1915—Vachel Lindsay (1879–1931) publishes *The Art of the Moving Picture*.

1916—Bray starts a cartoon series from the comic strip *Colonel Heeza Liar*, based on some of the traits of Theodore Roosevelt.

1916—Griffith releases *Intolerance*, which is 178 minutes long.

1916—The number of movie tickets sold each week in the United States reaches 10 million, and the number of movie palaces (theaters) is over 21,000.

1917—The International Feature Syndicate introduces *Krazy Kat*.

1917—Joseph Francis "Buster" Keaton (1895–1966) makes his first film, *The Butcher Boy*.

1917—Otto Messmer (1894–1985), later known for Felix the Cat, animates *The Charlie Chaplin Cartoons*.

1918—McCay creates *The Sinking of the Lusitania*, the first dramatic documentary cartoon.

1919—Walt Disney (1901–1966) and Ubbe Iwwerks (later Ub Iwerks) (1901–1971) form Iwerks-Disney Commercial Artists. The company goes bankrupt the next year.

1919—Pat Sullivan Studios releases the first Felix the Cat cartoon, drawn by Otto Messmer.

1919—The United Artists studio starts operations.

1919—Lee de Forest patents Phonofilm, a sound-on-film process.

1919—The Soviet Union nationalizes its film industry.

1919—The Tri-Ergon sound-on-film system is patented in Germany.

1920—Walt Disney produces and sells his first animated film. Milton Feld contracts Walt Disney to produce 12 cartoons, to be shown at Newman Theaters and known as Newman's Laugh-O-grams. The first is shown in 1921.

1920—Paul Terry (1887–1971) and Howard Estabrook introduce the Farmer Alfalfa character in Pathé's *Aesop's Fables* series.

1920—The number of people employed at Hollywood studios reaches 20,000, and the number of movie tickets sold each week reaches 35 million.

1922—Bray Studios assign particular animation tasks to specific departments and workers and also use some live-action editing techniques.

1922—Walt Disney and his employees produce Lafflets, a series of short films, incorporates Laugh-O-gram films, and releases the first Laugh-O-gram film, *The Four Musicians of Bremen*. Disney continues to work at his full-time job at the Kansas City Film Ad Company.

1922—On August 28, WEAF, in New York City, runs the first radio commercial.

1922—Marconi transmits short waves using a parabolic reflector behind an antenna.

1922—Herbert T. Kalmus, a 1915 graduate of the Massachusetts Institute of Technology, creates the Technicolor two-color process for movies. His wife, Natalie (1892–1965), publicizes and sells the Technicolor package deal to studios, thereby enabling Technicolor to monopolize the market until 1950.

1922—Ub Iwerks joins Laugh-O-gram Films.

1922—The first three-dimensional movie, requiring spectacles with one red and one green lens, is released.

1922—*Nanook of the North*, a 55-minute film thought of as the first documentary, is released.

1922—Fox Movietone News experiments with de Forest's Phonofilm sound process.

1923—In New York City, de Forest shows *Phonofilm*, the first sound-on-film motion picture.

1923—Laugh-O-gram Films, borrowing some of Max Fleisher's techniques, produces *Alice's Wonderland*, a combination of live-action and cartoon characters. After Laugh-O-gram goes bankrupt, later the same year, Walt Disney and Roy Disney (1893–1971) found The Disney Brothers Studio and start work on the Alice Comedies series.

1923—The Russian-born American physicist Vladimir Kosma Zworykin (1889–1982) invents the electronic iconoscope camera tube and kinescope display tube, another step toward television.

1923—Eastman's Kodak company introduces movie equipment for amateur filmmakers.

1923—The first neon advertising signs appear.

1924—Columbia Pictures starts operations, and MGM is formed.

1925—Western Electric markets Vitaphone, a sound-on-disc process.

1925—The Russian director Sergei Mikhailovich Eisenstein (1898–1948) creates the 65-minute film *Battleship Potemkin*.

August 1926—Warner Brothers' *Don Juan*, starring John Barrymore (1882–1942), is the first silent film released with Vitaphone music, played by the New York Philharmonic, and sound effects.

1926—The number of people employed at Hollywood studios reaches 300,000, and the number of movie tickets sold each week in the United States reaches 50 million.

1926—The German animator Lotte Reiniger (1899–1981) produces the first feature-length animated film, *The Adventures of Prince Ahmed* (*Die Abenteur des Prinzen Achmed*).

1926—Disney starts producing cartoons starring Oswald the Lucky Rabbit. The first Oswald cartoon appears in 1927.

1927—Warner Brothers releases 89-minute-long *The Jazz Singer*, starring Al Jolson (1886–1950). The first popular "talkie" uses Vitaphone technology for this mostly silent film with some talk and music.

1927—The French silent film *Napoleon* (235 min), directed by Abel Gance (1889–1981), is filmed in part-widescreen triptych.

1927—Fox Movietone News begins releasing sound newsreels using the Phonofilm sound process.

1927—Isadore (Friz) Freleng (1905–1995) starts working for Disney Studios.

1928—The Scottish electrical engineer John Logie Baird (1888–1946) shows the first television image.

1928—General Electric, Westinghouse, and RCA found RKO Radio Pictures Corporation.

May 1928—Disney releases *Plane Crazy*, the first silent film featuring Ub Iwerks' creation, Mickey Mouse. Disney patents Mickey Mouse the same month.

July 1928—Disney releases the Mickey Mouse film *Steamboat Willie*, which uses synchronized sound. Carl Stalling, later the Looney Tunes musical director, composes the score.

1928—*Lights of N.Y.* is the first all-talking film.

1928—The number of movie tickets sold each week in the United States doubles from 1926, reaching 110 million.

1929—Alfred Hitchcock (1899–1980) completes *Blackmail*, the first British "talkie."

1929—Disney releases its first Silly Symphony animation, *The Skeleton Dance*.

1929—The Marx Brothers' star in their first film, *The Cocoanuts*.

1930—Ub Iwerks leaves Disney. The company buys back his 20% share for $2,290.

1930—Disney releases *The Chain Gang*, the first film in which Pluto appears.

1930—René Clair (1898–1981) releases the first French sound film, *Sous les toits de Paris*.

1930—The Fleischer Studios release the first Betty Boop film, *Betty Boop's Prize Show*. The series runs until 1939.

1930—*Sinkin' in the Bathtub* is the first Warner Brothers cartoon.

1931—Goofy appears in his first Disney film, *Mickey's Revue*, although he is not named until the 1934 Mickey Mouse cartoon, *Orphan's Benefit*.

1931—Disney releases the first full-color Silly Symphony film, *Flowers and Trees*.

1931—Charlie Chaplin's film *City Lights* has a music-only soundtrack.

1932—Disney starts using the three-color Technicolor process for cartoons.

1933—The Fleischer Studios release the first Popeye cartoon, *Popeye the Sailor*.

1933—Willis O'Brien adds stop-motion animation and special effects to the live-action feature film *King Kong*.

1933—Disney uses three-color Technicolor in the cartoon *The Three Little Pigs*.

1934—The first drive-in movie theater opens in New Jersey.

1934—Donald Duck appears in the Silly Symphony film, *The Wise Little Hen*.

1934—Friz Freleng directs *Buddy and Towser*, his first cartoon for Warner Brothers.

1934—Mickey Mouse briefly appears in the black-and-white Laurel and Hardy film *Babes in Toyland*.

1935—*Mickey's Kangaroo*, with Mickey Mouse and Pluto, is the last black-and-white Disney cartoon.

1935—Warner Brothers hires Fred "Tex" Avery (1908–1980). His first Looney Tunes cartoon is *Gold Diggers of '49*, released the next year.

1935—Bob Clampett (1913–1984) creates Porky the Pig for Warner Brothers.

1935—Eastman Kodak introduces Kodachrome color film, and Technicolor introduces its three-strip process.

1936—Warner Brothers hires Mel Blanc (1908–1989) and Carl Stalling.

1937—Disney releases *Snow White and the Seven Dwarfs*, the first feature-length cartoon. *Snow White* is composed of about 477,000 drawings.

1937—Warner Brothers introduces Daffy Duck.

1937—The MGM animation studio hires William Denby Hanna (1910–) and Joseph Roland Barbera (1911–), the creators of Tom and Jerry.

1938—Chuck Jones (1912–) directs *The Night Watchman*, his first Warner Brothers cartoon.

1939—The Fleischer Studios release the feature-length cartoon *Gulliver's Travels*.

1939—John Vincent Atanasoff (1903–) and Clifford Berry invent the first digital binary machine, an ancestor of the computer.

1940—Disney employs Ub Iwerks as the head of the technical research division.

1940—Disney releases the feature-length cartoons *Pinocchio* and *Fantasia*. *Fantasia* has a musical score recorded in multichannel stereophonic sound and played by the Philadelphia Orchestra conducted by Leopold Stokowski.

1940—CBS demonstrates its color television system, which was developed by Peter Carl Goldmark (1906–1977), also the inventor of the long-playing record.

1940—George Pal (1908–1980), who worked on animated cartoons in Holland, comes to Hollywood and starts working for Paramount.

1940—Warner Brothers introduces Elmer Fudd and Bugs Bunny.

1940—Walter Lantz (1900–1994) produces the first cartoon with Woody Woodpecker.

1941—Tex Avery leaves Warner Brothers for MGM. Bob Clampett replaces him.

1941—Disney releases the feature-length cartoon *Dumbo* and the live-action film *The Reluctant Dragon*. *The Reluctant Dragon*, which changes to color from black and white, contains some animation sequences.

1941—The Fleischer Studios releases the feature-length cartoon *Mr. Bug Goes to Town*.

1942—Disney releases the feature-length cartoon *Bambi*.

1943—Warner Brothers releases the last black-and-white Looney Tune cartoon.

1943—John Mauchly (1907–1980) and John Presper Eckert (1919–) create the ENIAC computer.

1944—John Logie Baird, who showed the first television image in 1928, demonstrates three-dimensional color images.

1945—Warner Brothers introduces Pepé LePew, Sylvester, and Yosemite Sam.

1946—Disney releases the feature-length live-action and animated film *Song of the South*.

1947—The Bell Laboratories scientists William Bradford Shockley (1910–1989), Walter Houser Brattain (1902–1987), and John Bardeen (1908–) demonstrate their invention, the point-contact transistor. They win the Nobel Prize in 1956.

1947—The Hungarian-born English engineer Dennis Gabor (1900–1979) invents holography for which he wins the Nobel Prize in 1971.

1948—*Crusader Rabbit*, from Jay Ward (1920–1989) and Alex Anderson, is the first made-for-television cartoon series.

1948—NBC-TV turns down a *Dudley Do-Right* proposal from Jay Ward Productions.

1949—Warner Brothers introduces Wile E. Coyote and the Road Runner.

1950—The Peanuts comic strip, by Charles M. Schulz (1922–), appears for the first time in seven newspapers. Fifteen years later, the first Peanuts animated film is produced.

1950—Disney releases the feature-length cartoon *Cinderella*.

1951—Disney releases the feature-length cartoon *Alice in Wonderland*.

1951—John Hubley (1914–1977) produces his first independent film, *Gerald McBoing Boing*.

1951—Cinerama, a wide- and curved-screen movie effect, is introduced.

1953—Disney releases the feature-length cartoon *Peter Pan*.

1953—Disney releases *Toot, Whistle, Plunk and Boom*, its first cartoon produced in CinemaScope.

1953—Warner Brothers releases *Duck Dodgers in the 24 1/2 Century*.

1954—Color television broadcasts are shown regularly.

1954—ABC introduces the black-and-white *Disneyland* TV show, later renamed *Walt Disney Presents*. After being shown on all three networks, the show, filmed in color and named *Walt Disney*, ends in 1983.

1955—Disney releases the feature-length cartoon *Lady and the Tramp*.

1955—Disneyland opens.

1955—ABC introduces *Mickey Mouse Club*. The show runs for four years.

1955—CBS introduces the first all-cartoon Saturday morning show, *Mighty Mouse Playhouse*, produced by Terrytoons.

1955—Art Clokey is contracted to produce *Gumby*.

1955—For the first time, Otto Messmer is publicly recognized as the creator of Felix the Cat.

1956—CBS introduces Terrytoons' *The Heckle and Jeckle Cartoon Show*.

1958—Carl Stalling retires from Warner Brothers.

1958—Hanna-Barbera introduces the made-for-television animated series *Huckleberry Hound*.

1959—Disney releases the feature-length cartoon *Sleeping Beauty*, filmed in Super Technirama 70, a widescreen process.

1959—Disney releases the stop-motion short film *Noah's Ark*.

1959—John and Faith Hubley (1924–) release the animated film *Moonbird*.

1959—ABC runs the first episode of *Rocky and His Friends*, from Jay Ward Productions. In 1961 the show moves to NBC and is renamed *The Bullwinkle Show*. The series ends 1964.

1960—IBM mass-produces the transistor.

1960—Ub Iwerks wins an Oscar for a special-effects optical printer.

1960—Smell-O-Vision and in-flight movies are introduced.

1961—Ivan Sutherland, an MIT student, creates Sketchpad, a computer drawing program.

1961—Steve Russell, an MIT student, creates the first video game *Spacewar*.

1961—Ub Iwerks develops xerographic animation for Disney's *One Hundred and One Dalmations*.

1961—John and Faith Hubley release the award-winning animated film *Of Stars and Men*.

1961—Disney retires Donald Duck from short animated films.

1962—Bob Clampett Productions introduces *Beany and Cecil*.

1962—Hanna-Barbera introduces *The Jetsons Show*.

1963—Warner Brothers ends Looney Tunes.

1963—Disney releases the feature-length cartoon *The Sword in the Stone*.

1963—Academics use computer-generated films to illustrate scientific research.

1964—Disney releases *Mary Poppins*, a feature-length live-action and animated film.

1964—Robert Crumb (1943–) draws the first version of *Fritz the Cat*, later to become the first X-rated animated feature.

1964—Friz Freleng creates The Pink Panther™ for the opening title sequence of the live-action movie, *The Pink Panther*.

1965—*A Charlie Brown Christmas* is the first animated Peanuts television special.

1966—Gulf & Western buys Paramount, signaling the start of many more such mergers.

1966—CBS replaces *Mighty Mouse Playhouse* (Terrytoons) with *The Mighty Heroes* (also Terrytoons), produced by Ralph Bakshi (1938–).

1967—The first videotaped movies are sold for home use.

1967—Disney releases the feature-length cartoon *The Jungle Book*.

1968—*2001: A Space Odyssey*, from Stanley Kubrick, features HAL, the computer, and many special effects.

1968—The Beatles star in the animated film *Yellow Submarine*.

1969—Bill Gates (1955–) and Paul Allen report bugs in DEC PDP-10 software and are paid in computer time.

1969—Xerox opens PARC, the Palo Alto Research Center.

1969—Monty Python's Flying Circus is underway. American cast member Terry Gilliam (1940–) contributes animations.

1970—Disney releases the feature-length cartoon *The Aristocats*.

1971—Steve Wozniak and Bill Fernandez build a computer out of spare parts.

1971—Disney releases the animated and live-action feature *Bedknobs and Broomsticks*.

1971—Walt Disney World opens.

1972—Nolen Bushnell founds Atari and releases *Pong*, the video game.

1972—Ralph Bakshi produces the animated feature-length film *Fritz the Cat*, the first X-rated animated film.

1973—The live-action film *Westworld* uses computer-generated graphics.

1973—Disney releases the animated film *Robin Hood*.

1975—The microcomputer build-it-yourself kit is introduced.

1975—*Jaws*, directed by Steven Spielberg (1947–), uses mechanical sharks.

1975—Bill Gates and Paul Allen start Microsoft Corporation.

1976—Steve Wozniak and Steve Jobs develop Apple I, the first Apple computer, in March and start the Apple Computer Company.

1976—Microprocessors now control the operation of still cameras.

1977—Disney releases *The Rescuers*, the last feature film made by the original group of Disney animators, and *Pete's Dragon*, an animated and live-action film.

1979—George Lucas releases *Star Wars*, the winner of several Oscars for its imaginative technical effects.

1979—Lucasfilm forms its computer graphics division for enhancing motion pictures.

1979—Terry Gilliam contributes animations to Monty Python's *The Life of Brian*.

1980—Backed by Disney, Steven Lisberger, an animator, and Donald Kushner, a lawyer-turned-distributor, release the special-effects film *Tron*, about the world inside a video game.

1981—IBM introduces the IBM PC, with the DOS operating system.

1981—Disney releases the animated full-length film *The Fox and the Hound*.

1981—Xerox introduces the $16,000 Star, the first microcomputer with a graphical user interface.

1981—Microsoft begins work on the graphical user interface that will eventually become Windows.

1983—Woody Allen (1935–) completes *Zelig*, a film that incorporates images of Allen and other characters into old newsreels and photographs.

1983—Tom Brigham, a programmer and animator at the New York Institute of Technology, creates *morphing,* in which one character gradually evolves into another.

1984—Michael Eisner (1942–) becomes chairman and CEO of Walt Disney Productions.

1984—Apple introduces the Macintosh.

1984—The company Wavefront produces a commercial three-dimensional animation system.

1985—Disney releases the animated full-length film *The Black Cauldron*.

1985—Commodore launches the Amiga.

1986—Disney first uses computer graphics in its full-length animated film *The Great Mouse Detective*.

1987—Lucasfilm uses morphing in its full-length film *Willow*.

1987—Disney and Pixar start developing the Computer Animation and Production System (CAPS).

1987—*The Simpsons*, a series of short films by Matt Groening (1954–), is introduced on *The Tracey Ullman Show*.

1988—Bob Clampett Productions revives Beany and Cecil.

1988—The live-action animated film *Who Framed Roger Rabbit*, a production of Touchstone Pictures, Silver Screen Parners III, and Amblin Entertainment, is released.

1988—Don Bluth, a former Disney animator, directs *The Land Before Time* for Universal Pictures and Amblin Entertainment.

1989—Disney uses the CAPS system to produce *The Little Mermaid*.

December 1989—*The Simpsons* half-hour-long series premieres on the Fox Network.

1990—Disney releases the animated feature *The Rescuers Down Under*.

1990—Microsoft introduces Windows 3.0.

1990—Disney releases the feature-length film *Dick Tracy*, which uses many special effects.

1991—*Terminator 2: Judgment Day* morphs its villain.

1991—Disney releases the feature-length animated films *DuckTales: The Movie—Treasure of the Lost Lamp* and *Beauty and the Beast*, which receives the first best-picture Oscar for an animated film.

1992—Disney releases the feature-length cartoon *Aladdin*.

1993—*Jurassic Park* contains a herd of go-motion dinosaurs.

1993—Tim Burton produces the *The Nightmare Before Christmas*, a stop-motion animated film from Touchstone, a Disney division.

1994—The Tom Hanks film *Forrest Gump* uses digital compositing, in which scenes are created by overlaying various video sequences.

1994—Disney releases the feature-length cartoon *The Lion King*.

1994—*The Mask* combines cartoon effects with live-action shots.

1995—Pixar's *Toy Story* is the first completely computer-animated feature.

1995—Disney releases the feature-length cartoons *A Goofy Movie* and *Pocahontas*.

1996—Disney releases the feature-length cartoon *The Hunchback of Notre Dame* and the stop-action film *James and the Giant Peach*.

Computer-Based Animation

Computer-based graphics and animation have developed from several sources—photography, scientific research in academic and commercial laboratories, business and gaming computing, and motion pictures and animated films, as well as a tradition of both fine and commercial art. With computer-based graphics and animation programs, users can create a wide range of animations, from simple GIF animations to recent animated films such as the 110,000-frame *Toy Story* (1995). This appendix traces the history of computer-based graphics and animation.

THE BEGINNING

Computer graphics formally started in 1961 when Ivan Sutherland, an MIT student, created Sketchpad, the first computer-based drawing program. Sketchpad used a light pen with a photoelectric cell in its tip to draw images on a computer screen. The electronic gun on the computer screen actually communicated with the light pen, placing a cursor at the location of each electronic pulse emitted by the light pen. When the image was complete, it could be saved for use at a later time. While at MIT, Sutherland invented a computer-controlled head-mounted display (HMD), the first virtual reality (VR) system. The HMD displayed an image for each eye; this resulted in a three-dimensional effect (that is, a modern successor to the stereoscope).

The first computer-animated film *Simulation* demonstrated a gravity attitude control system for an orbiting satellite. Developed in 1963 by E. E. Zajac, a scientist at Bell Labs, the film excited interest from computer companies such as IBM, which soon released the 2250 graphics terminal.

In 1968 the University of Utah founded its computer science program. Its first head, David Evans, built a department that has been responsible for many landmarks in computer graphics and for training the founders of computer software and hardware companies such as Silicon Graphics, Adobe, and Netscape Communications. Ivan Sutherland became a professor at the University of Utah.

ADVANCING TOWARD REALISM

Computer-generated graphics programs can produce three-dimensional animations by calculating shadows and highlights, by showing every angle of an object, and by adding textures to foreground objects and the background. Designers who work with computer-aided design (CAD) and computer-based

313

three-dimensional (3D) graphics build their images on *wireframes*, skeletons made up of polygons to which they add textures and shading. Images have become more realistic as computer-based shading programming has become more sophisticated.

- *Flat shading*, the most elementary method in 3D graphics, uses a single color for the polygons.

- *Gouraud shading*, developed by Henri Gouraud at the University of Utah in 1971, calculates a range of colors with which to shade the polygons yet uses computer processing very efficiently. Gouraud shading is still in use today for smaller images.

- *Phong shading*, developed by Phong Bui-Toung at the University of Utah in 1974, is a sophisticated method for calculating a range of shading colors. Although the results look better, computing processing time increases a great deal. Today, graphic artists combine Phong shading (for the most realistic images) and Gouraud shading (to conserve computer memory).

- *Fractals*, described by Dr. Benoit Mandelbrot in 1975, are images that are somewhere between one and two dimensions. Using fractal geometry, a graphic artist can perform calculations to create random images that form irregular terrains and textures. Because nothing in nature is symmetrical or regular, fractal images look realistic.

- *Bump mapping*, developed by James Blinn of the Jet Propulsion Laboratory in 1976, adds indentations and bulges to a flat or textured surface, making the image much more realistic. Blinn also developed environment mapping, which draws front, back, top, bottom, left side, and right side views of the area adjacent to an object and applies the reflections of those six views to the object.

- *Ray tracing*, developed by Turner Whitted in 1980, uses a computer to calculate the path of every ray of light as it moves around a picture, reflecting off shiny surfaces and traveling through transparent and translucent surfaces until it either is absorbed by opaque or dull surfaces or goes out of the picture. Ray tracing produces extremely realistic scenes—reaching near-photographic quality—using extensive computer processing resources and time.

SPECIAL EFFECTS IN TELEVISION AND MOTION PICTURES

Both television and motion pictures started using computer-based graphics in the 1970s. Computer graphics hardware and software enabled special effect by manipulating and distorting scanned-in images. Television programs sponsored by Bell Telephone, CBS Sports, and others used short computer-generated program introductions and transitions between program segments. At the same time, moviemakers used special effects in films such as *Westworld* (1973), *Futureworld* (1976), *Star Wars* (1977), and *Tron* (1980). As better effects were needed, technicians invented new hardware and software, thereby enriching computer-based graphics as a whole.

PROGRAMMING ANIMATIONS

Today's animation programs and programming languages allow users to specify realistic and complex motion against lifelike backgrounds. With animation programming, a technician can control animation in many ways:

- Set an animation to run over a defined length of time.
- Set an animation to start and end at particular frames.
- Select an event that triggers the start of an animation.
- Program several animations to run simultaneously.
- Draw the important key frames, specify a series of actions—simple or complex—and let the program create the in-between frames.
- Automate special effects and the application of colors, patterns, and textures.
- Rotoscope succeeding images on the computer and then draw over the image to develop motion.
- Insert computer graphics and animations into live-action scenes.
- Select stock backgrounds and objects from a library of files.

Three-dimensional graphics programs allow animators to produce realistic-looking animations. For example, they can build objects as artists create sculptures. First, the skeleton is formed, muscles are added, and the object is overlaid with skin or another surface. To enable real-life motion, a technician may create a set of fingers, the rest of the hand, parts of an arm, and so on, and link them all. Then, when the program moves one linked object, the other objects move in harmony—all requiring many calculations and computer resources. Therefore, some full-featured three-dimensional graphics programs run on several networked computers.

ANIMATION ON THE WORLD WIDE WEB

Animation on the World Wide Web comes in three flavors: Common Gateway Interface, (CGI), Java, and GIF89a.

Common Gateway Interface

The Common Gateway Interface (CGI) allows those who visit a Web site to control a program running on the site server. The most common use for CGI is to enable users to communicate with databases. For example, a customer using an on-line shopping site fills in an order form, which is then sent by a CGI program to a database on the site server. After processing the order and updating the database, the CGI program creates and sends to the customer pages and/or messages about the order. Using CGI, a programmer can also create animations. The main drawbacks to CGI programming are that it runs on the Web server, using resources that might be better used in other ways, and that the site administrator must be concerned with server security.

Java Animations

Java is a programming language designed and developed by Sun Microsystems for use on the World Wide Web. When a user goes to a page, any Java *applets* (that is, programs) are downloaded to and run on the user's computer, thereby allowing other processing to occur on the Web server as well as eliminating security concerns. Typical Java applets communicate with databases, run small or large real-time multi- or single-player games, and display animated images and banners. The main disadvantage of Java is that not all browsers support it.

GIF Animations

The most popular choice for Web page animations is Graphics Interchange Format (GIF)—for two reasons. GIF files are relatively small, and they are very easy to create and animate. CompuServe developed GIF87a, the first GIF standard in 1987. GIF87a supported many images within a single file, which can result in animation. In 1989 CompuServe released GIF89a, the next standard, which incorporated features such as transparency and time delays between frames. For more information about GIF87a, refer to Chapter 1.

Index

NUMBERS

216-color palette, 5, 6–7
8-bit, defined, 4

A

adding frames, 16
adding intermediate frames, 16
Adobe Illustrator
    216-color Web swatch, 197
    adding text to an image, 217–18
    applying special effects, 225–26
    changing fill and stroke colors,
        199–200
    copying a selection, 217
    creating an image, 204–14
    cutting a selection, 217
    deleting a selection, 217
    deselecting a selection, 216
    displaying an image at its true
        size, 204
    drawing an image, 212–13
    Ellipse tools, 207–8
    fitting an image to the applica-
        tion window, 204
    flipping a selection, 221–22
    inverting a selection, 216
    modifying an image, 214–18
    moving a selection, 216, 219
    moving the artboard, 216
    Paintbrush, 204–5

palettes, 196-198
pasting a selection, 217
Pen tools, 211–12
Pencil, 206
Polygon tool, 208–9
rainbow star animation, 214
Rectangle tools, 206–7
reflecting a selection, 221–22
rotating a selection, 220
scaling a selection, 219–20
selecting an object, 215
selecting by color or style, 216
selecting several objects, 215–16
selecting an entire image, 216
shearing a selection, 220
showing the grid, 200–201
snail rule animation, 223–25
specifying stroke and line attrib-
    utes, 205–6
Spiral tool, 210
Star tool, 209–10
starting, 188–89
status bar, 198
supported file formats, 187–88
System swatches, 197
toolbox, 190–96
transforming a selection, 218–23
turning on the rulers, 201–2
using the Transform Each dialog
    box, 222–23
using the Web palette, 199
work area, 190
zooming in, 202–3

zooming out, 203
Adobe Photoshop
    adding text to an image, 175–77
    Airbrush, 158–59
    applying special effects, 182–83
    bouncing ball animation, 184
    changing canvas size, 173–74
    changing image size, 171–73
    changing the foreground and
        background colors, 142–45
    cool faucet animation, 185–86
    copying a selection, 169
    creating an image, 152–63
    cropping an image, 174–75
    cutting a selection, 169
    deleting a selection, 170
    displaying an image at 100%, 151
    Eraser tool, 159–60
    fitting an image to the applica-
        tion window, 151
    flipping selections or layers, 180
    inactivating a selection, 169
    inverting a selection, 169
    lighted rule animation, 162–63
    Line tool, 156–57
    modifying an image, 163–77
    moving an image, 169
    Paintbrush, 154–55
    painting an image, 160–62
    palettes, 137–40
    pasting a selection, 170
    Pencil, 155–56
    rotating a selection or layer, 180

317

scanning, 185
selecting a rectangular area, 164–65
selecting an elliptical area, 165
selecting an entire image, 169
selecting an irregular area, 165–66
selecting by color characteristics, 164
showing the grid, 145–47
Smudge tool, 157–58
starting, 130–31
status bar, 140–41
toolbox, 132–37
transforming a selection or layer, 179–82
turning on the rulers, 147
using the Brushes palette, 152–54
using the Color palette, 144–45
using the Color Picker, 142–44
using the Free Transform command, 182
using the Numeric Transform dialog box, 180–82
using the Swatches palette, 145
viewing an image at printed size, 151–52
work area, 132
working with layers, 177–79
working with paths, 166–68
zooming in, 148–49
zooming out, 149–50
algorithm, defined, 4
animated films and GIF animations, 13
animating
    by dragging, 24
    fade-ins, 22
    fade-outs, 23
    flexible objects, 24
    flickering objects, 22
    flipping objects, 20
    part of an image, 25
    revolving objects, 20
    rigid objects, 24
    rotating objects, 19
    speeding objects, 24

text, 21
with colors, 21
animation examples
    accordian, 271
    apple tree, 47–48
    arrow bend, 119
    bouncing ball, 184
    cool faucet, 185–86
    crazy HOME, 106
    Deborah's moon, 279–80
    flashing NEW sign, 58
    happy dog, 55
    lighted rule, 162–63
    lighthouse, 275
    movie marquee, 97
    orange-red-yellow NEW, 258
    rainbow star, 214
    rotating beach ball, 51
    snail rule, 223–25
    snapping scissors, 122
    square-square, 269
    teeth, 108
anchor points, defined, 135
animation file, saving, 15
animation speed, 16
animations
    designing, 14
    previewing, 16
    testing, 18
artboard, defined, 196
aspect ratio, defined, 101

B

background color
    defined, 38
    Web page, 8
Bezier curve, defined, 252
bit map, defined, 2
block, defined, 109
brightness, defined, 143

C

cache, defined, 13
caps, defined, 205
channels, defined, 140
checklist, planning and designing, 13
clip art, using, 12
closed path, defined, 166
color palette, defined, 5
Color Swatch, 38
color, transparent, 16
colors, RGB, 38
Composition Guide, defined, 35
compositions, defined, 29
CompuServe, 4
Copyright Act of the U.S., 11
copyright laws, observing, 11
CorelDRAW
    accordian animation, 271
    Bezier tool, 252–53
    Bitmap or OLE Object property bar, 267
    changing outline and fill colors, 246–47
    cloning a selection, 261–62
    color palette, 242–43
    Color roll-up, 244–45
    converting to a bit map, 267–69
    copying a selection, 261
    creating an image, 252–57
    Curve or Connector property bar, 252
    cutting a selection, 261
    deleting a selection, 262
    drawing an image, 256–57
    drawing page, 238–40
    drawing window, 238–40
    duplicating a selection, 261
    Editing Text property bar, 256
    Ellipse property bar, 254
    Ellipse tool, 254
    flipping a selection, 266
    Freehand tool, 252

Graph Paper and Spiral Tool property bar, 255
Graph Paper (Grid) tool, 255–56
grouping and ungrouping selections, 262
Knife, Eraser and Natural Pen Tool property bar, 253
mirroring a selection, 266
modifying an image, 258–62
moving a selection, 262–63
Natural Pen tool, 253
orange-red-yellow NEW animation, 258
pasting a selection, 261
Polygon tool, 254–55
Rectangle property bar, 253
Rectangle tool, 254
roll-ups, 240–42
rotating a selection, 263–64
scaling a selection, 265
scanning an image, 270
selecting a color palette, 245–46
selecting color options, 244–47
selecting objects, 259–60
showing the grid, 247
sizing a selection, 266–67
skewing a selection, 264–65
Spiral tool, 255
square-square animation, 269
standard toolbar, 231–34
starting, 229–30
status bar, 243
Symmetrical Polygon property bar, 255
Text tool, 256
toolbox and property bars, 234–38
transforming a selection, 262–67
turning on the rulers, 248
zooming an image, 249–51

D

designing an animation, 14
direction lines, defined, 166

E

effects
    animating by dragging, 24
    animating part of an image, 25
    color animation, 21
    fade-ins, 22
    fade-outs, 23
    flexible objects, 24
    flickering objects, 22
    flipping objects, 20
    revolving objects, 20
    rigid objects, 24
    rotating objects, 19
    rotoscoping, 25
    speeding objects, 24
    text animation, 21
emotions, showing, 26–27
end points, defined, 166

F

file size, minimizing, 14
file, saving an animation, 15
fill, defined, 195
first frame, 15
Fleischer, Max, 25
flickering, 16, 22
flyout, defined, 234
foreground color, defined, 38
formats, graphics file, 2
fountain fills, defined, 238
frame, first, 15
frames
    adding, 16
    movie, 12

G

GIF animations and animated films, 13
GIF
    defined, 4
    programs, using, 16–17
    programs, 18–19
GIF Construction Set
    applying transition effects, 126–28
    blocks, 109
    button bar, 111
    creating an animation from scratch, 124
    display area, 111
    editing a control block, 116–17
    editing a header block, 115
    editing a loop block, 116
    editing an image block, 117–18
    exporting an image, 121
    extracting a block, 121–22
    inserting objects in an animation, 119–21
    making a scrolling banner, 125–26
    managing control and image blocks, 123–24
    merging a file into an animation, 121
    preview box, 112
    starting, 110
    using the Animation Wizard, 112–14
GIF87a standard, 4
GIF89a standard, 5
GifBuilder
    choosing a color palette, 277
    creating an animation, 276–77
    creating an IMG tag, 281
    disposing of a frame, 278–79
    editing an animation, 277–81
    Frames window, 273–76
    getting ready to animate, 276
    looping an animation, 280

INDEX

optimizing an animation, 280–81
setting the interframe delay, 279
specifying a transparent color, 277–78
starting, 276
gradient, defined, 194
graphic resolution, 8
graphics file formats, 2
group, defined, 191

H

HSV, 39
HTML document, 17
hue, defined, 39
hue-saturation-value, 39

I

Illustrator. *See* Adobe Illustrator.
Image Composer
adding text, 57–58
apple tree animation, 47–48
applying art effects, 64–66
applying colors, 51–54
applying patterns and fills, 59–61
applying warps and filters, 61–64
centering Composition Guide, 43
changing Color Swatch color, 39–40
changing Composition Guide color, 40–41
Composition Guide, 37–38
creating a composition, 45–47
creating a sprite, 43–45
editing colors, 56–57
flashing NEW animation, 58
happy dog animation, 55
manipulating sprites, 48–51
panning, 43
placing Composition Guide, 43
rotating beach ball animation, 51

scanning a sprite, 66–67
starting, 29
status bar, 41
toolbar, 30–34
toolbox, 34–36
workspace, 36–37
zooming, 41–42
images, irregularly shaped, 8
inserting an animation in an HTML document, 17
interlaced, defined, 4

J

joins, defined, 205
JPEG, defined, 2

L

layer, defined, 133
Lempel-Ziv-Welch (LZW) compression, 4
limits, GIF animation files, 14

M

mask, defined, 137
Microsoft GIF Animator
controlling animations, 69–70
controlling frames, 70–72
creating an animation, 72
managing GIF files, 69
toolbar, 68–69
Microsoft Image Composer. *See* Image Composer.
minimizing file size, 14
motions, walking, 26
movie frames, 12
Muybridge, Edweard, 26

O

opacity, defined, 93
open path, defined, 166
outline pen, defined, 237

P

Paint Shop Pro
adding a border, 99
adding a chisel border, 103
adding a drop shadow, 102
adding a hot-wax finish, 104
adding text, 89–90
buttonizing an image or selection, 103–4
changing color preferences, 81–82
changing foreground and background colors, 82
changing opacity, 94
color palette, 80–81
copying a selection, 96
crazy HOME animation, 106
creating an image, 87–90
creating geometric shapes, 87
creating images for animation, 97
cropping an image, 100
cutting a selection, 96
cutting out a selection, 102–3
deforming an image, 104–5
deleting a selection, 97
drawing freeform shapes, curves, and lines, 88
drawing lines, 87–88
editing color palette, 82–84
enlarging the canvas, 100
feathering a selection, 93–94
filtering an image, 105–6
flipping an image, 98
image window, 80
inactivating a selection, 92
inverting a selection, 93

mirroring an image, 98
modifying an image, 90–97
movie marquee animation, 97
moving a selection, 95
moving an image or selection, 87
pasting a selection, 96–97
resampling an image, 101
resizing an image, 101
rotating an image, 98–99
scanning an image, 107
selecting a geometric area, 90–91
selecting a transparent color, 94–95
selecting an entire image, 92
selecting an irregular area, 91
selecting by color characteristics, 92
starting, 73–74
status bar, 84
style control bar, 77–79
teeth animation, 108
tool palette, 77–79
toolbar, 74—76
turning on the grid, 86
workspace, 79–80
zooming, 85
palette, 216-color, 5
paths, defined, 135
Photoshop. See Adobe Photoshop.
plug-ins, defined, 130
Piguet, Yves, 273
pixel, defined, 2
planning and designing checklist, 13–14
presets, defined, 232

previewing an animation, 16
Print Screen key, 12
programs, GIF animation, 18–19

Q

quality of movement, 16

R

raster, defined, 2
red-green-blue (RGB) colors, 38
resampling, defined, 101
roll-up, defined, 232
rotoscoping, 25-26
running animations in a Web browser, 18

S

saturation, defined, 39
saving an animation file, 15
scaling, defined, 2
scanner, using a, 11
scratch disk, defined, 141
screen-capture programs, using, 12
scripts, defined, 232
shareware, defined, 73
size, file, 7
splines, defined, 34
sprites, defined, 29
storyboard, 14
stroke, defined, 192

T

testing an animation, 18
text, animating with, 21
transparent color, 8, 16
transparent, defined, 4

U

uniform fills, defined, 238
Unisys Corporation, 4

V

value, defined, 39
vector, defined, 2

W

walking motions, 26
Web browser, running an animation in a, 18
Web page background color, 8

INDEX

CD-ROM Disk Contents

This CD-ROM disk includes the following folders and files:

mac_read.me—A text file, in Macintosh format, describing the contents of the CD-ROM disk.

win_read.me—A text file, in Windows format, describing the contents of the CD-ROM disk.

mac_anim—A folder containing a gallery of copyright-free animations created using GifBuilder, a Macintosh-based animation program, and readable by Macintosh computers and clones.

mac_pals—A folder containing two 216-color palettes: 216color.pal (for Paint Shop Pro) and 216color.aco (for Photoshop).

mac_pgms—A folder containing copies of trial and free programs that run on Macintosh computers and clones.Programs include the Adobe Illustrator Tryout, Adobe Photoshop Tryout, and GifBuilder 0.5 freeware.

win_anim—A folder containing a gallery of copyright-free animations created using GIF Construction Set, a Windows-based animation program, and readable by Windows PCs.

win_pals—A folder containing two 216-color palettes: 216color.pal (for Paint Shop Pro) and 216color.aco (for Photoshop).

win_pgms—A folder containing copies of trial, shareware, and free programs that run on Windows PCs. Programs include the Adobe Illustrator Tryout, Adobe Photoshop Tryout, GIF Construction Set 16-bit and 32-bit shareware, a Microsoft GIF Animator freeware version, Paint Shop Pro 16-bit and 32-bit shareware, and a trial version of Ulead GIF Animator.